BLUE SKIES AND SILVER LININGS
Aspects of the Hollywood musical

Bruce Babington and
Peter William Evans

To our families

BLUE SKIES AND SILVER LININGS

Aspects of the Hollywood musical

Manchester University Press

Published by Manchester University Press
Oxford Road, Manchester M13 9PL, UK
and 51 Washington Street, Dover, New Hampshire 03820, USA

British Library cataloguing in publication data
Babington, Bruce
  Blue skies and silver linings: aspects of the Hollywood musical.
  1. Moving-pictures, Musical — History and criticism   2. Moving-pictures —
  United States — History
  I. Title   II. Evans, Peter
  782.81'0973   PN1995.9.M86

Library of Congress cataloging in publication data
Babington, Bruce.
  Blue skies and silver linings.
  Bibliography: p. 248
  1. Moving-pictures, Musical–United States–History and criticism. I. Evans, Peter,
  1933 – II. Title.
PN1995.9.M86B3   1985   791.43'09'09357   84–25046

ISBN 0-7190-1739-4 cased

Acknowledgements

We gratefully acknowledge assistance, help and encouragement from the following: John
Banks, Catherine Annabel and Martin Spencer, at MUP; the Newcastle University
Research Fund Committee for a grant which enabled us to see films we might otherwise
have been unable to see; all the students over the last six years at Newcastle University's
Adult Education film classes, sponsored by the British Film Institute at the Tyneside
Cinema; the British Film Institute Stills Library; Maggi Hurt at the Tyneside Cinema;
Ron Guariento for much illuminating conversation; Andrew Tudor and Tony Badger for
suggesting material used in the chapter on *Hair*; Trevor Saunders; Iris Penny who helped
with Al Jolson; and, in a variety of different ways, Rosalie Novick, Trish Lis, Deborah
Marcus and Maggi Fielder.

Stills from *The Merry Widow, Summer Holiday, The Gold Diggers of 1933, Easter Parade,
  It's Always Fair Weather, On a Clear Day You Can See Forever* and *Hair*, courtesy of
  the MGM/UA Entertainment Co.
Stills from *Carousel*, courtesy of Twentieth Century Fox.
Stills from *Swing Time*, courtesy of RKO pictures.
Stills from *The Jolson Story* and *Jolson Sings Again* courtesy of Columbia Pictures.
We gratefully acknowledge help from Musicscape Ltd. in allowing us to consult *Hair:
  The American Tribal-Love Rock Musical*. Book and lyrics by Gerome Ragni and
  James Rado. Music by Galt MacDermot. Property of Tams-Witmark Music Library
  Inc., New York.

Designed by Max Nettleton
Typeset by Harvest Printers Ltd, Macclesfield

Printed in Great Britain by Bell and Bain Ltd., Glasgow

Contents

PART I

The genre

Introduction

Looking for the silver lining

In recent years, wider developments in art theory have turned criticism
of the Hollywood musical from an innocent enthusiasm into a sophisticated
area of expertise. Such developments have healthily questioned and rejected
the idea that some kinds of art (say, *Middlemarch*) are worth analysing, and
that other kinds (say, *Singin' in the Rain*) are not. It is no longer possible
seriously to dismiss musicals from the critical view. Indeed, given on the one
hand the extreme aestheticism of the genre and, on the other, the way it so
clearly embodies ideas of love, happiness and freedom as conceived in the
society from which it comes, both the critic whose interest is primarily
formal and the critic whose interest is primarily ideological, will as likely as
not find themselves agreeing as to its centrality and importance in the
American cinema. There are battles that no longer have to be fought, and we
simply take for granted here that large body of critical work which has
naturalised the ideas that the Hollywood cinema produced an enormous
body of significant art, that popular culture is a field worthy of the most
intensive study, and that the musical, as much as the gangster film, the
western or the European art film, raises complex issues which can only be
dealt with by complex approaches.

This said, it must also be admitted that these have attracted their own
devotees of pretentiousness, whom the more traditional and lighthearted
enthusiasts have not been slow to satirise. While much of the writing in the
recent British Film Institute anthology of essays on the musical which he is
parodying is not really fair game, Clancy Sigal's strictures on the solemnities
of the new critical theologies are timely warnings for anyone too hastily
abandoning the terrain of pleasure and entertainment for the regions of
ideological deconstruction.

On deeper analysis, it appears, Busby Berkeley, Vincente Minnelli and
George Sidney become auteuristic 'activists of *mise en scène*' of a genre whose
nodal points of textual ideology, historically mutated and syntagmatically

demarcated by studio *équipe* into coded unities, are best seen as self-referential *discours* diegetically ritualised in a kind of optical politics whose mediatory function is structured paradigmatically according to Lacan, Althusser, Metz, Wollen and probably Freud and Jung as well. Poor Busby!

Practised by the clumsy and pretentious, the method can clearly lead to much madness, but Sigal's witty parody of the extremities of critical jargon does not obliterate the fact that the musical, so closely identified with 'escapism' and 'fantasy', has largely produced an escapist criticism – the domain of the coffee-table critics, content to allow glossy stills from the most popular films to tell their own stories. Film makers themselves, however, knew that there were more difficult and important things to be said, even European artists like Renoir and Truffaut whose high seriousness was not in doubt. As Truffaut writes of one of the many musicals we might have chosen to analyse in this book:

> As I left the theatre after watching *Love Me Or Leave Me*, a psychological American musical, or if you prefer, a dramatic comedy with singing, I thought how apt Jean Renoir's remark was: 'There is no realism in American films. No realism, but something much better, great truth . . . ' If we had to list the most shattering and moving scenes in movies, we would have to cite many of these Hollywood 'singing comedies'.

In highlighting the absence of realism in Hollywood films generally, not as a defect but as a positive merit, Truffaut and Renoir together touch on a subject that has gripped those writing recently on the musical from the standpoints of structuralism and semiology. The best of such writing has tried not to lose sight of the questions of pleasure and entertainment (so much more difficult than they seem on the surface) as it tries to understand how the musical, in its own distinctive ways, expresses its truths and formulates its meanings.

In an influential article first published in *Movie*, 'Entertainment and Utopia', Richard Dyer was one of the first to show how Hollywood musicals strive through both 'representational' and 'non-representational' elements to promote an idealised 'utopian' view of life. On this reading, musicals seek to arouse, especially through the song and dance that distinguishes them from other kinds of films, feelings of energy ('capacity to act vigorously'), abundance ('conquest of scarcity'), transparency (qualities like sincerity), community ('togetherness, sense of belonging') and intensity ('experiencing of emotion directly'). This process is achieved as much by 'non-representational' formal elements (e.g. colour, rhythm, musical and dance patternings) as by the more easily describable 'representational' elements (such as character, plot and themes). Dyer's work is important for two reasons. First, it says that if the genre is 'escapist', its 'escapism' is not merely trivial. Musicals give such intense pleasure to so many people (even structuralists and semiologists) because they lead us into worlds where qualities lacking in our lives and the societies in which we live them have a freer rein. Second, it links together the formal and thematic qualities of the musical with precise historical and ideological elements, both of which provide contexts of meaning over and beyond the constraints of any single film. In other words, although musicals, through their emphasis on movement, rhythm, pattern, indulge our pre-cultural, hedonistic, freedom-seeking desires, there is a way in which these basic needs and their gratifications are harnessed through the narratives to the demands of ideology. The best criticism of recent years, seeking to unravel these interrelated threads, has not been afraid either to recognise the brilliance and complexity (and indeed the value) of the musical's art, or to pinpoint the way in which these qualities are sometimes bound up in a regressive ideology.

The task, though potentially exhilarating, is by no means as transparently simple as Clancy Sigal would have us believe. The musical's art is elusive, surprising, protean, while the ideology that speaks through it is contradictory, inconsistent and unreliable. The way through these labyrinthine and interconnected passages is by concentrating both on entertainment, as Dyer has done, and on pleasure itself. We do not only have to ask why we find the dancing of, for instance, Astaire and Rogers so satisfying, or the power of voice and vulnerability of persona so appealing in Judy Garland, but also whether in finding them pleasurable we are being anchored in attitudes that are to some extent either regressive or subservient to dominant social and sexual assumptions. It is not inconceivable that what we find pleasurable may also turn out to be ideologically crippling. But that is ultimately as true of, say, the nineteenth-century novel as of the Hollywood musical.

However, in so far as it does seem to be more than usually committed to the celebration of 'pre-cultural' tendencies, the musical is a genre particularly suitable for the study of the balance in art between the desire for the innocent pleasures of harmony and form, and the acquiescence, sometimes unwitting, in the authority of ideology. Such an approach does not necessarily imply that one is exclusively looking in the musical at the ways these pre-civilised elements are systematically sabotaged by culture (western bourgeois culture in this case), nor that one is looking for civilized sensibilities and subtleties of thought by which to judge – in some idealistic way, either conservative or radical – the moral value of any particular musical, but, that in looking at the musical with the same theoretical and critical apparatus until recently restricted to the study of 'high' art, we can achieve a materialist reading of its mechanisms that is sensitive as much to the explicable as to the mysterious aspects of pleasure in art.

The musical, of all the Hollywood film genres, seems at first sight to revel most exuberantly in the exposition of its own artificiality, but as Jane Feuer argues in another largely helpful but constricted British Film Institute book, one would do well to be wary of looking for exact parallels with the modes of operation of modernist, Brechtian or Godardian texts, all of which through their distancing techniques, call for greater awareness on the part of reader or audience of the ideological and formal conditions of artistic illusion.

The comparison she makes is an interesting and valuable one, but the conclusions she reaches seem to us too simple as far as they apply to the musical and, incidentally, in so far as they refer to the modernists or radicals, too indulgent. Feuer argues that for every step of 'demystification' that the musical takes, another is taken towards 'remystification'. In other words, every instance that allows the audience to see into the artificiality of the spectacle is followed by another to restore the conditions of illusion. This succeeds, in her view, in destroying all sense in the audience of the experimental, arbitrary and conventional nature of artistic and social forms. In her view, Brecht and Godard seek by contrast to encourage such a conviction.

Though in many respects appealing, this description is ultimately unsatisfactory, for all art, even the most radical, is in some ways shaped in its reception, regardless of authorial intent, by the audience's desire for wholeness. We need look no further than Freud for an argument that the search for patterns, order and beauty figures prominently in our complicated responses to art. But this does not mean that moments of disruption and interrogation, along the route of the narrative, cannot be understood and used – consciously or unconsciously – as opportunities for reflection and self-awareness. Of course the musical sometimes masks its conditions of production and conceals the difficult beneath the effortless. Of course one should look for the silences, gaps, elisions and inconsistencies of the text to see how ideology helps shape the musical's meanings. Indeed the whole enterprise of looking at how culture silences or represses different social and psychological perspectives, is nowhere more fascinating than in the musical, and criticism of the genre has very much benefited from approaches postulating that key areas of knowledge are hidden or distorted in art for political purposes. But in doing so we should neither ignore the evidence of what is actually there, nor naively assume that the musical is mere propaganda. It is, rather, a genre that gives us the contradictions as well as the certainties of thought, the individual as well as the collective, the positive as well as the negative sides of the culture that produces it.

So, in scrutinising our enjoyment of musicals, our attention in subsequent chapters will fall not only on their historical links, formal structures, narrative patterns, dialogue and use of stars, but also on the traditions of popular song and dance. In a paraphrase of what Roman Jakobson, one of the earliest and most influential of structuralist critics, wrote about poetry, Robert Scholes remarks:

> the principal way in which the poetic function manifests itself in poetry is by a projection of the paradigmatic and metaphoric dimensions of language onto the syntagmatic. By emphasising resemblances of sound, rhythm, image, poetry thickens language, drawing attention to its formal properties and away from its referential significance.

Though too reductively formalistic, these remarks have a bearing on the musical which, leaving aside only for a moment its ideological contexts, is in this sense perhaps the most poetic of film genres, emphasising and celebrating as no other the very rudiments of film's poetic, formal resources. Each of these resources is in its own right a subject of infinite complexity, and we shall argue henceforward that the musical's use of popular song, orchestration, dance routines and so on, is not only as complicated as that in opera or ballet, but also as relevant as the analysis of, say, seventeenth-century stage comedy or the nineteenth-century novel, to the whole question of the relationship between art and life.

Whys and wherefores

Despite the constant stream of coffee-table histories of the musical and the recent flurry of more analytical activity, a new book on the musical needs no apology, especially when it is, like this one, orientated towards the detailed reading of particular films.

It is a curious feature of work on the genre that theoretical writing has far outstripped serious writing on individual films. The historical reasons for this strange and distorting imbalance can be traced to the inherent difficulties of writing about a kind of film in which convention and 'non-representational' signs are so important. As contemporary film criticism developed through its various phases, first of *auteurism,* then of genre study, then of structuralism and beyond, large numbers of films were written about in almost all of the genres from these differing perspectives. But this hardly happened at all with the musical. There were, of course, from time to time, suggestive comments and helpful insights, but the only single piece of writing about a musical film that comes near to anything like a full reading – i.e. a reading that attempts, if not to exhaust, at least to suggest the full semantic complexity of the text – is Andrew Britton's discussion of *Meet Me In St Louis*, hidden away from the majority of readers in a not easily available Australian film journal.

The trend of serious criticism towards 'poetics' – the effort to describe what may be true of many or all works rather than what is unique to the individual – has been very marked in the last few years. In the study of most genres this generalising approach could build on much pragmatic work on individual films so that theorising did not proceed in a vacuum, but could draw on a large range of specific studies to aid its systematising and check its possible arrogances and simplifying tendencies. In these cases the proper symbiotic relationship between the study of individual films and the attempt to establish general rules worked well, but in the case of the musical it hardly existed and, as a result, the simplifying tendencies of much of the theoretical work is that much more evident. Though the recent books published by the British Film Institute, by Jane Feuer and edited by Rick Altman, contain much serious writing to which we are indebted, they tend towards simplification, towards the announcing as universal of what are only partial truths about the musical. Such a tendency is inevitable if you stop, or have not even started, testing generalisations against the idiosyncratic complexity of specific films, since the generaliser is always at risk from the temptation to simplify the particular fact into the framework of a generative theory, the more dazzlingly simple the better. This should not be taken as a statement against theory, since this book clearly attempts to add to a general theory of the musical in many ways, but as an assertion of the necessity of studying individual films. The symbiotic relationship, the double process, is necessary and productive. Theory, which can emerge only from a knowledge of individual films, gives us tools to investigate and understand the single film text, while study of the individual text in turn refines those tools, allowing us to escape from too simple models which restrict our understanding.

A year or two ago it seemed almost passé to write, as we do in this book, about single films. Some influential critics, rather superficially and arrogantly, talked about such a focus as mere 'fetishism' of the text. The suggestion here was that to write about a single film (or other work of art) was to surrender to a bourgeois idealism in which the cultural phenomenon – seen as a virgin birth, haloed and nimbused with mysterious perfection – was cut off from all its social determinants and material relations. Such a barren practice, where it exists, might properly be labelled a fetishism – a distraction through a set of false meanings (or, at least, unquestioned and unexplained ones) from more real ones. But in writing about specific films we have at all times attempted to see the single text within as large a network of determinants, relationships and communicated meanings as possible. This has meant that we have chosen the films we discuss not only to illustrate the chronology of the musical (working through from the thirties to the seventies) but also to be systematically representative of the most important subtypes of film within the genre (e.g. the backstage musical, the pastoral musical, operetta, and so on). Thus, for instance, in discussing the two Jolson films, we have tried to develop a general theory of the musical 'biopic' with reference to many other films. We have also tried to analyse the appeal of Jolson's performance style and the nature of Larry Parks' remarkable imitation of it. In addition we have pursued in a particular narrative such basic material of the musical as the relation of art to life and the mechanics of self-referentiality, as well as the more local material of Jolson's Jewishness as it is handled by the film. Our aim has been to make every chapter similarly 'busy', with special attention – for this is a quintessentially American genre – to the relation of the films to an American cultural context. If the cost of this is the loss of the sustained analytical rigour that a much narrower project with commensurately narrower ambitions might boast, it is a cost we have calculated and are willing to pay. Our aim has been to consider the films in such a way as to suggest as much of their complexity as possible, and in a mode of address that can offer something both to the film specialist and to lovers of the musical unfamiliar with the sometimes difficult movements of contemporary criticism, but looking for ways to sharpen their own experience.

To return to the quotation from Clancy Sigal with which we began. We cannot really ignore – though we must surely attempt to civilise and make communicable – the techniques of deeper analysis, the problems of ideology and aesthetics to which the major theorisers of human behaviour and aesthetics are of course relevant. Poor Busby! And poor reader! if the end result is a banality rendered protectively opaque by a vocabulary that does not try to explain itself to the intelligent reader. But poorer Busby! And poorer reader! if we try to get by without Metz and Freud, without 'optical politics' and a precise attention to the many intricate systems of meaning that operate in the musical. Of course these films are entertainment, but entertainment is made out of meanings. Busby and Astaire and Rogers are seemingly perennial entertainment because they mean many things to many people. If we took Clancy Sigal's amusing riposte for substance rather than a warning against the abuses of methodical study, we would be nailed eternally to the coffee table, caught in a kind of writing that is accepted as the 'natural' way to talk about musicals, and which, in essence, does nothing but convey gossip and prejudice. Here is a passage from a recent book on the subject which is by no means the worst that has appeared and which is in certain respects quite useful.

It might have been a Liza Minnelli decade, except like Streisand and Andrews she made more nonmusicals than musicals, and has also fallen victim to the ignorance of contemporary moviemakers, most notably in *New York, New York* (1977), Martin Scorsese's big-band romance with Rober De Niro as a saxophonist (Georgie Auld dubbed his axe) and the look of the 1940s constantly outfitted in attitudes of the 1970s. Look, if you want to do an oldie, do it; what is this 'commentative museum' approach supposed to express other than contempt for the old forms?: in which case, why revive them?

It is informative to look briefly at how this series of statements works and how, in fact, it consists of little else than a tone of authority, built up by a number of deceptive (probably unconscious) strategies, but never by sustained argument. Note, for instance, the completely arbitrary reference to the fact that the jazz player Georgie Auld dubbed the music. This is true information about the film, something that in different contexts it might be useful to know, but put down here the only purpose it serves is to show the reader that the author knows more than he or she does. What it really says is that someone who doesn't know that Georgie Auld did the dubbing has no right to question the whole range of judgements of someone who does, someone, moreover, so intimate with the world of popular music that he calls a saxophone not a saxophone but an 'axe'. Such details pave the way for the last, very prescriptive sentence which begins: 'Look, if you want to . . .' which is calculated to suggest a common sense man talking to other common sense people, an author so firm and admirably uncomplicated in his attitude that you can almost see him personally dressing down that ignorant moviemaker, Martin Scorsese! All this confidence, which may at first sight seem impressive, is, in reality, quite empty. The negative judgements made depend not on an argument but on a series of unexamined prejudices and the repression of any conflicting views or evidence. There is, for instance, no mention of the facts that many filmgoers and analysts think of *New York, New York* as a major and innovative musical, or that Scorsese's use of seventies hindsight on forties forms (often expressed in images of nostalgic beauty), can be seen as something quite other than contempt for the old forms. We will not continue to labour the point, but the deceptive 'common sense' of this kind of writing is quite as dangerous as the kind of pretentiousness that Sigal mocks, in fact we think even more so.

Finally, we ought to say a brief word about our choice of films out of the enormous number of Hollywood musicals that we could have analysed. A desire to embrace the chronology of the musical, to exhibit its most important sub-types and, of course, to do justice to most of its major stars, directors and other creative personnel provided an underlying logic, though restrictions of space made for the occasional casualty – the omission, for instance, of a film by the major contemporary director of the genre, Bob Fosse. Within these constraints we have felt free to choose according to our likes, which is as it should be, since analysis comes best out of passion. We particularly regret not writing about *The Eddy Duchin Story*, *Meet Me in St Louis*, *Love Me Tonight*, *Cabaret* and *New York, New York*, but every act of choice means something not chosen.

Our bias has clearly been toward musicals that illustrate the complexity of the genre rather than its simplicities. Has such a bias given a false view of the musical, based on a few peak films? Would a book that instead of the films considered here, moved through, say, *Broadway Melody of 1929*, *Whoopee!*, *Babes in Arms*, *The Toast of New Orleans*, *Million Dollar Mermaid*, *Grease* and others, be a very different book? In some ways we think yes, in others no. Films like the latter would tell us a great deal about the conventions of the genre, would be equally susceptible to ideological analysis, but would perhaps be less rewarding from the viewpoint of aesthetic density and innovation. However, it may be that even here there would be surprises. The Jolson films, for instance, on which we did choose to focus, are not usually regarded, even by *aficionados* of the musical, as approaching significant art, yet close examination has made us feel otherwise, and certainly reveals films surprisingly concerned with meditating a series of questions about the relation of art to life.

Our own criteria of representativeness and aesthetic density have allowed us to write about what we find most interesting, to demonstrate the genre in its most complex workings, and also to escape where we want to from the straitjacket of a choice determined solely by commercial popularity. Though most of the films we write about were very popular – with only *Summer Holiday*, *It's Always Fair Weather*, *On a Clear Day You Can See Forever* and *Hair* falling outside the category of mass successes – we wished not to be wholly bound by a procedure that would force us to disregard that very real phenomenon, the important film under-appreciated in its own time which, in retrospect, is seen to be a major and representative work. In looking at the films we have chosen from the vantage point of greatest intellectual reward, we have tried to preserve a double perspective; both to ask in what terms the film was made and first viewed, and to ask in what other terms a later audience and criticism might view it. In keeping with the same principle, we have used where we feel appropriate the various insights of history, sociology, psychology and general cultural study and, of course, the various formulations of modern film theory (*auteurism*, genre study, structuralism, psychoanalysis and ideological deconstruction). Whenever an approach has seemed relevant and productive, likely to explain the feelings of pleasure we and so many other viewers have had from these films, we have put it to use.

2

Reading a musical –
Easter Parade (1948)

The voice of the genre

This chapter, the most detailed reading of a musical in the book, is designed to act as a bridge between the general principles that have just been outlined and the readings of particular films that follow. Before we move to necessarily more economic procedures, it attempts to suggest something of the full complexity with which musicals may be structured, especially at the less obvious levels.

The choice of *Easter Parade* (Charles Walters, MGM, 1948) was dictated by a question we asked ourselves early in the writing of this book: which of all the musicals we found interesting would we find it hardest to write about? Which seemed to offer in its cinematic pleasures the least foothold for the analyst? The answer we came up with was *Easter Parade*, a highly popular film, familiar to many viewers both from the cinema and from repeated showings on TV; a film never written about analytically, yet widely enjoyed, even loved, and in this combination of the known, but unarticulated and therefore in some sense not known, very representative of the Hollywood musical.

Though every film bears the pressure of its social context, still it is a film where such traces are difficult to see, and it certainly has no overt social problematic inscribed in it as, say, *Gold Diggers of 1933* has with its Depression content. Neither is it a clear candidate for the kind of revelation of a shadowy undertext, either consciously put there or unconsciously manifested, such as the one Andrew Britton uncovers in *Meet Me in St Louis*. Nor is it comparable in strong narrative and character-psychological interest to a film like *On A Clear Day You Can See Forever*. On the last point, *Easter Parade* with its *sixteen* different numbers – where many major musicals have as few as four or five – hardly has the narrative space for complicated plot developments or psychological nuances. In fact it seems to consist most fundamentally of its songs and dances. So if it is anything more than a happy ragbag of Irving Berlin tunes, if it develops coherent meanings and pleasures, it would seem that a great deal must be carried by the semiotics of the song and dance performances of its stars and the way these are integrated into the pattern of the whole film.

Another foothold that *Easter Parade* fails to offer is the security of a major author. Unlike its predecessors in 1948 from the Freed Unit, Mamoulian's *Summer Holiday* and Minnelli's *The Pirate*, it cannot with conviction be fitted into a discourse based on an author's style and thematics. Charles Walters was a successful director of musicals, but not even the most extreme *auteurist* seems ever to have been tempted to construct a theory of his idiosyncratic authorial voice. Thus *Easter Parade* reminds us in a salutary way of what is often forgotten when dealing with musicals by exceptionally strong stylists like Minnelli and Lubitsch, that the musical is the most diverse, heterogeneous and collaborative of genres. To give an instance: in *Easter Parade* the dance numbers were divided between Walters and Robert Alton, an equally notable choreographer, while – as in any Astaire film – the star's own dancing was in large part self-designed. And *Sheer Accident* might be given an important credit too as co-author, in that the last-minute, enforced substitution of Astaire for Gene Kelly could not but substantially alter the film's meanings. Lastly, another part-authorial factor is highlighted when the titles present the film as 'Irving Berlin's *Easter Parade*', suggesting the primacy of the songs for both producers and audience. Indeed, because *Easter Parade* – like such films as *An American in Paris* (based on the Gershwins' songs) and *At Long Last Love* (on Cole Porter's) – is built around a large number of pre-existing songs that did not originate in a single narrative, its narrative possibilities are to an interesting degree determined by the songs rather than the other way round. Such heterogeneous origins do not necessarily produce incoherence, but the kinds of coherence produced are unlikely to be quite those of the most intricately narrativised and (relatively) homogeneously produced musicals.

Indeed, we might risk the hyperbole that in *Easter Parade*, with its excess of numbers, its accentuated play on star personae, the amount of meaning conveyed through the conventions of the different styles of song and dance in which its characters perform, it is the musical genre itself which speaks, even more clearly than in the more personally inflected films of Minnelli, Lubitsch and others. This is what makes it so interesting to analyse, and also so difficult, for while it is usually stated as a truism that the numbers are the real centre of a musical, commentators really tend to be much happier the closer musicals approach ordinary narrative.

Narrative, star personae, deep reading

The most obvious sources of pleasure in *Easter Parade* are of course the Berlin songs, the personalities of Astaire and Garland (together for the only time), and, to a lesser extent, those of Ann Miller, Peter Lawford and the comical Jules Munshin, the choreography and the nostalgic costumes and décor of 'golden age' pre-first world war New York. Few people would come away feeling that narrative complexities rivalled these as primary causes of their satisfaction. This does not, however, mean that the narrative is non-existent or without significance. Like most classical Hollywood films it is full of artful rhymes and parallels and its story of an ageing dancer's professional and emotional death when his partner leaves him and his subsequent 'resurrection' through the young woman he teaches to dance, reminds us that the most common love-story plots of musicals have their far distant basis in myth and ritual. In this film such origins are nearer than in most, with ritual overtly gestured at in the title, and the Greek myth of Pygmalion and Galatea (reworked again in *My Fair Lady*) clearly active when you think about it. Astaire (Pygmalion) fashions a dummy (Galatea/Garland) as his partner and she comes to life. Of course various intricacies are added to this base. *She* refashions him; a previously transformed statue Nadine Hale (Ann Miller), is added to the story, her leaving precipitating Don Hewes' search for a new partner, but also inhibiting it as she continues to haunt him professionally and emotionally; and there is also the presence of Johnny Harrow (Peter Lawford), Don's friend who is in love with Hannah Brown (Garland), so that we get that basic situation of hundreds of musical comedy plots where the difficult erotic economy of two men and one woman has to be resolved, in this case by the union of the minor figures played by Miller and Lawford.

Allusive, then, and reverberative the narrative may be, but it is still in ordinary terms scanty, until we see that its design depends less on cause and effect and linear inventiveness than on a conceptual and structural virtuosity which invents spatial structures, many of them closely linked to the film's title image, the *Easter Parade* – signifying renewal and innocence on the one hand and, more mundanely, on the other, fashion, modishness and display. These ideas are particularly embodied in the songs and dances which are structured in relation to each other within the film, even where they have their origin outside it, Irving Berlin numbers that have been selected and specifically *re*designed for their capacity to contribute to the story. For instance, the number 'Shakin' the blues away' signifies certain things as a song divorced from any film context. Worked into *Easter Parade*'s network of meanings, it takes on certain other meanings, many of them quite distinct from those generated when Doris Day (instead of Ann Miller) sings it in *Love Me Or Leave Me*. Placed within the plotline of the story about a performer's metamorphosis from a sophisticated, sexually vulnerable narcissist into a more 'natural' self, they reflect and comment on alternative styles of living: to give the most polar instances, the life of sophistication and excitement exemplified by Nadine set against the creative humility of Hannah. The action is made to flow out of these numbers not just in simple chronological structures, but in alternative ways, so that, for instance, 'Drum crazy' is introduced at the start not so much to point to Don's frame of mind at that moment in his life as to reveal something hidden in him. The number delineates a potentiality in him and prepares the way for his eventual union with Hannah rather than Nadine. The point is that it is there, in the song and dance, that the most intense meanings are registered. If you look for them primarily in the elliptical non-musical narrative, thinking of the numbers as pure spectacle (which they clearly cannot be since they employ referential signs), you will be disappointed.

The title *Easter Parade* can, then, be seen as an overarching image which the numbers, even more than the narrative, explain. In accordance with this, the film, which is full of small-scale symmetries and rhymes, is also on the largest scale symmetrical. By the time it ends, the meanings of the image have been resolved through the intervention of the numbers, so that when the Easter motif is reprised, the mythic sense of revelation connected with Easter, dimly present throughout the film, coincides with the surface psychological and theatrical success-story resolutions. There are two Easter Parades: the first, near the beginning, in 1912, shows Nadine as the star of the procession; the second, in 1913, shows her place taken by Hannah.

The Irving Berlin numbers of course rely heavily on the idiosyncratic interpretations of Astaire, Garland and Miller. As always, the values stars bring to Hollywood films through the multi-faceted forces of their personae, are dominant in character construction, even more so here with this film's lack of interest in discursive complexity. If Don Hewes had been, as originally planned, Gene Kelly, things would have been altered by the different force of Kelly's persona. As it is, the radical difference in Astaire's is played upon to produce meanings that could not possibly be present in a Kelly film. To be more precise we should be referring to Astaire's persona in the 1940s, which tends to be more vulnerable than in the 1930s, with the loss of Ginger Rogers and the search for a new partner (Rita Hayworth, Joan Fontaine, etc.) common knowledge to every film fan and intriguingly built into the plots of some of his films.

The film also relies on a duality in the Astaire image that runs through his films right from the thirties to the fifties. Debonair, sophisticated, discreetly tyrannical on the one hand, and impish, anarchic, flexible on the other. Equally it also depends on the small-town girl-next-door qualities of the early, untraumatised Judy Garland, in particular, here, still not too far distant from 'Over the rainbow', qualities of waif-like innocence, vulnerability and warmth, qualities very different from the gloss of Ann Miller's supremely bodily presence.

But in *Easter Parade* there is a further twist to the Astaire role to be equally developed in other films as he ages into the 1950s. Much older than Kelly, a young man to Garland's young woman when he stars with her in *For Me and My Gal* (1942) and *The Pirate* (1948), Astaire is here given a paternal function so that he is, for Hannah and the audience, both father and lover. In the real world, forty-nine (and, if 'ageless' never looking exactly younger than that) to Garland's twenty-six, Astaire's age allows the film to play with a mock crisis. Is he past it? Did he really 'die' when Ginger Rogers left? Such concerns merge effortlessly into those surrounding the character Don Hewes and his relationship with Hannah Brown and Nadine Hale, till the double focus seems a single one.

Easter Parade is at bottom a renewal myth. Of course, its Easter is a very secularised version of the prototype, like Christmas in *Meet Me in St Louis*, stripped of its formal religious resonances so that what is left is a vague aureole of communal and seasonal feeling as meaning shifts from the religious to the secular sphere. Its resurrections are of feeling and attitude as well as worldly success, its modes those of urban musical comedy. But the basic pattern announced by the title is strikingly embodied in the ageing male redeemed by a young woman connected with the pastoral world, and the overarching image of the metropolis filled with a parade in which people wear new clothes and bonnets decorated with flowers, like the earth apparelled in new clothes in traditional poetic imagery.

Of course, by no means every musical gestures so openly towards the meanings of ritual and myth, so that in this respect *Easter Parade* might be thought untypical, especially of the many musicals whose values seem completely urban and contemporary. But this is not really so. The hundreds of musicals we have watched reveal basic patterns, not only in their conventions of song and dance, but in their plots and concerns. These are almost invariably in the classical musical some variant of what is called by critics the 'New Comedy', the basic comic plot movement handed down from Plautus and Terence in Rome to the Renaissance and then later bourgeois comedy, in which the heterosexual couple overcome obstacles to their union. The variation on such basic patterns over more than two thousand years of western art is the subject of the literary critic Northrop Frye's great book *The Anatomy of Criticism*. Very often in the musical such plots are connected to stories of theatrical success, the rise of performers from nothing to stardom, or their fall and re-emergence (*Easter Parade* cunningly includes both), and the successful putting on of a show. Such 'backstage' materials are unique to the musical, but many other aspects are not, and a look at Northrop Frye will convince the reader that many of the concerns of the musical are contemporary inflections of the traditional ones of western narrative and dramatic comedy, just as the stock characters of musical comedy are contemporary versions of traditional types representing basic psychological and moral positions.

This does not, of course, mean that those who made most musicals thought of Fred Astaire in the context of Roman comedy or of his union with Rita Hayworth, say, at the end of *You Were Never Lovelier* in terms of fertility patterns. The makers will have produced what seemed 'right' to them in the immediate traditions in which they wrote. If questioned about an effect, they would probably have said 'It feels right' and left it at that. But of course 'It feels right' is a statement of effect that presupposes unspoken causes. Those inclined to think any other explanation pretentious have only to ask *why* does it 'feel right?' to bring back the necessity of the more radical explanations which are the business of the analyst. And it would be, on reflection, very strange if such explanations – whether biased towards the aesthetic, the ideological or the psychoanalytical – proved altogether different to those we give to the kinds of 'high' cultural products to which it seems natural to give 'deep readings'.

'Deep readings' of *Easter Parade* might imply three different things. First, the recovery of basic patterns underlying its story, in this case, as we have suggested, mythic and ritual ones, attached to the basic pattern of New Comedy. Such elements may be seen as also particularly susceptible to psychoanalytic readings. Second, tracing the multiple codes of meaning that intersect in the film – e.g. what the characters say, look like, wear, how they dance and sing, the functions of décor, places, objects in the film, etc – and how these are attached to and in part produce the oppositions and relationships that generate the meanings of the story. Finally, there is a third kind of deeper structuring to be revealed, what has been referred to in the previous chapter as 'ideology', the way in which the film naturalises certain assumptions, presenting a certain view of the world and cancelling others. Our concern with *Easter Parade* crosses all three levels, but is particularly addressed to the second, since at this point in the book our main project is to show how musicals make their meanings and less to question the 'progressiveness' or 'regressiveness' of such meanings from the standpoint of a particular politico-philosophical critique.

If even a few of the ramifications opened up by these different levels of approach are pursued, it will be obvious that rather than stretching the film to fit a long chapter, a discussion that started out with the intention of being exhaustive will in fact be highly selective. Accepting this, what we have done is at least to gesture towards comprehensiveness by bringing into our description of the film *all* of its numbers, and by giving them priority over the narrative – a priority they clearly have in the film – in our demonstration of the way the film produces at least some of its meanings.

Ideology

But as we scrutinise form we shall consider its ideological elements: the way in which the patterns, colours, shapes, music, dance and narrative are made – consciously or unconsciously – to reinforce, however discreetly in parts, a set of assumptions about life, a point of view that is not merely the film's but that also of a sizeable proportion of a whole society. As Terry Eagleton points out,

> It is far more subtle, pervasive and unconscious than a set of explicit doctrines: it is the very medium in which I 'live out' my relation to society, the realm of signs and social practices which binds me to the social structure and lends me a sense of coherent purpose and identity. Ideology in this sense may include the act of going to church, of casting a vote, of letting women pass first through doors . . .

Yet, as Eagleton goes on to argue, Althusser's view of ideology, which the quoted paragraph in some senses summarises, as something consistent, all-embracing and unproblematical, has in recent years been increasingly under challenge. We are careful ourselves, though to a large extent inspired by Althusser's overridingly helpful insights, constantly to note the contradictions and tensions developing through the interaction of art and life.

Ideology in this sense is, therefore, clearly distinct from the range of themes around which the narrative of a film may be organized. Some films (say Luis Buñuel's *Viridiana*) seem to recognise more fully than others the way ideology underpins social behaviour, and the thrust of the film is towards exposing how ideology creates social meanings. Others, like *Easter Parade*, not nearly as implicitly polemical, while ignoring ideology as a theme, seem to reflect even so the frustrations as well as the celebrations of a culture's way of seeing, organising and labelling a social structure's created realities.

While it may not, at a deep level, seriously question, as *Viridiana* emphatically does, the roles men and women are expected to play both in private and in public, *Easter Parade* frequently shows the struggles of characters fitting into their ideological roles. Expected to be courteous, confident, dominant, concerned primarily with the serious issues of life, men in this film sometimes do display these qualities, but at other times strain to live up to stereotype. Don Hewes has a wilder, anarchic self hidden beneath the ideological exterior; while Johnny, too, seems keener on playing the silly ass than on making a conventional success of himself.

The same tensions apply to the women in the film. Ideologically, the film is consistent with offscreen realities in denying them positions of economic power. Women with talent are allowed to display it – as Nadine and Hannah clearly do – but whatever gifts they possess are seen, from one point of view, as best governed by men, since vanity or fragility – venerable ideologically-motivated attributes traditionally imposed on women – can sometimes jeopardise or make more vulnerable their chances of success.

And yet in Nadine's excess of vanity there is an element of rebellion and self-sufficiency which counteracts male dominance; while in Hannah's trials and ordeals in her relationship with Don Hewes the film seems to be undermining the very image of male ascendancy that elsewhere it seeks to promote. Sometimes, too, such films may surprise us by bursting the bounds of their ideological constraints, as where here in *Easter Parade*, suddenly, towards the end, the idea of sexual equality is taken up with unexpected seriousness by allowing Hannah to assume the traditional male role of dominance over Don, something presented to the audience without irony as pleasurable and natural.

While not consciously interrogating the ideological categories into which men and women are slotted, while remaining tolerant of associations between women and, say, flowers and primary colours in dress, or men and, say, action, rationality and business acumen in careers, while not overtly questioning such institutions as marriage or the economic structures of capitalism, and while projecting the image of a white, middle-class world as an ideal of normality, *Easter Parade* nevertheless invariably exposes the inconsistencies and complications of such ideological patterns and assumptions, however deeply ingrained they may be, however utopian they may seem.

A route map of Easter Parade

Number 1   'Happy Easter' (Sung by Don as he shops for flowers and a hat for Nadine, with some interpolations from other characters.)

Number 2 — 'Drum Crazy' (Sung and danced by Don in the toyshop as he wins the toy rabbit he wants to buy away from a small boy.)

Narrative segment 1 — Don arrives with gifts at Nadine's. She breaks the news that she is leaving to go solo. He turns down her idea that he could dance with someone else. (*Motif of Don's dependence on Nadine; motif of the couple versus the solo performer.*)

Number 3 — 'It Only Happens When I Dance With You' (First version, sung by Don and Nadine, as Don tries to persuade her to stay.)

Narrative segment 2 — Johnny enters: Don leaves angrily. Nadine tells Johnny that she has split with Don because of him. (*Motif of Nadine's desire for Johnny and his resistance*). At a homely Italian restaurant bar Don drinks and talks to Mike the barman. When Johnny arrives Don claims that he could teach any girl to dance like Nadine. He approaches one of the chorus-line – Hannah. (*Motif of the Pygmalion myth.*)

Number 4 — 'I wish I was in Michigan again down on the farm' (Sung by Hannah to the restaurant audience.)

Narrative segment 3 — On *Easter Sunday* Don waits to rehearse Hannah, regretting his impetuosity of the night before. Obliged to keep his word because she has given up her job, he rehearses her disastrously. When he acts out desire in his dancing, Hannah momentarily thinks it is real. (*Motif of Hannah's love for Don.*) Later, during the Easter Parade, they see Nadine, but Don does not tell her who she is. Hannah says 'Isn't she wonderful!' (*Motif of Hannah's inferiority to Nadine.*) Don promises that Hannah will take her place and put Nadine's 'nose out of joint'. Taking Hannah shopping he chooses for her, overriding all her preferences and announcing 'There is no more Hannah Brown! There is only Juanita!' (*Motif of his repression of Hannah's true self both as person and performer.*) When Hannah protests, he makes her take a test to see if she is the type who turns men's heads on the streets. She surprises him by doing so, with a grotesque expression that he cannot see.

Number 5 — Dance (Don and Hannah/Juanita's stage debut in the Nadine and Hewes style, is a comedy of her dancing errors.)

Narrative segment 4	Johnny meets Nadine for dinner in the restaurant presided over by François. She is pushy about marriage and he is evasive. (*Motif of Johnny as the 'Professor'.*) Johnny hopes to reconcile Don and Nadine and leaves the two together when Don arrives. Nadine resists Don's approaches and says he has made her look ridiculous by training his 'seamstress' to be a poor copy of her. Don realises she is right and rushes off. (*Motif of meals and restaurant and the joke of François' exasperation with the diners who never get round to eating because of their emotional problems.*) By contrast, Hannah is seen paying for a meal at a drugstore. The rain prevents her from walking and Johnny tries to pick her up. (*Motif of Johnny's unsuccessful love for Hannah.*)
Number 6	'I'm just a fella' (Sung by Johnny to Hannah and then by Hannah to Johnny.)
Narrative segment 5	Hannah, escaping from Johnny, arrives late for rehearsal. Don tells her – against her protests that the decision was his – 'You've been trying to be something else'. He decides that 'There is no more Juanita! From now on you're just plain Hannah Brown!'
Number 7	'I love the piano' (Sung by Hannah for Don, then danced by Hannah and Don. Begun in rehearsal/ended in performance.)
Number 8	'Snooky Ookums' (Sung by Hannah and Don in performance.)
Number 9	'Ragtime violin' (Sung by Don, danced by Hannah and Don in performance.)
Number 10	'When the midnight choo-choo leaves for Alabam' (Sung and danced by Don and Hannah as an audition for the Ziegfeld Follies.)
Narrative segment 6	Don and Hannah are about to be offered contracts by Ziegfeld, but Nadine arrives to announce that it is her show. Hannah recognises her from the Easter Parade and asks Don if he was in love with her. He does not answer clearly and Hannah goes off. As she calls a taxi, Johnny arrives and she agrees to a dinner date. Later Don comes to Hannah's hotel room to tell her that he has refused the contract – 'It's got to be all ours – we're not sharing it with anybody'. Johnny arrives for his date with Hannah and Don looks unhappy. (*Motif of Don's unacknowledged feeling for Hannah.*) In the same

restaurant as in narrative segment 4 Hannah and Johnny talk about Don. Hannah confesses her love and laments that Don's interest in her is 'strictly business'. Johnny suggests to her that Don is still in love with Nadine and declares his own love. Earlier in the scene, when they are wondering what to order, François demonstrates his famous *Salade François*, but again the diners leave without eating. Meanwhile Don, dressed rather dingily and looking defeated, goes into the foyer of the Follies and gazes at Nadine's portrait.

Number 11	'Shakin' the blues away' (Nadine sings and dances solo, with offstage chorus, for the Follies.)
Narrative segment 7	Don, who has been watching her, leaves. Johnny receives a phone call from Hannah who is worried about Don's depression at the Follies' success. Don arrives with the news that Dillingham has signed them. Hannah reminds him that they will be opening a year after they first met and of his promise to take her to the Parade. Don suggests a celebratory dinner and asks her to pick him up at his apartment. When she arrives it seems he has planned a romantic meal, but it turns out he only wants to talk about work. Hannah angrily tells him he is just 'a pair of dancing shoes'. He kisses her. Looking around the apartment Hannah sees the sheet music of the Nadine and Hewes hit 'It only happens when I dance with you'.
Number 12	'It only happens when I dance with you' (Second version, sung by Hannah to Don.)
Narrative segment 8	Don very obliquely declares his love. (*Motif of Don's vacillation.*) Later, the opening night of Dillingham's revue.
Number 13	'Steppin' out' (Sung and danced by Don with Creole men and women dancers in a New Orleans honkytonk setting for the Dillingham show.)
Narrative segment 9	Essie (Nadine's maid) who has been sent to spy, tells Nadine that Don's number was not a success. (*Motif of Nadine's jealousy.*)
Number 14	'A couple of swells' (Sung and danced by Hannah and Don for Dillingham's show.)
Narrative segment 10	Hannah and Don receive congratulations. Hannah asks Don to take her to the restaurant bar where they first met, but Don

has made a reservation at the Follies. Essie tells Nadine that Hannah is a failure. Later Don and Hannah enter the Roof Garden to applause which upsets Nadine.

Number 15 'The girl on a magazine cover' (Male singer with a series of tableaux. Then Nadine dances with a chorus line of men.)

Narrative segment 11 Nadine forces Don to dance publicly with her. Hannah watches and leaves abruptly.

Number 16 'It only happens when I dance with you' (Third version, danced by Nadine and Don for the roof-top audience.)

Narrative segment 12 Don runs after Hannah. Hannah goes to the restaurant bar where she talks to Mike.

Number 17 'Better luck next time' (Sung by Hannah to Mike.)

Narrative segment 13 Don catches up with Hannah at her hotel where she accuses him of being in love with Nadine and of using her to spite his former partner. Don admits it, but says that he has changed. 'How was I to know you'd be the most wonderful girl in the world?' Hannah has locked him out of her room but, moved by what he says, opens the door. Don, however, has gone, moved along by a suspicious house detective. She thinks he does not care for her, and Don is unaware of her softening. A little later Johnny visits Hannah and selflessly encourages her to take the initiative with Don. He himself accepts that his fate is to be with Nadine, and rings her to tell her to prepare for the Parade. Next morning, as Don is dressing, various gifts arrive – flowers, a hat, an easter egg, a live white rabbit – followed by Hannah who hurries him up, reminding him of their date.

Number 18 'Easter Parade' (Sung by Hannah and danced by Don and Hannah in Don's apartment. Then sung by Don and then, lastly, by an offscreen chorus, in the Easter Parade itself.)

The numbers

'Happy Easter' and 'Drum Crazy': (man about town as Pied Piper)
The opening asserts the film's formal priorities by conveying almost all its initial information through the numbers, with only a brief narrative moment when Don arrives at Nadine's interrupting the musicalised flow of

the first three numbers – 'Happy Easter', 'Drum Crazy' and 'It only happens when I dance with you'. It also introduces Don Hewes on his own as he tours the shops to buy Easter gifts for his 'honey'. The juxtaposition of the first two numbers establishes a basic duality in Don's character that much of the rest of the film will play on. The first, 'Happy Easter', shows him as the perfectly adjusted man about town, very much at home in what becomes identified later in the film as Nadine's milieu of expensive fashion. His ease – which, retrospectively, becomes slightly ironised when Nadine announces she is leaving him – is the same whether greeting passers-by or deciding which of the mannequins wears the right hat for Nadine. He is very much the epitome of the image of Astaire abstracted in the audience's memory from a dozen films; finely but not flashily dressed, urbane, at home in any situation. This image will soon be a little undermined since, rightly or wrongly, Nadine is about to do the unthinkable, abandon him, but at the beginning it is one the audience knows well and (like Don) feels comfortable with. It is the second number that is more surprising. 'Drum Crazy' seems completely outside that register as it releases more anarchic impulses, a curious drama that amounts to a contest between two wilful children: in one corner a little Lord Fauntleroy of about nine, and in the other a more determined and cunning child of forty-nine. This clash of wills focuses on the desire of each for a large toy Easter bunny. Clearly Don wants it as a gift to signify his love for Nadine, but at a figurative level (clarified by Nadine's collection of pets that she 'wears' with various outfits), it draws attention to the fact that he is somewhat in the grip of convention and lifeless fashion. It is appropriate therefore that when by the end of the film he has been released from too great an immersion in this world, his desire for the toy rabbit is symmetrically rhymed by the gift of a living Easter rabbit from Hannah.

With the laws of condensation that operate in the dreamlike world of numbers, the toy rabbit and Don's battle with the child can generate opposite meanings, not bound by laws of contradiction. On the one hand it is an infantile battle for a silly object, but on the other it positively releases elements of the child who should be father to the man. Cheating the real child, Don revels in his own recaptured childishness. In some ways the number recalls Kelly's 'I got rhythm' number in *An American in Paris*, with the grown man entertaining children. But whereas the Kelly number is all sentiment, Astaire has something of the malice of a Pied Piper as he leads the child into a military routine the end of which is immobility and defeat. Don, as the piper, calls the tune, whisking the rabbit away from the spellbound victim. Throughout the number Don is the master of improvisation, capable of magical metamorphoses, as when drumsticks become flutes at his touch. For all its virtues, the elegant self of the opening number and the great dance duo 'Nadine & Hewes', may have forgotten what is here so suddenly released.

'It only happens when I dance with you' (the spectre of Nadine)

Reprised not only once but twice, this is the most extended example of a number carrying meanings given only shorthand treatment in the narrative. First danced by Don and Nadine as he tries to prevent her going solo; then sung by Hannah and inspiring an indirect declaration of love from Don; its final appearance is a disruptive use by Nadine when she persuades Don to dance with her again, in front of Hannah. Positively embodying the metaphoric equivalence that binds together love-making and dancing in so many films, it is also associated with more troubled feelings – with Don's dependence on Nadine, his loss of her, the question of whether Hannah can replace her, and Nadine's continuing power over him.

Though the lyrics and music taken on their own are unproblematically affirmative, different dramatic contexts problematise them. The first version is in fact a disruptive dance of failure by Astaire in which Don tries to entice Nadine back into the world of his dancing and in which she continually refuses the dance. Hannah's version of the number also has troubling elements. Though Nadine is not literally present as on the first occasion, her presence haunts this one. From one point of view indeed the reiterated number belies the sentiment of its lyrics and becomes a series of representations of Nadine's blocking of the relationship between Don and Hannah. Here her spectre is raised when Hannah looks at a piece of sheet music which has her portrait with Don on the cover and remarks 'She's very beautiful'. Although he has just kissed her, Don spends half the number facing away from her, meditating. His eventual declaration, in reply to Hannah's vulnerable self-doubting look, is passive and oblique – 'Why didn't you tell me I was in love with you?'

At the third appearance of the number Don has insisted on celebrating his and Hannah's success for Dillingham by going to see Nadine perform, a choice which testifies to Nadine's power. While the lyrics assert that dancing and lovemaking are one ('That trip to heaven till the dance is through'), Nadine's forcing Don to dance publicly with her in front of Hannah denies this. The big-band sophisticated swing version of the number that they perform is full of the 'mirror' steps that denote complete emotional unity between the partners, but Nadine's reasons for dancing are purely to reassert her own stellar and erotic predominance over Hannah.

'I wish I was in Michigan' and 'Better luck next time': (a new-fashioned old-fashioned girl)

The narrative makes no attempt to establish biographical information of even the most rudimentary kind about Hannah Brown. Like most characters in most musicals she has an archetypal outline which the richness of a star persona fills in with kinesic particularity and emotional density. Like Vera-Ellen as Ivy Smith in *On The Town* and Ruby Keeler as Peggy Sawyer in *42nd Street*, Hannah Brown is the unspoiled girl trying to make it on Broadway, fusing urban and pastoral values. Complexity arises when, within this outline, are traced various aspects of Judy Garland known from other films – the ubiquitous qualities particularly associated with her that Dyer defines as 'transparency' and 'intensity'; the values of vaudeville from 'Be a clown' at the end of *The Pirate* (released just before *Easter Parade*); the innocence and freshness of Esther Smith in *Meet Me in St Louis* and, before that, Dorothy in *The Wizard of Oz*.

Though the narrative does not tell us where Hannah is from, *she* does in her first song, 'I wish I was in Michigan again, down on the farm'. If this is not literally true, it has an important figurative truth that links her to all the positive associations of small-town life in American mythology (see chapter 6). It is important to the renewal-cycle underpinnings of the narrative that Hannah has this relation not only to small-town culture (viewed nostalgically as unalienated), but to Nature itself, the farm.

But these values are not given in a simple form. They are negotiated through the urbane mode and attitudes of her performance. This is immediately apparent in the emblematic white pinafore she puts on over her pink chorus girl costume (a colour scheme that will be symmetrically rhymed with the white and pink she wears for the final Parade). The pinafore proclaims homely values, but, as comically overt iconography, it underlines an unmistakable self-consciousness. The nostalgia of the number is not undermined by the comedy, but complicated as it is mediated through comic effects (e.g. the rhymes 'wish again/Michigan' and 'I miss the rooster/The one that used to/Wake me up at 4 am'). Whereas in 'Better luck next time' (below) the young Garland's primary quality of 'transparency' operates relatively straightforwardly on a number of basic pathos, here it acts upon comic nostalgia and nostalgic comedy. She means what she says, but the way that she says it is far from simple. In this way the dichotomies invoked – pastoral (the farm) versus urban ('Your great big city') and nature versus art – are already complicated in the act of expression. Hannah, though committed in memory to the country, is committed by presence to the city, thus acting out for the audience their relation to the ideal of the agrarian republic.

Her song is not an item of simple feeling, but one of sophisticated feeling recalling simple feeling.

Various physical elements embody and extend what the lyrics say. For example the combination of her sophisticatedly naive costume with the rather unexpectedly formal dress of the orchestra. Moving round as she sings, she makes contact with the small interior audience, even sitting on a table belonging to a middle-aged couple. Significantly, she is first seen performing in an area where there is no demarcation between performer and audience, establishing an image she retains even when she ascends to the proscenium stages of Broadway. Hannah as performer therefore seems to break down the divisions between theatre and life, between role-playing and sincerity. We know she is acting, but yet in another sense she does not seem to be. In her the theatre seems to be returned to the community as she acts not to an abstract audience but one that she seems to know individual by individual. She is 'natural' rather than artificial, but the number consciously plays with the paradox that the natural is embodied by artifice – the kind of self-consciousness found in many musicals, but particularly apt here.

Proximity is not only extended to the interior audience but to a fellow artist as she puts her arm round the trombonist, an image of partnership that will play in various ways through the film against Nadine's values of solo display. Together they improvise a jazzy, sophisticated version of the song, again a highly complex mediation between urban forms and pastoral nostalgia. The significance of this is verbally clarified later on (narrative segment 6) when Don says to Hannah: 'Some people dream of a little farm to settle down on, a spot all of their own. That's what we want, only our spot's on a marquee – Hannah and Hewes in blazing lights!' In the mythic workings of the musical Broadway and Michigan can be one!

'I wish I was in Michigan' contains all the elements of the Garland persona as it is modulated into Hannah Brown, except one, her capacity for deep emotion. This aspect is foregrounded in the later part of the narrative as Don fails to respond adequately to her feelings. 'Better luck next time', like Hannah's version of 'It only happens', is an address to a character within the film, but it becomes very much an occasion for interior thoughts and, like the other number, is visually constructed so that she both sings to the character and is face to face with the audience, giving the impression that she is speaking straight to them – a feature of the use of Garland in many films. When she starts to sing, the intimately approaching camera cuts Mike the barman out of the frame for the duration of the number, until its close when she drops forward crying and the camera gently retreats to show Mike still listening. Apart from the movements at the beginning and end, the frame is simply static for the whole number, a medium close-up of Hannah's face and shoulders. Since the restaurant background is defocused, there are no objects to vie for attention with the minute facial kinesics that register her emotion or her single rapt action of running her fingers round the edge of a glass. The one complicating element is her costume which, for this most emotionally open and vulnerable moment, is the most sophisticated that she wears in the whole film, a dark green gown with emerald earrings and a pendant. Here the costume exists in a more oblique relation to her mood than as its mirror. Its sophistication is a sign not only that she has crossed into Don's world, but that she has attained outward polish without losing her own values. Additionally, as befits her role in the pastoral renewal myth, the colour symbolism distantly associates Hannah with her origins in nature. Green, white and of course brown predominate in her costumes as against the fiery reds and oranges of Nadine's.

The number is also part of the film's bringing together of two contradictory ideas of love which it manages to hold in a paradoxical unity. The cue for Hannah's song is Mike quoting:

> For every rose that withers and dies,
> Another blooms in its stead.
> A new love waits to open its eyes
> After the old one is dead.

To which Hannah replies

> I'd like a new lucky day, that would be nice.
> But this comes just once in a lifetime, not twice.

For Hannah love is a unique, unrepeatable phenomenon and she asserts the fantasy of one first and lasting love in the face of Mike's pragmatism. But for Don, who has been in love with Nadine and 'danced with dozens of others the whole night through', love is recurrence, reawakening, a proving of the truth of the words on the sampler. The close of the film manages an agile feat of paradoxical wish-fulfilment when it brings together these mutually exclusive categories, also presented as 'male' and 'female' views of romance.

'I'm just a fella, a fella with an umbrella' (Johnny: 'I've got to take an old Psychology exam'. Don: 'You'll flunk it')

At first glance Peter Lawford's role in the film looks rather insipid, like his bland romantic roles in films like *Royal Wedding* and *The Boy From Barnardo's*, and although he is clearly the more handsome of the two, he, in the role of Johnny Harrow, lags well behind Don Hewes as a serious lover. Even so, there are some interesting implications to his involvement with the other characters: Nadine's attraction to him; his failure to woo Hannah away from Don; and his relationship with his closest friend, Don. Johnny's single number draws together all these strands of interest.

Johnny's appeal for Nadine is equivocal. On the one hand, she presumably finds his good looks more compelling than Astaire's ageing and rather irregular features. On the other hand, not being a dancer, or anything very much except a habitué of the evanescent world of restaurants, swanky cars and fur coats, he can at once be a mirror for her narcissism and an echo for her status as star performer. This being so, he can eventually be cast in the role of unquestioning idolator that vain women like Nadine expect their lovers to be (though, to be fair, he does resist his fate for most of the narrative). Don is no use to Nadine because he takes himself too seriously, is essentially her rival and even her superior, certainly attempting to dominate her as he signs contracts on her behalf. By contrast it would seem that Johnny is the perfect partner (whether he knows it or not) for the egocentric Nadine, ready to worship at the altar of her beauty and creative talents. But, in any case, the boyish, immature lover has no real chance with a woman bent in some complex way on finding a partner who may remind her of her father. Hannah's quest for an older man is clearly a major obstacle for Johnny and he soon discovers that she can only think of him as a brother. However, his gentleness, coupled with an evident rootlessness and lack of purpose, do arouse sympathetic feelings in Hannah.

There are many traces of Don in Johnny's personality – one of the many sets of parallelisms and oppositions between the main characters – especially in his clumsy attempt to impose himself on Hannah. Johnny indeed sometimes looks like an inferior version of Don, a social and ideological husk deprived of inner qualities. Like Don, Johnny is also going through a process of metamorphosis, only instead of moving from one professional state and emotional condition to another, he moves from one unsatisfactory University degree course to another (from law to psychology to medicine) and is nicknamed by Don, who cannot, any more than the audience, take Johnny as a student seriously, 'Professor'. Don, of course, is the true 'Professor' in the old jazz sense of musical maestro. Johnny mirrors at a superficial level Don's search for himself, but Don's progress is marked by his partnership with Hannah who offers him a chance to find the sources of fulfilment, while Johnny's retardment is symbolised by his eventual submission to Nadine. These and other issues are given expression through the 'Fella with an umbrella' number.

From the slightly suffocating gentility of a restaurant we switch to a street and find Hannah leaving a drugstore where her lunch has consisted of a lowly roast beef sandwich. At least there is some sustenance in plain food. In a sort of prefiguration of Buñuel's *The Discreet Charm of the Bourgeoisie* none of the four major characters that we see at the smart restaurant is ever capable of starting a meal, so busy are they trying to cope with their problems.

It begins to pour with rain. A country girl takes shelter. Out pops a gallant to rescue her from the menace of the elements. He appropriates a sunshade from a fruiterer, bringing with it some of the qualities of the produce it was sheltering. Johnny will therefore be this natural, protective, innocent boy for this girl who has 'saved her love for a rainy day'. And yet there is something factitious about it. Johnny is merely posing since he is obviously not a country boy, literally or at any level.

Like Don, Johnny takes an object from the world around him and transforms it into a prop for his magical tricks. Moreover, Johnny attempts to manipulate Hannah in a way reminiscent of Don's early treatment of her and, as far as one can see, of his habitual attitude towards Nadine. Johnny refuses to allow Hannah to make up her own mind. At first he tries to call for a taxi, regardless of Hannah's protest that she only has a buck. Next he dashes off to find the umbrella and escorts her down the street. This is the law of male arrogance in action. Such a law, admittedly, offers protection (Hannah is nearly knocked over by the crowd, the manhole closes just as she reaches it and she rushes to the shelter of Johnny's umbrella after a slight scare), but it is also capable of blighting the development of those it considers vulnerable through a misguided application of the instinct to protect. In the film's final number, 'Easter Parade', Don's 'resurrection' is causally linked with Hannah's own self-assertion.

The medley and 'A couple of swells': ('Be a clown!')

Hannah begins her career with Don as a ridiculous imitation of Nadine, the mock-exotic 'Juanita'. When Nadine attacks him for this, he realises his error (though he attempts to put the blame on Hannah). Hannah's transformation begins when she arrives to rehearse and he asks her to sing to him. But instead of accompanying her on the piano as expected, he starts pumping with his feet. His apartment, which is decorated with many cultural objects, including what looks like a medieval statue and a frieze, also contains a pianola. The pianola stands for the energies of vaudeville as against Don's commitment with Nadine to a more rarified ballroom style, though, as elsewhere in the film, such an opposition does not remain a rigid one, but tends to reconciliation – i.e. Don's sophistication learns from Hannah and Hannah takes from Don in a total style made of the marriage of the best of both.

As Nadine's shadow, Hannah/Garland has been made over into a *dancer*.

She has literally been robbed of her voice. Though Garland is a competent dancer, the audience knows that to dance is not her destiny. Garland's vital identity is bound up with her voice, so that her transformation in 'I love the piano' is not only a movement to vaudeville values (which are complicatedly conflated in her with the pastoral), but to a predominance of the voice. Only then is dance allowed.

'I love the piano' develops similar elements of cultural mixing to those found in 'I wish I was in Michigan' (whose music it closely evokes). Here, surrounded by Don's 'high' art objects which contrast with the mechanical ragtime energy of the pianola, the lyrics of the number are both a celebration of vaudeville over other kinds of art and a reconciliation of them with the world of classical music. So when Hannah sings that she knows 'a fine way/ To treat a Steinway', the effect is double. The finest way to treat a Steinway is clearly to beat out ragtime on it, but the very invocation (however irreverent) of the instrument as best of its kind, grants it respect, and when she also sings of how she loves to hear Paderewski 'the longhaired genius play', the invocation of Paderewski calls up a figure who because of his cult status can easily be reconciled as a star within the musical's values. Although Don's progress as a performer in the story is a loosening up towards more popular styles, the film wants to associate him with a sophisticated embracing of art, something also attached to the Astaire character in *Funny Face* and *The Band Wagon*.

As Hannah sings, Don applauds, and they dance a vaudeville routine – a dance which transmutes via a temporal and spatial cut to its continuation in stage performance as the first of a medley of song-and-dance numbers that has several functions. First, the medley allows the *new* Hannah and Hewes to be shown economically in a wide-ranging display of their talents. Second, because the medley begins in rehearsal, moves through on-the-road performances and ends with an audition for the Ziegfeld Follies, it shows the progress of their act to the point where it receives the highest accolade (although Don in fact rejects Ziegfeld's offer because Nadine is the show's star). Third, the four different numbers are a summary of the various values that Hannah and Hewes have discovered in themselves and for their audience. There is no need for these acts to emphasise the known, primary qualities associated with Astaire and Garland, his detached grace, her emotional 'transparency'. Instead they focus on what is understood to be brought to the duo by Hannah – the energies of popular theatre.

The acts are interrelated in various ways. The most obvious is that the first and third ('I love the piano' and 'Ragtime violin') are based around musical instruments. Comic, sophisticatedly low, athletically virtuosic, these routines turn the musical instruments (in the 'serious' music world almost sacred objects) into physical parts of the performance, by jumping on and over the piano and by treating the violin as the lyrics suggest – 'Lay right on it. Rest your chin upon it'. 'Snooky Ookums' and 'When the midnight choo-choo leaves for Alabam' are a pair of rather unconventional love songs. The first is a parody of 'sweet nothings', while the second, where the reason for catching the train is to see 'my honeylamb', is really an explosion of energy, picking up the mechanisation of the piano in the rehearsal number and transforming it into the energy of the train which Hannah and Hewes mimic in their dance. This connection with mechanical energy that is seen as wholly positive is augmented by a prefiguration of the negroid elements associated with primitive energy in 'Steppin' Out' and 'Shakin' the blues away', with the train significantly bound for the black South. The lyrics' mimicking of a drum beat in the repeated 'Álabam, Álabam, Álabam' echoes 'Drum crazy' as did Hannah's ecstatic 'P-i-a-n-oh!-oh!-oh! in 'I love the piano', all asserting percussion, pulse and (heart)beat.

In numbers 1 and 3 the larger than life vaudeville costumes integrate simply with the comic values of the pieces. But in 'Midnight choo-choo' the costumes do not simply match the mood. Here both are dressed in suits, crossing sophisticated dress with the primitive and mechanical. Their dress in 'Snooky Ookums' is also sophisticated. Here, at first thought, it is an expression of the performers' amused superiority to the lovers' silly baby-talk. But, more profoundly, the number's balance of affection over criticism continues an important motif in all the medley numbers, initiated in 'Drum crazy' – the necessity of (metaphorically) becoming a child again (Easter rebirth), also present in the sophisticated babytalk of 'The midnight choo-choo'.

The famous 'A couple of swells' occurs later than the medley as a number from the first night of the Dillingham show, rivalling Nadine's success for Ziegfeld. It is a curious idyll in which two tramps stroll along Fifth Avenue, asserting that they would be stars of the social world if they had the money, which they have not. With all social reality expelled, the tramps become, like the blacks gestured to in the film's negroid allusions, bearers of a vitality and reality behind social appearances, a kind of comic version of 'the foul rag and bone shop of the heart' as pursued by the democratic arts.

'A couple of swells', like the medley, reduces eroticism to a minor feature of the pair's interplay, their humour contrasting with the sensuousness of Nadine's numbers. Indeed here Garland impersonates a man. Neither Astaire nor Garland are blatantly sexual performers, though their quieter erotic potential is released at the narrative's end. What is primarily dramatised is a set of attributes – their humour, irony, energy for life, etc. – without which, we are told, the erotic is sterile.

'Shakin' the blues away' and 'Steppin' out': (Voodoo Queen and King Creole)

These numbers are placed together because they show us the individualistic self-expression of the two performers who, before and after Hannah's intervention in their lives, struggle for supremacy in an undeclared war of professional and psychological rivalry. In the 'Blues' number the vampish Ann Miller gives an exultant display of her fundamental drives and values. Released from her bondage to Don, she indulges her most sensual instincts for exhibitionism. We discover that this narcissistic drive is governed by two impulses, continually held in tension: primitive urges and urbane ambitions. Voodoo and Chic are the star signs that despotically rule over a willing slave to fame.

The *mise-en-scène* warns us immediately before her entry that her act is to be a study in self-absorption. The only decorations are grey drapes, so there is to be no distraction from the star's self-unveiling. 'There's an old superstition', etc., she begins to sing and then, as the orchestra leaps into swing rhythm, she strips off an unnecessary garment, in a gesture that is both a tribute to her own indiscretion and to the discerning taste of the spectators at the theatre who have paid to admire or envy those singularly voluptuous lower limbs. As the pace of the music quickens, she reaches the full ecstasy of an act which has taken on the qualities of some sort of swingtime Rite of Spring.

> Do like the voodoos do,
> Listenin' to a voodoo melody;
> They shake their bodies so, to and fro,
> With every shake a lucky break . . .

The twin implications of these witty, mocking lyrics are, first, that they express jubilation at the release of primitive erotic instincts, and, second, beyond the meaning that Nadine intends, that they warn against total commitment to the pursuit of sexual gratification, since that is bound in the end to lead to subjugation by forces beyond rational control. The moral philosophy is conventional, but the form is delightful. 'Shakin' ' (surrender to the body) will lead to 'a lucky break' (quality of life). But as the emphasis is on luck, sexual gratification may do little more than place the devotee of the erotic life in the hands of fortune.

The whole number is full of creative contradictions. From one point of view, it would be foolish to deny that both male and female audiences enjoy Ann Miller's extravagance and brazen upholding of the pre-eminence of physique. Nadine is a character who would easily attract men with even more circumspection than Don Hewes. From another point of view, though, we are embarrassed by this image of excess and vulgarity (noticeable in even so small a detail as the alluring and slightly tasteless floral designs in black at the tops of her tights), because of Hannah's display of other values, alternatives to such a naked display of libido, a display that is, in Nadine's case, at least, unreal. Though Nadine sings of animality, of the primitive, we know that finally she is orchideous and remote from the jungle. The only animals she knows are the lapdogs she 'wears' with her various outfits. Nadine is only playing at the voodoo life, for riding over everything with her is the drive for display and applause in an oversophisticated and devitalised world. Offstage her sexuality and desire to marry Johnny seem very conventional. Like Johnny she has glitter, but little substance.

The Creole setting of Don's only solo stage number links it directly with Nadine's. In the phrase 'Steppin' out' we are given the essence of the Astaire persona, here perfectly adapted to the narrative demands of the film. 'Steppin' out' is to be suitably and expensively dressed for love. 'Steppin' out' is grace and elegance, without which love in the city at the highest levels of sophistication would falter and die. Here, as in 'Shakin' the blues away', the star performs without a partner, and is consequently transfixed in an attitude of self-revelation. But, unlike Nadine's, Don's entry on stage is proclaimed by an already forming group of dancers. Nadine dances alone as a declaration of her victory over all. She has withstood the trials and tribulations of competition and now stands isolated, a diva among mortals. By contrast Don's number contains more overt signs of vulnerability.

The number enacts a pantomime more complex than the lyrics, in fact in some places subversive of them. As distinct from what the lyrics say, the drama of the dance shows us Don losing his baby (so that, as in the first version of 'It only happens', he is far from invulnerable). A Nadine-like seductress then takes over his life and treacherously steals his cane. It takes little imagination to see that in an environment that evokes the threats and exhilarations of the sexual (a New Orleans honkytonk house), Don's cane is a graphic representation of his own virility, and that the sexual for him contains the dangers of humiliation and emasculation. But the loss of the cane is only a brief nightmare of mutilated masculinity and the force of the nightmare softens when his cane, its usefulness to the seductress over, is restored to him. Indeed the part of the number most remembered by audiences has Astaire triumphantly dancing in slow motion with the cane while the mass of the performers dance at normal speed.

Within its more obvious suggestions of a release of sexual energy associated with his movement towards Hannah, the number tells us that a man of talent will never be free from danger. Though his costume in the number is predominantly white, and therefore a sign of purity, there are splashes of red in more hidden areas (waistcoat, tie and socks) and these are the signs of his continuing susceptibility to passion – a thing both good and bad, creative and destructive. The reds recall Nadine, and Don is still under her power when he makes Hannah celebrate their success by watching her perform at the Roof Garden. Once there, he finds himself 'Steppin' out' into the old routine at Nadine's insistence, while Hannah looks on forlorn, knowing that she can never match the sensuality of the voodoo madonna.

'The girl on a magazine cover': (Nadine as 'Calendar girl')
Hannah and Hewes' stage costumes are as often as not comic, culminating in those of the tramps (where a radically deglamourised Garland even has her teeth blacked out). Nadine's second stage number at the Follies, which follows the tramp number performed for Dillingham, is an antithetical celebration of the glamorous artificial image, in the particular form of demure cover girls of magazines for the leisured middle classes – *McCalls, Vogue, Ladies Home Companion*, etc.

An anodyne vocalist sings that he is in love with the girl on a magazine cover and searching in real life for a 'little girl' who fits this ideal. Inspecting a line of faces, who in turn look at him and smile, he apparently rejects them as unsatisfactory. These 'real life' women then give way to a series of ingenious *trompe l'oeil* tableaux in which other women, placed within framed painted backgrounds, represent the covers of different magazines of 1912.

In the first tableau the singer stands by a seated girl who is posing for a magazine cover, to which an artist is putting finishing touches. The cover image then steps from the frame of the *Delineator* magazine in a movement that suggests the Pygmalion motif of the main plot, and joins her 'real life' model, looking at her while being regarded by the singer. As the two women sit, the image who has been brought to life smiles confidently, while her 'real life' model, eyes cast down, conveys shyness and inferiority. Interpretation of the small-scale kinesics of the singer and the two women is anchored by the lyrics in which the male singer stresses the difficulty (but unquestioned desirability) of finding a real girl equal to the cover girl. Thus it is clear that the singer's looks convey greater interest in the icon than its original, and that the contrast in the girls' behaviour suggests the model's inferiority before her own image.

The set of magazine cover tableaux that follows moves chronologically from February 1912 to November 1912, omitting only September, with models dressed in seasonal outfits. All this is the prologue for the appearance of Nadine as the epitome of the image, stepping from the cover of *Harper's Bazaar*. Her dramatic appearance in flaming scarlet and white dress, with a huge fan of scarlet feathers, curiously breaks the sequence, since she is a repeating image for August 1912, rather than the expected completion of the year (December) or one of the spring or summer months of the next year (1913). The logic for Nadine as August is that as a performer she is identified with (sexual) heat. But – as distinct from a number of the other girls who are placed in exterior summer or winter scenes – she steps from an interior (a dressing room?) which places her as a figure of artifice rather than nature. Her odd placement as a *repetition* of August *1912* might suggest that her mid-summer of posed sexuality, with suggestions in the costume of a fan dance, is a regression, exciting but finally sterile. In 'Shakin' the blues away' her performance was wholly individual, without accompanying dancers. This we have read in terms of her individualism, which the film places as inferior to partnership. Here she does have accompanying dancers, but, as she said to Don at the Ziegfeld audition, this is *her* show. The men around her are the most conventional chorus-line figures imaginable, functioning solely as her props, so that the performance becomes in real terms another solo display. At one point she gravitates to the singer, whose song now addresses her as the ideal cover girl, but quickly returns to the generalised adoration of the group before the spectacle ends in a tableau of *Magazine of Beauty* 1912. This culminating picture reinforces the way the number develops the film's concern with images, both on and off stage. The oppositions/relations between artifice and naturalness, individualism and partnership, between overt sexuality and a sexuality modified by sentiment and wit, play with great force in Nadine's performance, very much grounded in the Pygmalion (painter and model) tableau which begins it. Nadine, the number seems to say, is a Galatea created by male desire who steps from the frame to fascinating life. But, finally, her coming to life is factitious since life for her is all image. She is a Galatea who turns back into a statue.

Within the number there is also a certain ambivalence in the way celebration of the cover girls and an associated high bourgeois lifestyle signified by the magazines go hand in hand with a critical use of the same things to place Nadine as a fetishistic object. The number and the film thus both celebrate

---

Easter Parade: The girl on a magazine cover, Ann Miller, a female Narcissus framed by aesthetics and ideology.

HARPER'S BAZAAR

EEN
CENTS

and criticise the making of images in both art and life. The lyrics of the title song speak of the couple being snapped by the photographers on Fifth Avenue, and the Parade itself is an occasion for a kind of show and theatre of the self. Here, as onstage, an opposition exists not simply between artifice and nature, but between display as an expression of relationships that go beyond the self (with partner, with community, with ritual), and display that is an overconcern with the self. Thus the offstage Nadine poses narcissistically with her Russian wolfhounds for the photographers in the earlier Parade, while in the later Parade Hannah gracefully waves to the cameramen and then pulls a reminiscence of her funny face from an earlier moment in the film (narrative segment 3), demoting the image of sultry glamour and promoting one in which humour and self-irony are constituents of the ideal self.

'Easter Parade': (Galatea and Pygmalion, New York, 1913)

At the end, as at the beginning, a number carries the narrative, here the process of the awakening of Don and the extension of the onstage partnership into marriage. Narratively it proceeds from Johnny's acceptance of his roles as brother to Hannah and partner to Nadine. It is he who encourages Hannah to question her conventional idea that Don must decide. This leads her to send Don the gifts he receives in the following scene. Here, to a symmetrical echoing of the 'Happy Easter' music that opened the narrative a year previously, arrive first flowers and then boxes containing an Easter egg and a befrilled top hat containing a live white rabbit. The audience, of course, guesses that the flowers are from Hannah, but Don obtusely seems not to know. He thinks they have been sent to the wrong apartment, not recognising that the flowers and hat parallel the ones he bought Nadine a year back, and that the white rabbit, petted by Don and his Chinese servant, Sam, and called a 'little fella', replaces in a kind of comic resurrection the toy one he also bought for Nadine ('A bunny for my honey').

Hannah's arrival begins a series of role changes as she humorously rebukes him for being late, 'just like a man', reminds him imperiously of their date, and instructs Sam to get Don's jacket. Dressed in white, carrying a huge flowered hat, Hannah is the most conventionally feminine and beautiful she has been in the film, yet from this point on she appropriates large elements of the conventionally masculine role with a deft wit to which Don responds with a mixture of surprise, some alarm and eventual pleased acceptance of this disruption of the last vestiges of the master/pupil, father/daughter hierarchy which has dominated their relationship.

Because it invokes an ideal of the equality of the sexes (however transgressed this may have been in practice), and because it is embodied in the persons of Astaire and Garland and all the pleasurable forces of the musical, this dominance of Hannah's which might in other circumstances be threatening, could give pleasure to its original audiences. It consists of many particular items: her stance with folded arms and then with arms akimbo as she circles Don, inspecting him approvingly ('Very nice'); her winking at him; her blocking of his way before she starts to sing to him, the first of a sustained series of moves in which she physically directs him (recalling the first rehearsals and performances where he directed her masterfully and her movements were faltering). Once she even dares stand behind him, encircling him with her arms, appropriating one of Astaire's own dance positions (which can be seen in the first version of 'It only happens').

The lyrics she sings are addressed to a woman by a man, but in Hannah's version the sexual roles are reversed. It is she who calls Don 'pretty' and remarks upon *his* 'Easter bonnet' (the top hat). Don's reactions constitute the other interacting half of the number, twin responses that exist in tension until the final resolution – surprise on the one hand, and pleasure on the other. Like Hannah's new dominance, Don's reactions exist in a complex context of humour, self-consciousness and self-irony that makes a reading of their interplay difficult to pin down, but much of it is built around a comedy of embarrassment mixed with delight on the part of the male who is turned into the object of desire. Twice, though, his intensified consternation causes an increase of tension in the drama of the number. Don takes off his hat to polish it, removing the frill ('with all the frills upon it') before tapping it back into place at a jaunty angle. If this is a reassertion of undermined masculine authority allowed to disintegrate almost too far, it quickly modulates again into acceptance in the dance into which Hannah leads him. The second moment of tension follows fast as Hannah actually places Don upon her knee, a position from which he hurriedly extricates himself with a shocked look and a negative palms-down gesture. But again this gives way to an accepting smile and, joining arms, the pair execute a little mutual routine up and down the steps that lead to the door. Here, in the last of the reversals, it is Hannah who holds the door open for Don, a gesture which he accepts, throwing up his cane (*c.f.* the 'Steppin' out' number: Hannah's self-assertion hasn't destroyed his virility) and catching it.

Finally the couple walk towards the viewer and Don sings the lyrics in their original form to Hannah, presenting her with a wedding ring. As they walk, Hannah poses for the photographers with a humorously grand sweeping gesture and a reminiscence of her funny face. The lyric is then taken over by the offscreen chorus and the camera lifts to give the panorama of the Parade on Fifth Avenue, prominently taking in St Patrick's Cathedral in the final image. If the most obvious significations here are the idea of marriage and the calling up of a famous local landmark, nevertheless the shot reinforces the ritual rebirth structure of the story. In the other sunken mythic allusion that plays into the film, if Don is Pygmalion and Hannah is Galatea, not only does Pygmalion create Galatea, but she recreates herself and, finally, Pygmalion as well.

A short note on some textual complexities

Different ways of looking at works of art reveal different things. Looking at *Easter Parade* we have largely been interested in the way the numbers contain potential meanings that are readable in systematic and coherent patterns. Views of art which assert coherence above everything else, as in the model of the work of art as an 'organic' entity (a plant, a body), have lately fallen into disfavour, giving way to models that stress contradiction and unevenness alongside partial coherence. The most influential models in contemporary literary and cinematic criticism are markedly influenced by Freud's explications of the work of the mind in dreaming, which of course lays great emphasis on contradiction, condensation and displacement, and interrogates the text (in this case the dream) to reveal its hidden meanings rather than accepting its surface statement. Where the older theories and newer ones meet is in their assertion that no detail is insignificant, that the text (dream, novel or film) is meaningful in all its details.

We do not propose to argue the case through here, but simply to ask what attitude one takes to the less overt complexities it is possible to read in the narrative? If every detail is the product of a choice (conscious or unconscious), if every one could have been replaced by other elements, each can be interrogated for the meanings (surface or deep structural) that it is part of. For instance, why are the characters in the film named as they are – *Don Hewes, Hannah Brown, Nadine Hale, Johnny Harrow*? With peripheral characters like Sam and François the relatively simple answer is probably satisfactory. François is a generic, rather pretentious waiter's name, summing up the character immediately, though part of the comic thickness of the part is in the way Jules Munshin's very American persona relates to it. Likewise, the joke about Don having a Chinese servant named Sam asserts something

---

'In your Easter bonnet/With all the flowers upon it/You'll be the finest lady (feller) in the Easter Parade'. Astaire and Garland step out at the film's end in the faint aura of mythology and resurrection narrative.

about the relation of the American to the exotic, in this case an optimistic view of the film's ability to americanise the outlandish, though of course it should not be forgotten that Sam is a servant. Part of the joke may also be the allusion to another more famous Sam, the black nightclub performer in *Casablanca* (1942). But the names of the primary characters who intersect with so many more of the film's important thematics can be shown to have a series of more intricate relationships with some of the patterns of meaning produced in the film. Who thought (consciously or unconsciously) of those meanings? Do audiences – as distinct from analysts – pick them up? What is made of them? These are questions too complex to pursue here. Our demonstration is simply that they may be found in the text, however they are to be explained.

The deflection in *Hewes* from the expected *Hughes* of course marks him as slightly different, what we would expect of the hero and Astaire, but of course any one of a thousand similar skewings could have done the same. Why this one? A sub-system, established elsewhere as a powerful presence in the film, within which the peculiarity of the name might be seen to function, is the *pastoral*, so that connotations of *hewing* (i.e. cutting wood) relate to the more overtly pastoral connotations in Hannah Brown and Johnny *Harrow* (the agricultural instrument). Even Nadine's surname, *Hale* (healthy, etc.) might be seen to belong to this set. This distribution of connotations does not seem to be consciously worked, in as much as it does not discriminate along a system of positives and negatives as we expect it to: i.e. it doesn't follow the logic of giving pastoral connotations to the names of characters associated with the positive pastoral values and anti-pastoral names to those who represent anti-pastoral values, but instead distributes similar meanings through all the names. If we want to resolve this from the characterological point of view it has to be in terms of Johnny and Nadine being deceitful or superficial, and functioning ironically, while those attached to Don and Hannah are positive. When Nadine's surname of *Hale* is read in terms of its verbal meaning of to drag or constrain, an obvious logic is at work, since in certain terms that is what she clearly does to Don; but when Johnny's surname of *Harrow* is seen in terms of another subsystem of meanings closely related to the pastoral, that of Easter – as in the action of Christ *harrowing* Hell – the significance is clearly not to be attached to Johnny and is more satisfactorily read as a displacement, an echo, of a general concern throughout the film. This kind of unconscious structuring will not be surprising to anyone familiar with Freud's *The Interpretation of Dreams* or *The Psychopathology of Everyday Life*. The Easter motif even seems to find a further displacement in the curious comedy of the waiter François' *Salade François* (narrative segment 6) which has an indubitable, if obscure, place in the film's sequence of food references (the swish restaurant where nobody manages to eat, Hannah's drugstore sandwich, the importance of restaurants in the narrative generally, Don's dinner for Hannah at his apartment which we never see eaten (narrative segments 7 and 8), Hannah's gift of an Easter egg – food as a symbol of re-birth – at the end of the film. François' salad, to labour the point, is made not of sweets or meats but of vegetation, and as such is the essence of the green world of nature. Such a significance seems unconscious because of its peripheral displacement. That is, although it is a version of the film's already sunken 'resurrection' interests, it appears in a form so obscure and so comic as to conceal it.

PART II
Three from the thirties

Gold Diggers of 1933 and the Busby Berkeley backstage musical

Upstaging the depression

Gold Diggers of 1933 has an unusually close relationship to precise historical events for a musical. *Easter Parade*, the subject of the last chapter, and *Swing Time* and *The Merry Widow*, the subjects of the two that follow, are much more typical of the genre in their apparent imperviousness to contemporary social conditions. If a film like *Easter Parade* tells us things about the post-war forties – as, on reflection, it surely does – it is in a multitude of indirect ways; through the styles and modes of its stars, through its assumptions about relationships and goals, through its post-war nostalgia for a pre-first world war 'golden age' and so on. But *Gold Diggers of 1933*, although on closer inspection revealing elements just as fantastic as the nostalgic products of MGM at a later date, is that rare thing, a musical that strongly invokes contemporary political happenings (as well as styles and attitudes), reflecting and in part creating a mythology out of the midflow of history.

The moment is the great Depression of the early thirties, and more particularly the Democrat victory in the election of November 1932, the inauguration of Franklin D. Roosevelt on 9 March 1933, and the promise and emergence of the 'New Deal' legislation combating the worst effects of the economic catastrophe. Warner Brothers had already picked up the phrase from Roosevelt's platform speech – 'I pledge myself to a new deal for the American people' – to give a topical buzz to the advertising of *42nd Street*, the enormously successful musical completed around the time of the election and then released to coincide with public enthusiasm at the inauguration. The poster of the film announced it as 'A New Deal in Entertainment'.

Opportunistic though this appropriation was, Warner Brothers had, in fact, committed themselves to supporting Roosevelt, in marked contrast to other studio heads. Louis B. Mayer of MGM, for instance, was prominent in

Californian Republican politics and a friend of President Hoover, while Harry Cohn was an admirer of Mussolini. The Hollywood production hierarchy (though by no means all the actors, writers and directors) were extremely conservative politically, most of them looking with horror on the New Deal. This was understandable, given their dependence on the banking industry, and the psychological factor of their rise as self-made heroes of capitalism from the ghetto to the top of the hill made almost inevitable an identification with the more extreme end of the ideology of private enterprise. What it was in the Warners' make-up that encouraged them to break this pattern has never been satisfactorily answered, but the result was Harry Warner's instruction that the studio was to support Roosevelt's campaign, and the later incorporation of the NRA emblem of the blue eagle into the title cards of Warners' films, as well as a general commitment to a cinema that reflected the experience of the Depression shared by many millions of Americans, and contained many literal and figurative references in support of the New Deal. The extent of Warner Brothers' commitment to government interventionism on a revolutionary scale should not be over-estimated. As writers like Andrew Bergman and Nick Roddick have made clear, the films that emerged from the studio managed to make criticisms of the abuses of the system that produced the Depression, and to exhort to social action, without attacking such cornerstones of prevalent ideology as the belief in thrusting individualism and free enterprise. And the Warner Brothers, like the other studios, strongly opposed Upton Sinclair in his radical EPIC campaign for Governorship of California in 1934, a campaign which attacked excessive profits in the movie industry. As Bergman is acute at pointing out, films of the period are very good at presenting the atmosphere and effects of the Depression, but less good at analysing its causes, typically finding scapegoats such as the gangster or corrupt capitalist (i.e. abusers of an otherwise reasonable system), highly visible figures on whom blame could be placed, rather than on the less visible deep economic and social structures.

Nevertheless, in spite of their ultimately conservative tendencies, numerous Warner Brothers films do engage with the reality of social and economic tumult as experienced by the common man and woman, most obviously in the 'topicals' like *I Am A Fugitive From A Chain Gang*, most subversively, perhaps, in the gangster films like *Little Caesar* and *The Public Enemy* (which consciously or unconsciously dramatise the gangster as the dark *doppelgänger* of Horatio Alger's heroes), and most surprisingly in the series of musicals that begins with *42nd Street* (1933) and then *Gold Diggers of 1933* (1933), *Footlight Parade* (1933), *Dames* (1934) and *Gold Diggers of 1935* (1935). All these musicals involved the dance direction (and in the case of the last the complete direction) of the brilliant cinematic choreographer, Busby Berkeley, with the direction of the narrative (with the exception noted) in the hands of highly competent 'house' directors – noted for expertise in various genres, for hardboiled treatments and narrative efficiency – Lloyd Bacon, Ray Enright and, in the case of *Gold Diggers of 1933*, Mervyn LeRoy.

Gold Diggers of 1933 was in preparation as a story treatment in November 1932, and emerged as a final shooting script (though it was substantially altered in the shooting process) by February 1933. Shot in forty-five days, it was in the cinemas and being reviewed by June 1933. The making of the film and its release thus coincide with the height of expectation leading up to the first legislation of the new Congress, and both the anxieties and expectations of this period are refracted in it. An early remark sets the tone when Fay Fortune explains the closing of the show with the words, 'the Depression, dearie'. At another point early on Trixie Lorraine's wisecrack when the producer Barney Hopkins announces that his new show will be about the Depression is 'We won't have to rehearse that'. The film begins with the announcement that 'The long-lost dollar has come back to the fold' (a too premature optimism) and ends with the acting out of Barney's idea of converting into 'the show business' the material of 'wailing, wailing – men marching, marching' in the number 'Remember my forgotten man' (the words 'forgotten man' also have a Rooseveltian source, from a speech of April 1932 when he was governor of New York State).

In a brilliant article, Mark Roth has very persuasively read the series of films from *42nd Street* to *Gold Diggers of 1935* not simply as entertainments but as films with a profound meaning for their original audiences. The fundamental point of his argument is that the films are 'rituals' whose ingredients had such appeal because they acted out a reaffirmation of American ideology – that peculiar interaction of the ethos of egalitarianism, reinterpreted to mean equality of opportunity rather than equality of status, and the open market – to which the audience were deeply committed, but which seemed to be failing them. In the backstage, putting-on-a-show plots of all the films he finds a homology with, if not near allegory of, the call made by Roosevelt for a momentary social cohesion, with its temporary downgrading of individualism, needed to fight the slump. The theatrical community, all pulling together to achieve the aim of the successful show, parallels the greater community which ought to be similarly united in their attempts to achieve the greater show of a democratic and flourishing America. And in *42nd Street* and *Footlight Parade,* where the figure of the show's director is given great importance (in *42nd Street* the ailing but brilliant Julian Marsh, played by Warner Baxter, in *Footlight Parade* the dynamic Chester Kent, played by James

Cagney), he argues very plausibly that there is an image of the leader who will take the nation out of the wilderness – Roosevelt himself, who actually appears as an icon, along with the NRA eagle and the American flag, in the 'Shanghai Lil' number in *Footlight Parade*. The argument is capable of embracing not only such overt signs but also the basic mode of Berkeleyan dance spectacle (*le système Berkeley* as a French critic rather grandly puts it), which features not individual dancers such as Astaire and Rogers or Chevalier and MacDonald in the great intimate waltz number in *The Merry Widow*, but a seemingly endless set of units, each one part of a greater whole, combining together into patterns ordained and controlled by the choreo-grapher – in other words, enacting on the plane of dance formation the social cohesiveness demanded by the ideology of the New Deal. Barney Hopkins (played by the unidealistic, hardbitten Ned Sparks) may, like the Warner Brothers themselves, be opportunistic in his vision of a successful show based on the Depression, but the film – like the show within the film – is more than merely opportunistic, giving expression to a set of problems and ten-sions, as well as the 'ritual' of optimism brought to the fore by the recent economic collapse, which will be examined in the sections that follow.

Berkeley at Warners: sex, geometrics and significance

Obsessed by geometrics and female flesh, Berkeley was a naive surrealist who owed nothing consciously to that intellectual tradition, or indeed any other, though his eye for cinematic detail was sharp enough to include a pastiche of Sternberg in the 'Shanghai Lil' number in *Footlight Parade* and allusions to Lang's *Metropolis* in both *Gold Diggers of 1933* and *Dames*. Inheriting the native showbiz tradition of the rarified girlie show from the Ziegfeld and other Follies (which it is estranging in a salutary way to see as the vulgar inflection of the fine art tradition of display of the female body), he turned it into a carnivalesque riot of unfettered images. Various movements have seen Berkeley in different ways. Devotees of 'camp' (he is included in Susan Sontag's compendious definition of that sensibility) have claimed him. He has been seen (in the French tradition of attending to the American cinema with the utmost seriousness) as almost the exemplar of purely cine-matic imagery. And, recently, feminist criticism has seen in his use of the vacuous faces and pliant bodies of his massed chorus girls a heightened instance of the cinema's too frequent portrayal of the female as mere sex object rather than intelligent subject.

We are now used to the notion that many of the older Hollywood profes-

sionals were intuitive craftsmen and untheorising pragmatists rather than self-conscious explicators of their work. We should therefore no longer feel that there is something suspect in reading beyond Berkeley's naive comments about his art (mostly to the effect that he simply gave the audience what it wanted, ingenious spectacles with pretty girls) for further significance. All three views mentioned tell us something valid about the extraordinary spectacles he produced, though taken separately each is insufficient. 'Camp' Berkeley certainly is, if by camp we mean the flaunting of excess, a collision of vulgarity with style and the elevation of bad taste to a principle. But any such definition itself needs further defining. It is the very ability that Berkeley has to move so directly into the realm of the 'tasteless' (one thinks above all of numbers like 'Pettin' in the park' in *Gold Diggers of 1933*, 'Honeymoon Hotel' in *Footlight Parade* and 'Shuffle off to Buffalo' in *42nd Street*) rather than just the sentimental, vivacious or energetic, that is one of the grounds of his significance. Prurient and leering he may often be, but at a certain level of imagination he is not controlled by the usual censors of an internal rather than external kind. Up to a certain point the voyeurism of 'Pettin' in the park' is commonplace; views of girls reclining so that the audience look up their nyloned legs, girls' shadows undressing behind a screen after the rainstorm. But the presence in both instances of the leering dwarf/child (played by the midget, Billy Barty) pushes both moments into the realm of the unsettling. In the first instance he grins knowingly at the audience, teasing them with their voyeurism, as he prepares to lift the screen. In the second he scampers on all fours after a ball that has nestled by the legs of a reclining girl. There is something very disturbing about the condensation of infant and mature voyeur into the same figure. It is most unlikely that Berkeley ever read Freud, but the second image of the infant peering at the place of his and the audience's origins with such curiosity has no better commentary than Freud's essay on 'The Uncanny' with its statement of the attraction/repulsion the male feels for the female genitals.

The second, formalistic, view of Berkeley also has a real but limited truth to it. Whatever one's ideological position, it seems impossible, if one is interested in the potentialities of the cinema, in the arrangement of images in motion, not to respond with excitement to his work. In a smaller way, he belongs with Eisenstein, Griffith, Norman McLaren and a few others as a master of cinema as dynamic, kinetic experience, generating wonder at the

---

Gold Diggers: voyeurism foregrounded. The leering dwarf-infant (Billy Barty) teases the audience in 'Pettin' in the park' with a promise of female nakedness. Freud's 'infantile sexuality' uncannily joined with adult knowingness.

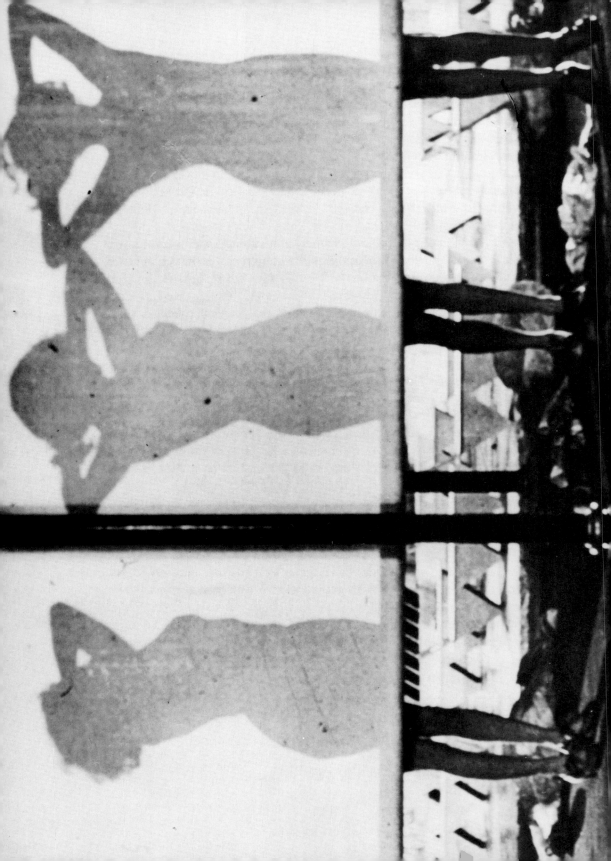

audacity of his spatial imagination as it dissolves the proscenium stage solidity into a vertiginous world of shifting planes, ambiguous dimensions and extraordinary patterns of metamorphosis. To say this is to assert that a great part of the delight in a Berkeley number is formal, a truth that tends to be neglected by criticism that concentrates exclusively on questions of the ideological content of art.

Yet, though Berkeley's images cannot be wholly explained in terms of their ideological content, they are not ideologically innocent. This is the point that has been made by a number of feminist critics, the most important of whom, Lucy Fischer, has discussed the way in which (in *Dames*, but the point applies to all the films) the numbers present a series of hyperbolised female stereotypes, making explicit, as it were, attitudes present, but more hidden, in less excessive films. It is impossible to escape Berkeley's sexism but, equally, it is neither so simple nor so unitary as is sometimes thought. A too simple concentration on it may lead to a neglect of the complexity of numbers that are not so fundamentally based on questions of sexuality, such as the 'social realism' numbers: 'Remember my forgotten man', 'Lullaby of Broadway' from *Gold Diggers of 1935* and '42nd Street' from *42nd Street*. It may also lead to an excessively simple reading of those numbers very much built around the display of the female, to the simple enumeration and condemnation of a variety of phallocentric tropes (most notoriously the camera journeying through a tunnel made of the legs of the chorus girls) at the expense of asking whether any further play of meaning takes place. Of Berkeley's ogling imperial tendencies, the most intelligent thing to say, it seems to us, is that they exist, alas, but closely tied in with other aspects of his genius, the mainspring that often releases meanings that are by no means so simple and conventional.

Berkeley's career was not, of course, limited to the Warners films we are considering. He made less substantial musicals at Warners both before (e.g. the Eddy Cantor vehicles such as *Whoopee!* in 1930 and *The Kid from Spain* in 1932) and after (e.g. *Gold Diggers of 1937*), and then worked for a long period at MGM. In this later period at what had by the forties become the major studio for musicals, he worked in conditions that suited him less, operating with more restricted budgets, in films that were designed to exhibit stars, like the young Garland and Rooney, rather than spectacle, and within an ethos where the primary talents were committed to the integrated musical rather than the backstage type. Nonetheless, in terms of sheer spectacle (with the

---

Flaunting female flesh and the Depressed Male Look

added resource of colour), some of his later work is as extraordinary as any he produced. The one large-scale aquatic spectacle in the Esther Williams vehicle *Million Dollar Mermaid* (1952) uses colour in what is almost a preview of psychedelia, and the Fox film of 1943, *The Gang's All Here*, could be seen as the pinnacle of both the sexual and the abstract urges in his work. The former reaches its apotheosis in 'The lady with the tutti-frutti hat', where gargantuan bananas carried by chorines plunge rhythmically into strawberry centred patterns made by other girls; the latter in 'The polka dot polka' where the designs, at one point viewed through a kaleidoscope, are no longer erotic, or even human, but momentarily attain total abstraction in a rush of changing patterns akin to the abstract experimental cinema associated with figures like Len Lye and Norman McLaren.

It is also true that many of the typical Berkeley images are present in the early films (*The Kid From Spain*, especially, has some very intricate patterns of visual metamorphosis). Berkeley's work, early, middle and late, is in its essentials similar, but different production and narrative contexts tend to allow it a more or less interesting and more or less developed release. If – as we and most observers believe – the very best of his work was done in the few films under consideration, it is not simply because the sudden revival of the musical in audience favour begun by *42nd Street* prompted Warners to give him large budgets for his numbers. It is also, more complicatedly, because Berkeley's obsessions were placed within a kind of musical that not only allowed such spectacles a major part but were also powered by the social consciousness that sprang from the Warner Brothers' half political, half commercially opportunistic highlighting of Depression material which other studios mostly chose to ignore. Two things happen as a result of this. In the other Berkeley films the splendour of the numbers overwhelms the lightness of the narratives. Who would remember *The Kid From Spain* or *The Gang's All Here* for anything but the numbers? Whereas in the Warners' films, extremely knowing and witty narratives specialising in hardboiled humour, innuendo and a sophisticated recognition of the character types they are playing with, surround the numbers. Since these narratives centre on questions of sexuality, economics and backstage spectacle in a more than simply conventional fashion, they may be said to intersect with Berkeley's almost identical obsessions (sex, economics, spectacle) in a far more intense way than happens elsewhere, causing significant relationships examined in the last part of this chapter. Secondly, the context of Warner Brothers' commitment to Roosevelt presses Berkeley into the production of certain numbers which differ from those he made either earlier or later in their terpsi-chorisation of urban social material (the breadlines, poverty and World War I scenes of 'Forgotten man', the urban frenzy, culminating in a killing in '42nd Street' and the scenes of wild pleasure-seeking set against the grind of work in 'Lullaby of Broadway' in *Gold Diggers of 1935*). In both instances, in the latter overtly, in the former obliquely, the specific meeting of Berkeley's genius with a social context and a studio in some measure responsive to it produces, for a short while, a unique inflection both of Berkeley's art and of the backstage musical.

Backstage

The backstage musical is a series of closely related plot-forms encompassing a multitude of minor variations. A show is launched successfully, a performing career is followed (shading, if the basis is factual, into the 'biopic'), performers meet and love in that metaphoric equivalent of perfect performing and perfect relationship that is so common in the musical. Many more than half the musicals ever made are of the backstage type – from *The Jazz Singer* and *Broadway Melody of 1929* to *The Rose, Cabaret, Fame* and *Nashville*.

The reasons for the dominance of this type are several. Conservative producers, rightly or wrongly thinking of conservative audiences, found in it a type of musical in which no imaginative grasp of convention was required. All the singing and dancing could be realistically motivated by the fact that the characters were professional singers and/or dancers either performing or rehearsing. Their dread (surely over-estimated) that mass audiences might respond, as they could to opera, by refusing the convention that people sing their feelings, also produced a kind of film in which it was not necessary for the numbers to have an especially complex relationship with the narrative material. A success and love story with a few intimate and spectacular numbers, would be enough, and such an undemanding form would work well for mass production. Such an argument, though, only stresses the lowest common denominator. More affirmatively the sub-genre offers audiences all the fascinations that the meta-theatrical mode gives in films like *Les Enfants du Paradis* and *The Red Shoes* as well as Hollywood instances like *All About Eve, A Double Life* and *Two Weeks in Another Town* – entry into the glittering world of backstage, a view not merely of the glamour of an exciting and creative profession, of fame and applause, but of the traditional meta-theatrical themes of acting versus sincerity, of masks and roles, of appearances and realities. These are themes deeply embedded in traditional classical theatre, especially from the Renaissance onward, but given a special ethos in the world of the musical – at its most irresistibly simple in the lyrics of 'There's no business like show business', and at its most complex in the neurotic performance worlds of films like *Cabaret* and *All That Jazz*, made by the modern master of the sub-genre, Bob Fosse. Not only this, the dominant sub-type in the history of the musical is, as Jane Feuer and others have extensively argued, an exceedingly sophisticated, self-conscious, self-referential and self-celebratory kind of art. At one level this can be seen as the self-sustaining of the mythology of 'entertainment' by the industry; at another a source of intense formal pleasures in the recognition by audiences of the manipulation of conventions. Finally, there is the larger equivalence, always there but occasionally, as in the Berkeley–Warners films, given especial contemporary relevance, of the performing world and life, in which the former provides more heightened, more exciting images of the trials and tribulations of ordinary existence, and in which we can find our own equivalents of 'first night nerves', rising from chorus line to stardom, the profits and perils of success and adulation, and the values not only of talent and fortune but also of durability and hard work.

   This parallelism is, as we have seen, powerfully present in the Berkeley– Warners films. But there are other ways in which these films develop possibilities latent, but not often realised, in backstage stories. To say that the Berkeley musicals are more realistic than most is to use a notoriously slippery term. It is, however, a useful shorthand if we take it to mean, in this specific context, a relatively developed interest in presenting (for some, though not all of the time) a deglamourised picture of actual theatrical work and institutions; the theatre, that is, as a workplace and the product of social forces, rather than as a glittering parthenogenetic spectacle.

   At the simplest level, *Gold Diggers of 1933* shares with its predecessor and successors the slightly proletarian feel cultivated by many Warners films of the period. This is something manifested not only in the tacky, unglamorous sets (a happy combination of aesthetic rightness and studio thrift) but also in the stars and supporting players that inhabit them, as far removed as possible from the more glamorous worlds of MGM, Paramount and the RKO musicals. There may be little analysis of the working class to be found in Warners' films, which remain fundamentally committed to entrepreneurial individualism, but there was clearly a mass appeal in their roster of players – Cagney, Ned Sparks, Una Merkel, Ginger Rogers and others, most with something of the common touch, a brashness, a cockiness, a street-wisdom and not too scrupulous energy about them. This, we remember, is the time that the large, homely and elderly Marie Dressler was a great box office star, a time when, for millions in trouble, glamorous values might be secondary to more fundamental ones. *Gold Diggers of 1933* is, for all its many fairytale elements, full of touches that register a sense of the conditions felt by the majority of Americans.

Unlike most backstage musicals, the Berkeley–Warners films emphasise the difficulties of finding the material means to put on the show. Shows do not just happen. They are part of a capitalist entertainment industry requiring money from backers who expect profits in return. Many backstage musicals, building their plots round the staging of a show, need in those plots blocking mechanisms to make the final triumph difficult. In *The Band Wagon,* for instance, the show chosen is the wrong kind of show, with the wrong director and tension between the male and female stars. Sometimes finance is one of the difficulties, but usually only in a formal and superficial sense. In the Astaire-Rogers films such problems are almost non-existent in a chicly deco and decorous world which tends to evade the Depression which Warners, with their Rooseveltian leanings, incorporate into their musicals. The Berkeley films are stories of a fairytale success, from poverty to riches, from the chorus line to stardom, but they are 'rituals' (to use Roth's term) which refer to economic realities even while they transcend them more easily than happens in the real world. It is typical of the films' *mélange* of glamour and realism that while the problem of getting money is a constant worry, it is often actually gained through channels that owe more to the conventions of comedy than to mundane likelihood. This is the case in *Gold Diggers of 1933* where Brad Roberts just happens to be the heir, Robert Treat Bradford, incognito, who puts up the $15,000. The solution owes nothing to realism, but much that surrounds it does, e.g. the invasion of the bailiffs in the opening number, the image of the names of the theatres that have closed near the beginning of the film and so on. Images crowded together at the beginning of *42nd Street* enact economic realities with especial force when we are given two significant closeups, the first of Dorothy Brock's Equity contract and the second of a director's contract to which a hand (before we have seen a face) puts Julian Marsh's signature. In both cases the images stress the show's genesis in a world of contracts, the legal structures of entrepreneurial capitalism. In *Footlight Parade* the producer Chester Kent (James Cagney) is presented not just making stage shows, but producing a specific product for a newly evolved market brought on by the advent of talking pictures. Indeed, in *Footlight Parade* not only is the atmosphere of the factory present as the cast frantically rehearse 'units', but Kent's idea is of an assembly-line product that can be played at many sites rather than one, entertainment as a mass industrial product.

These films also emphasise the instability of the theatrical profession and the struggle for jobs. At the beginning of *Dames*, the Joan Blondell character is out of work because a show she has been in, put on by an unscrupulous producer, has folded. In *42nd Street* the great Julian Marsh who may be fatally ill, comes back to direct the show not solely because of his creative drive, but because of his need for financial security. *Gold Diggers of 1933* acts out such instability with great dramatic force when the brilliant Berkeley number that opens the film, 'We're in the money', a paean to the recovered powers of capitalism that announces the defeat of 'Old Man Depression', is cataclysmically thrown into disarray by the arrival of the bailiffs announcing the show's bankruptcy.

If shows require capital, they also require the labour of rehearsal. Jane Feuer's thesis that the musical, in pretending to be unalienated folk art, must above all give an illusion of spontaneity, is true of the majority of backstage musicals. These may occasionally gesture at the work of rehearsal and the accumulation of skills, but they hardly foreground them. In the Astaire–Rogers films, for instance, when a number is performed in rehearsal, it will be as perfect as any other. But the Berkeley–Warners films, more than any backstage musicals before Fosse's *All That Jazz* (where the final show is never seen, only the rehearsal process), stress the business of rehearsal. If the labour of the acquisition of technical skills is largely ignored (since audiences, rightly or wrongly, would have considered, and would still consider, such representations boring), the sheer grind of the process is not. *Gold Diggers of 1933* does not stress this as much as *42nd Street* and *Footlight Parade*, but even so it does show us the most brilliant of the numbers, 'Pettin' in the park', in rehearsal, shot from angles that de-emphasise pattern and spectacle and concentrate on the physical activity that underlies the 'magic'. And before the 'Shadow waltz' and 'Forgotten man' numbers, there are behind-stage shots of technicians at work, girls choosing costumes and warning shouts being given for the performers, all of which emphasise, at least momentarily, the mundane base on which the brilliant spectacle is erected.

There is one other area where certain problems are raised and dwelt on in a way very different from other backstage musicals. *Gold Diggers of 1933*, like the other films of the series, makes a series of connections between economics and sex that link the intertwined love and stage plots. As the girls exchange their bodies for financial security, so the show's success is largely bought by the display of female bodies for the audience. As the Dick Powell character sings to a meeting of backers of his show in *Dames*:

What do you go for?
Go see a show for?
Tell the truth, we go to see those beautiful dames.

We spend our dough for
Bouquets that grow for
All you cute and cunning, young and wonderful dames.

Dames are necessary to show business.
Dames, without you there would be no business.
Your knees in action,
That's the attraction.

Whether we see the lyrics as naively self-betraying or more consciously constructed as commentary, they certainly underline the crucial place of the female body and the predominance of 'the male look' in Berkeley's spectacles. What we have in the Berkeley films is a curious mixture of extreme invitation to this (hence the feminist interest in and attacks upon him), mixed with a curious insistence (intelligently noted by Lucy Fischer) on drawing attention to the very voyeurism that is invited. Only in the exceptional *Dance Girl, Dance* (1940), directed by a woman, Dorothy Arzner, is a character – Judy O'Brien (Maureen O'Hara) – allowed to turn on the audience of ogling males and berate them for their actions and assumptions. The Berkeley films' reaction is rather different, a kind of ambivalence operating within a largely celebratory attitude. Nevertheless, their intelligence is such that they raise such problems, rather than simply sweep them away.

The narrative: sex, love, money

In *Gold Diggers of 1933* the three heroines, Polly, Carol and Trixie pursue love relationships that move towards the economic security of marriage to a wealthy man. At one pole there is a rather anodyne 'true love' represented by Polly and Brad (Ruby Keeler and Dick Powell), in which all economic problems are solved by the conventions of sentimental comedy. So Polly falls in love with Brad, thinking him to be a penniless songwriter, though, happily, he turns out to be a 'Boston blueblood'. At the other pole there is Trixie trapping the elderly lawyer, Peabody, into a marriage where, plainly, her only satisfactions will be monetary. Placed between these in the spectrum of feeling is the relationship between Carol (Joan Blondell) and Brad's older brother, J. Lawrence Bradshaw (Warren William), which crosses romance with the reality principle and *vice versa*, and ends with Carol, the goodhearted gold digger, finding a more realistic romance than Polly's, as well as money.

This trio of heroines is discovered at the opening of the narrative innocently in bed together and reluctant to get up to another debt-ridden day. The narrative's main movement is to get them back to bed in a way that will guarantee them security for life. As in Elizabethan stage comedy, the triad of pairings represents different aspects of love – but love always connected (even where the film heavily represses the implications, as with Polly and Brad) with economic security.

Though Ruby Keeler as Polly is the sentimental heroine, she is hardly the focus of the most intense audience sympathy and identification. That, really, is Joan Blondell as Carol, who shares something of Trixie's tough realism along with a susceptibility to romance, and who also represents in the final 'Forgotten man' number, to quote Barney, 'The spirit of the Depression'. The only one of the 'cute and cunning, young and wonderful dames' excluded from the rewards of matrimony is Fay Fortune (Ginger Rogers, before she became Astaire's partner), who is punished for threatening the erotic-economic success of the heroines by her 'chiselling'; for treating sex too overtly as a bargaining commodity. Though this distinction is enforced by the film, it is in fact, illogical, and with it the division the film wants to impose between acceptable (gold-hearted) and unacceptable (cold-hearted) gold digging. It is difficult to see how Fay's attempt to snatch Peabody is any more predatory than Trixie's. Indeed the distinction is sustained wholly by the fact that the rhetoric of the film persuades us to sympathise with Trixie rather than with Fay. A similar ambiguity tends to accompany the analogous plots in the other films of the series. The variation in *Gold Diggers of 1935* is particularly interesting. In that case the sentimental plot involving Dick and Ann (Powell and, in this exceptional case, not Keeler but Gloria Stuart) where the money problem is easily solved because Ann is an heiress, is paralleled by the activities of Dick's ex-fiancée, Arlene, who, when told by Dick that she deserves the 'finest man in the world', replies 'Till he comes along, I'll take a rich one', and hooks the much-marrying playboy, Humboldt. There is also Betty Hawes (!) (Glenda Farrell) who specialises professionally in eliciting and then profiting from the proposals which for the other girls are the end of their search. She traps the asexual millionaire Moseley T. Thorpe by getting him to write what he thinks is the lyric of a love song, but which she can use as a statement of intent in a breach-of-promise suit. The moment trenchantly intersects the sentimental and the economic, with the unsuspecting lyrics a parody of numbers like 'I only have eyes for you' and 'The shadow waltz'. Having got her evidence, she then sings, in intricate intertextual parody of the opening of *Gold Diggers of 1933*, '*I'm* in the money,/ The skies are sunny,/*I've* got a lot of what it takes to get along.' Glenda Farrell's marked (generic Warners' blonde) resemblance to the early Ginger Rogers is played upon here to deepen the force of the changing of the optimistically oriented 'we' of the original lyrics into this atomistic variant. In the earlier *Footlight Parade* (made just after *Gold Diggers of 1933*) the function of Betty Hawes as the most 'chiselling' of the women is divided between Chester Kent's unscrupulous ex-wife and his fiancée, Miss Rich, another breach-of-promise specialist. These characters, far more than Arlene or the cheerfully pragmatic 'Anytime' Annie (Ginger Rogers) and Lorraine (Una Merkel) of *42nd Street*, are presented as cold and ruthless. Nevertheless, though one tendency of all the films is to mark a moral division between what good girls are forced to do and what bad girls go too far in doing, between acceptable and unacceptable methods of keeping afloat, another antithetical tendency (as we remarked of Trixie and Fay in *Gold Diggers of 1933*) is to blur such distinctions, since the behaviour of the less sympathetic figures is only an extension of the battle waged by more sympathetic ones, and their breach-of-promise settlements, etc., can be read as a parodic version of the heroines' quest for the economic haven of marriage. In fact the film really wishes to have it both ways – using the amoral characters to criticise the conventional ones, but also invoking 'true love' to criticise amorality.

It is interesting to see how *Gold Diggers of 1933* flirts with the idea of prostitution, about which there are various jokes (e.g. Fay: 'If only Barney could see me in this dress'. Trixie: 'He wouldn't recognise you') and references running through the text (e.g. Trixie's suggestion to Brad that if he doesn't go on stage to save the show the showgirls will have to sell themselves). None of this, of course, touches Polly, but there is a very curious scene in which Trixie and Carol talk about their economic positions of a year ago. On the one hand the dialogue seems to want to establish that they have engaged in swapping sex for financial support. On the other, because their anecdotes take a form that suggests fantasy, they are protected from the full implications. Thus Carol remembers a penthouse on Park Avenue and Yardley soap, while Trixie talks of taking 'a couple of hundred dollars' from the 'pants' pocket' of someone she addresses as 'Big boy'. The logic of the situation leads one to think it true, while the details of the exposition suggest a joking fantasy.

What the producer Barney Hopkins calls 'the mush interest' (to Brad: 'You and Polly would make a swell team – like the Astaires – you'd be a knock-out for the mush interest') is thus only a part of the whole socio-economic plot and an ambivalent part, as much criticised as affirmed. This is true of the whole sequence of films. For instance, in *42nd Street*, Ginger

Rogers and Una Merkel exchange an idiot face when they first meet Ruby Keeler, and later, in the number 'Shuffle off to Buffalo', holding the fruit of knowledge, a peccant apple and ribald banana, they parody the lovers with such lyrics as

> Matrimony is baloney,
> She'll be wanting alimony
> In a year or so.

> When she knows as much as we know,
> She'll be on her way to Reno
> While he still has dough.

Intriguingly *Gold Diggers of 1933* seems to recognise that the Powell and Keeler figures belong to a different order of unreality than the others when it arranges it so that neither of them performs in the great closing Depression number. Instead they are seen offstage after their wedding as if to emphasise that they do not belong in such a panorama of the real. Yet at the same time they are obviously important to the film and we should attempt to plumb the depths of their rather dated 'klutzy' appeal.

Powell's is perhaps the slightly more complex persona. In the deeper comic pattern he is the *adulescens* (the young lover figure) by long descent from Plautus and Terence and later European comedy, combined with his typical role of the show's 'juvenile' star as well as songwriter here (and producer in *Dames*). The ancient aspect of the character was wittily recognised (consciously or unconsciously) in the casting of him as Lysander in the Warners film (made by Reinhardt and Dieterle in 1935) of *A Midsummer Night's Dream*. His position in *Gold Diggers of 1933*, attached to the vibrant world of popular music, is typical. He describes the Boston Symphony as playing the kind of music you listen to if 'you're half dead'. As the *adulescens* is often opposed by restrictive older figures, so here he gets his way against an initially stuffy older brother. In a curious way he represents an overt sexiness, palpably there in numbers like 'Pettin' in the park', where love is defined as taking 'a little exercise', and 'Young and healthy' in *42nd Street* where he sings the memorable lyrics

> If I could hate ya,
> I'd go away;
> But it ain't my nature,
> I'm full of vitamin A.

But this sexiness is always firmly controlled in the narratives of the films by his attachment to the virginal Ruby Keeler – ('There goes Lord Fauntleroy with the village maiden', wisecracks one of the girls in *42nd Street*). It is emblematically satisfying that his very first appearance in the whole cycle is where Ruby Keeler, in *42nd Street*, misdirected into his dressing room, finds him stripped to his underclothes, as if to express his latent sexuality, while the scene is, at the same time, largely innocent. In the narrative of *Gold Diggers of 1933* he and Keeler act out, as Mark Roth says, a populist sentimental version of the Horatio Alger success myth. But in the numbers, Powell's sexuality, which, in the narrative is channelled into his love for Polly, flies apart into separate sentimental and erotic manifestations, in the first case 'The shadow waltz', in the second 'Pettin' in the park'.

Ruby Keeler, his partner in four of the five films, is a simpler presence, consistently in both the numbers and the narrative. Though limited, simple is perhaps not quite the word for this persona, since it manages to combine aspects of passive virginity and romantic adoration with a spunky, go-ahead commitment to making it as a star. But we have only to think of her appearance in *Gold Diggers of 1933* – the checked skirt, the belted cardigan, the chaste hair style – to know that her sexuality poses no threat of any kind. Whereas the other girls are seen in suggestive ways (Trixie in the bath, Carol putting her stockings on), Polly never is, and even the name 'Polly Parker' sounds extra innocent, like something out of a Gilbert and Sullivan operetta. This aspect of her is underlined when J. Lawrence actually calls her a child before correcting himself ('You're the sort of child who – sort of girl – who's not cheap and vulgar like people of the theatre'). Brad too speaks to her as if she is a child when he promises that he will get the money for the show. When she asks him how, he jokingly says that he will turn his ring and make a wish, as if she still believes in fairytales.

As we have stressed, the Polly/Brad strand of the love plot is only a part of the whole, and Polly's innocence is countered by the cynicism of the wise-cracking and predatory Trixie. The timing of the film, just before the more rigid enforcement of the Censorship Code in 1934 (which affected, among other films Lubitsch's *The Merry Widow*, discussed in a following chapter), made possible a verbal assault on good taste in a series of variations on a joke connected with Trixie. She christens the family lawyer, her object of seduction, Faneuil H. Peabody, 'Fanny' (i.e. in the vulgar American phrase 'a piece of ass'). Peabody is a 'fanny' to her since his money has the same drawing power as her 'fanny', her sexuality; i.e. his money is his sexual attraction. When he buys her the lugubrious lapdog to which he bears a remarkable facial similarity and Trixie, to the consternation of the seller, insists on naming the male dog 'Fanny', the joke is further developed, culminating in her extraordinary statement that she will now 'have two little fannies'.

Occupying the middle ground, Carol, the narrative suggests, has experienced the necessity of selling herself (something supported by her appearance as the brave-hearted street-girl in the 'Forgotten Man' number), but survived with some ideals intact. She agrees to Trixie's plan to humiliate and fleece J. Lawrence by making him think that he has spent the night with her while drunk, but quickly decides against cashing the cheque for $10,000 that he gives her, framing it and hanging it on the wall instead. We are in no doubt that Trixie would have spent the money. The narrative closure rewards Carol by providing the best of both worlds, money and love in the same man.

The narrative of *Gold Diggers on 1933*, more verbally daring and witty than the majority of musicals, acts out many significances, some of them, as we shall see, further acted upon and complicated by the numbers. In its backstage and group ethos, where the girls (except in the vital matter of men) share their opportunities and give each other support, it suggests the communal energy and pulling together that will defeat the Depression. In its pervasive interest in the interrelation of sex and economics it both accepts as normal and to some degree critically investigates, the power structure by which women barter their bodies for male economic gifts. It also acts out, in rather deceptive terms, the myth of social mobility, that fundamental tenet of American free enterprise ideology which, even in the middle of capitalism's worst disaster, can argue against the need for a radical, as distinct from a makeshift, reorganisation of the economic sphere. Three lower-class girls meet with and marry into the upper-class financial aristocracy. The latter, rather than being seen as oppressors, are revealed as stuffy but ultimately goodhearted. This – though it omits from its consideration the vast middle sectors of American life – seems to demonstrate the openness of the social structure and allows a redistributon of wealth and a merging of the classes without disturbance and major change. Only at isolated points do slippages occur which for a moment suggest that blame might be attached to the owners: where, for instance, Barney says to Brad, 'You've got class', and the statement reverberates with more connotations than the speaker intends, or when Trixie mistakes Brad for the Toronto bank robber, with the unspoken comparison between bankers and bank robbers. But the fissures are healed as soon as they are created. It is, of course, illogical that the marriage of three sexually attractive girls to three members of the banking establishment should argue beyond the particular to the general, but that is the effect – a statement that society can somehow rearrange itself without a revolutionary alteration of the system. It is, in fact, with its faith in mobility, its images of classlessness and of a communal solidarity that does not clash with the ethos of individualism, an oblique symbolic acting out of the renovatory (rather than revolutionary) politics of the 'New Deal'.

The numbers

Integration or non-integration?: le système Berkeley
It is often stated that these films make no effort to integrate the two levels
of narrative and number. The plots are usually seen as trivial, merely a peg on
which to hang the bizarre dance spectacles on which the films' reputations
rest, spectacles without any real attachment to the narrative context in which
they are placed. Exceptionally, a few critics (most notably Roth and Fischer)
have questioned this over-simple viewpoint, Fischer talking of the 'Centaurian'
construction of *Dames*, and Roth finding a general parallelism between the
mode of the numbers and the politics of the films. We would press the point
further and argue in detail against the consensus view that sees these films as
merely an extremely primitive form of the genre, whose clumsiness is soon
replaced by the development – subtler in every respect – of the musical integrated by the principle that the numbers reflect in their linear progression the
psychologies and relationships of the main characters. We would hardly
deny that this 'great tradition' of the musical (running from Lubitsch and
Mamoulian, through the Astaire–Rogers films to MGM in the '40s and '50s)
has been the most innovative and productive sub-type in the history of the
genre. But it is important to recognise that this is not the only form that
narrativised musicals (as distinct from a non-narrativised type such as the old
plotless revue film) have taken or may in the future take. It is possible to see
the Warners–Berkeley films not just as a laughably primitive form of the
genre (kept from disappearance simply by the fact that Berkeley worked on
them), but as possessing their own logic of integration.
Since the typical structure of these films tends to bunch the spectacles
into the last third of the film (where they appear as the numbers of the
'show'), significant sustained linear interaction is, in any case, impossible.
What we have instead is what may be described as a series of metaphoric
explosions that produce meaning in their collision both with each other and
the narrative material of the film. These meanings are produced not – except
in a few cases – to delineate the progress of the hero and heroine's relationship, but on a more thematic plane, not by the intimacy of soliloquy or duet,
but through a spectacular mode that employs multiple tropes of elaboration,
hyperbole, parody and subversion. So, to take a typical example from *Gold
Diggers of 1933*, if you look to anchor a number like 'Pettin' in the park' in a
rationale such as the illustration of character psychology, you will look in

vain. Its rationale is that it produces a cluster of images and actions that contradict the sentimental, romantic view of sexuality embodied in the Powell
and Keeler characters, and makes heightened play with the themes of love,
appetite, the law, the place of the female and voyeurism (to name a few),
developed in a different way in the plot-line. Originally, the curious structural design of the films, with their flurry of numbers at the end motivated by
the opening of the show (though *Gold Diggers of 1933* compared, say, with
Footlight Parade, has a much more linear dispersement of its spectacles, with
one opening the film and another at about midpoint) may have been as much
an industrial decision as anything else, the Warners' factory's realisation of
the time-saving benefits of one director working semi-autonomously on the
numbers while another (LeRoy, Bacon or Enright) handled the plot. For this
the loosest possible linear integration may well have been an advantage. But a
close look at the films reveals that while they may lack the kinds of integration
we are used to (based, as said, on the expression of individuals' psychologies
and relationships), the numbers do gather up and excitingly hyperbolise
material from the narratives to a degree which argues that the films' production in autonomous parts must (like many Elizabethan plays) have been
tempered by intimate collaboration. This is most dramatically seen in the
intense relation between number and narrative at the very opening of the
film, which is not simply an alteration of number and narrative but the brutal
rupture of the spectacle ('We're in the money') by plot realities (bankruptcy,
the precariousness of Depression show business).

But there are also many examples of intricate thematic relationship on a
more intimate scale. For instance, in the dream-like logic of the 'Pettin' in
the park' number, Trixie appears as a policewoman who bars Polly's way. At
the end of the narrative, having just married Peabody, she appears backstage
in the same costume, reinforcing the metaphor of Trixie's dual relation of
manipulation of and subjection to the patriarchal law. As the most cynical of
the girls, she follows its logic to the furthest extent, using it to secure financial
rewards for herself, but is its victim in that the cost for her is the renunciation
of all her sexuality. In another instance there is a marked, almost schizo-
phrenic, effect produced by the juxtaposition of the cloyingly sentimental
moment when Polly and Brad murmur their love backstage with the radically
desentimentalised display of sexual drives in 'Pettin' in the park' which
follows on immediately. And perhaps the most interesting of all is the
extreme contrast between the way Ginger Rogers appears in the 'We're in the
money' number and in the narrative. Hers is the last image in the credit
sequence which emblematically introduces the stars and characters as if they
were faces on coins. From that there is a cut to her in extreme close-up

singing 'We're in the money'. This view of her is very different from that given in the credits (dressed up to the nines) and in the narrative where she is a predatory, competitive figure. In the number all is affirmation, openness, almost innocence, alive with the slightly common, endearing charm Rogers radiates at the beginning of her career, rather as if the Lady Pecunia of Renaissance allegory were played in a modern inflection by Daisy Miller. But the 'Fay' – the benevolent fairy of the number – bringing 'fortune' in the secular gospel of the nation's recovery, appears in the narrative in a harsher, less optimistic light, actually identified as 'the wolf' by one of the girls as she enters their apartment. Fay's surname is much played upon by Peabody in a series of puns – 'Miss Fortune'/'misfortune'/'my good fortune'. We see her plummet from a symbol of utopian liberty and happiness, the positive embodiment of 'fortune' itself, to the mere fortune hunter of the plot, characteristically associated with disguise (in a film full of disguises) from the moment she first enters in dark glasses.

The film's numbers consist of four major spectacles, the opening 'We're in the money', 'Pettin' in the park', 'The shadow waltz' and the closing 'Remember my forgotten man' – the last three are parts of the *Forgotten Melody* show, the first the dress rehearsal for a show aborted by bankruptcy. A fifth number 'I've got to sing a torch song' is more domestic and conventional, sung by Brad, composing at the piano, to Polly, and filmed in a conventional two-shot format.

If the four major numbers are considered in pairs, a system becomes apparent. The first and last, the pre-narrative opening and post-narrative close, openly invoke the material of the Depression. The middle two, however, are centred on the other major thematic of the film, sexuality. Each of the items of the pairs is, simply speaking, the obverse of the other. 'The shadow waltz' with its iconography of nighttime, moonlight, poolside reflections, flowers, violins, white evening dress and gowns, etc., embodies 'true love', ideals of romance and monogamy. As such it is wholly different – except in the pervasive Berkeleyan element of the use of masses of participants to make spectacular patterns – from the brash daylight world of 'Pettin' in the park' where relatively unsublimated sexual drives are on display in a panorama of carnality. Treated as a pair, the numbers are related by opposition; dramatising antithetical definitions that the film balances simultaneously, love as romantic desire and love as the play of sexual drives. In both, the same pair of lovers (Brad/Powell and Polly/Keeler) metamorphose into a seemingly endless series of other pairs. But whereas in 'The shadow waltz' such splittings and reflections celebrate the centrality of the monogamous couple, the context of the second suggests that the pairs are infinitely interchangeable in anonymous couplings, in the domain of appetite rather than sentiment.

Whereas Keeler and Powell dominate the numbers concerned with the world of Eros, Ginger Rogers and Joan Blondell are the leading presences of the two numbers that belong to the domain of Plutus, numbers dominated by the economic concerns of the Depression and recovery. These numbers are equally antithetical. 'We're in the money', an ode to a repaired capitalist economy, is dominated by a décor of giant dollar pieces, whose legend 'In God we trust' expresses a providential confidence in the return of the economic cycle to prosperity. It is danced by nubile showgirls whose bodies, especially the sexual areas of breasts and crotch, are clothed in smaller versions of the same currency. It is also based on ingenious tropes celebrating the powers of money, as, for instance, when the girls are lined behind Ginger Rogers in such a way that all but their arms are invisible, metamorphosing her into a many-armed Hindu goddess of plenty. Strangest of all is the casual surrealism of Ginger Rogers' scatty variation on the lyrics when she sings them in 'Pig-Latin' (a language system that distorts words with the addition of extra syllables), in a kind of pentecostal ritual of speaking in tongues to celebrate the return of heat to the frozen economy, or a latter-day version of the lines Ben Jonson gave to Volpone on the powers of gold – 'the dumb God that givest all men tongues'. This spectacle, interrupted by the entry of the bailiffs, is economic fantasy disrupted by economic realism. Its twin, which symmetrically closes the film, 'Remember my forgotten man', moves away from a downbeat economic realism which acts out Depression misery in a Hopper-like townscape, to an optimistic climax in which the realism is shaped into a moment of symbolic extravagance which echoes the appearance of Maria before the suffering workers in Fritz Lang's *Metropolis*, with Joan Blondell, prostitute and Madonna, female symbol of the Republic and 'spirit of the Depression', saluted by the masses. These men, previously seen as soldiers and then in breadlines, have marched forward rather threateningly from the back of the stage towards the audience. As ex-veterans (something clearly established by the lyrics and visuals) these 'forgotten men' must have reminded the audience of the Bonus Expeditionary Force, claiming war pensions not officially due until 1945, 20,000 of whom camped in Washington in June 1932. A serious disturbance in which a policeman, firing into the crowd, killed two men, resulted in the extraordinary decision to use infantry, cavalry, tanks and teargas (under the command of General MacArthur) to clear the area. As men recalling these marchers move forward threateningly, they stop and turn, kneeling imploringly towards Joan Blondell with the plea 'Remember your forgotten men'. Here, as distinct from the opening spectacle, the fantasy of this number is based upon the realistic world of the narrative – in fact upon a more depressed social picture than is ever shown in the stylised comedy of the plot – incorporating it and defusing its threat, investing it with hope.

Eros and Plutus

The title of Barney Hopkins' new show, '*Forgotten Melody*', clarifies the film's dual levels of significance in at least two ways. While highlighting the grimness of Depression life in 1933 it simultaneously recalls what Herbert Marcuse has called the past 'time of gratification and fulfilment'. The new show is partially about forgotten men – the war veterans who now loiter on street corners, queue up for soup, and drift towards oblivion – but also about recapturing the forgotten melodies, rhythms and pleasures associated with Eros, an all but defunct deity, ignored by a world with neither the time nor the energy for sexual gratification, but, even so, reincarnated here in *Gold Diggers of 1933* in the 'Pettin' in the park' number. Marcuse puts it like this:

> From the myth of Orpheus to the novel of Proust, happiness and freedom have been linked with the idea of the recapture of time: the *temps perdu*. Remembrance retrieves the *temps perdu* which was the time of gratification and fulfilment. Eros, penetrating into consciousness, is moved by remembrance; with it he protests against the order of renunciation; he uses memory in his effort to defeat time in a world dominated by time. But in so far as time retains its power over Eros, happiness is essentially a thing of the past. (*Eros and Civilization*)

However, as 'We're in the money' (the number from the dying show) reminds us, the instinctual and passionate tendencies are not totally buried under the economic constraints of the times, even though, at the narrative level, almost everyone is preoccupied by the struggle for survival. Consequently, when the world is released from the severest financial pressures – as Brad steps in with his $15,000 – a show can once again give space to revelry and celebration of life, and, as we look into *Forgotten Melody* and Busby Berkeley's numbers, we see how an injection of wealth leads to freer celebrations of courtship and love. Even the great 'Forgotten man' number is not merely a litany to ex-soldiers tossed on to dungheaps by an uncaring society, but also a hymn to a goddess of love.

While, in the eyes of austerity, 'We're in the money' is a wishfulfilment number about renewed prosperity that barely masks the paranoia of life without money, 'Pettin' in the park', a number in a show with a sound financial basis, swerves away from the combined themes of money as catalyst and the cruder associations of women and materialistic value, to a view of women from the perspectives of love, courtship and marriage.

One of the most striking features of the number is the way it replaces Ginger Rogers with the demure Ruby Keeler. The number introduces us to a comic but threatening world of sex. The park – the site of various forms of 'pettin' ' – is clearly a place where sexual instincts are liberated. The caged apes, seen canoodling in closeup, are there to remind us of the park's real business, more animal than spiritual. We move from the apes to three singing policemen, who have picked up the theme of 'pettin' ', but seem to mock it sceptically. But the more tolerant camera looks for and finds other couples, young and old, black and white, seated on benches rocking to the rhythm of their heartbeats, who seek relief from social laws and yield themselves up to Eros. This law is embodied by the anarchic and rather unnerving dwarf/infant with his peashooter (rather than bow and arrow) who leaps out of his pram and rollerskates expertly away from the policemen who frustratedly chase after him, losers in the contest between the laws of instinct and social repression.

As officers of the social law the policemen can be expected to scoff at love. When Polly, after a row, leaves her suitor's taxi and is therefore compelled to make her own way home, they point her in the direction of the 'Roller skate service for girls who have to make their own way home', jeering and laughing, seeming, like Trixie who is also here in the guise of a policewoman, in the economic and ideological pay of society, to gloat over the fracas and disappointments of desire. But the knowing Cupid frustrates these killjoys, leading them a merry chase and actually skating through their legs in Berkeley's self-parody of his most notoriously phallocentric shot through the chorus girls' legs. This done, he takes us on a tour – in the natural settings of sun, snow and rain – of sexual pleasures through silk stockings, suspenders, naked flesh and a series of suggestive shapes. This culminates in a gesture that establishes his solidarity with Dick Powell/Brad. The Cupid offers Brad a tin opener to cut into Polly's provocative tin shield of a blouse, allowing the victory, through love's ingenuity, of instinct over reason.

As played by Ruby Keeler, Polly is the nation's pure sweetheart. Her lilting tone of voice and calf-like expression have given the persona away well before she appears for the first time in the number. When she does make her first entrance in the stage show, to sit, with a mixture of coyness and daring, beside Brad who reads a book entitled *Advice to Those in Love,* she may seem mummified in the wraps of ideological repression. Yet the traces of independence, rebellion and excess have not been quite erased from her identity. She can join in Brad's song with lines like 'Oh my!' (rhyming with 'Pettin' on the sly'), her reproachful refrain 'Bad boy' is as much admiring as admonitory, and eventually she takes the initiative with the words 'Come on, I've been waiting long/Why don't we get started', thereby leading Brad to expect more from her later on. In due course Brad is disappointed when, we presume, she draws the line at too serious 'pettin' ', hence the fight in the taxi. But, chastened by her ordeal of going home alone as a punishment for taking the desired quality of demureness too far, she finally returns to Brad's embrace, surrounded by a multitude of similar lovers, and seems not too disturbed by his final and successful attempt to remove all physical barriers to his sexual progress.

The logic of the number runs something like this. Men seek sexual gratification, as do women, though in a more covert way since they are required to balance desire with reluctance. If men's desires are too much frustrated, then they punish women by withdrawing their courtesy, their veneer of gentleman-liness, and make their dames/damsels go home unescorted. And while some women are militantly virginal, 'career girls' making no capitulation to male demands – like the hostile troupe of suited young women who pour out of the roller-skate depot, all heading unaccompanied for home – Polly is redeemed in male eyes by her vulnerability and sweetness, both qualities that combine with her innate pert sexiness to create the dated charm that Ruby Keeler embodied.

Brad, of course, conquers Polly who, it is implied, becomes a co-celebrant of the Cupid's religion of love. In the next number he exalts her beauty and a much more ethereal version of desire. In this, 'The shadow waltz', he is transformed from the informally dressed, slightly cocky boy from an ordinary neighbourhood trying his luck in a city park, into a shining knight of love, singing loftily (operetta fashion as distinct from crooning) in the stylised romantic setting of a daydream. Brad is dressed in glimmering, eye-aching morning dress, while Polly is transformed from the shy but smart little stenographer-type and is now dressed very elegantly in a somewhat futuristic design. Yet, curiously, there is a reflection in the chic 'Shadow waltz' costume of her earlier suit of armour from the park. Now she wears an alluring creation with a shimmering metallic motif that matches the metallic effect of her blonde wig, and these together make one conscious of the several numbers' continuing ideological association between women and exchange value, e.g. coins ('We're in the money'), armour protecting the precious jewel of virginity which is both desired and resented by the male ('Pettin' in the park'), and now gold-plating ('The shadow waltz'). Like the equations in Renaissance poetry between women and precious metals and stones, Polly as 1930s America's virtuous domesticated woman is imaged in terms of materialistic worth.

She is one of the numbers' versions of America's ideal of 'real' womanhood. Among other things the film traces the quest by three men for 'real' womanhood, as Peabody's words remind us: 'First time in my life . . . Real love . . . true love . . . with a real woman'. Trixie is not of course, in any of the senses Peabody misguidedly means, a 'real' woman. She is, on the other hand, the film's spirit of unsentimental comedy, alive to the weaknesses of suckers, particularly rich male ones. But where Trixie is the character who perhaps too cynically sees through the follies and hypocrisies of society, not to protest against them but to manipulate them to her own advantage, the third of the trio, Carol, is, like Maria in *Metropolis*, the nation's Madonna, its intercessor, rising above the Depression to lead its male victims to redemption through love.

She may be 'cheap' (the money metaphor again), and 'vulgar' (like the Virgin Mary before her, chosen from the common people), but she is undoubtedly, in the terms proposed by the film, most men's notion of a 'real' woman. Rather than Polly's ingenuousness and Trixie's ingenuity, she possesses a radiant, outward-going sexuality. While in 'Pettin' in the park' Trixie takes on the masculine role of a cop and Polly is the girl-next-door, later mixed up with the idealised virgin beauty of 'The shadow waltz', Carol is presented as the ideal woman, both sexual and maternal; in some senses capable of taking the initiative (as she puts down the cop who tries to move the hobo veteran along), but ultimately investing her strength in a man (like those strong, suffering heroines of the 'woman's picture', Joan Crawford and Margaret Sullavan). The costume and make-up are again primary expressions of this ideology and attitude of mind. Joan Blondell as Carol stands confidently in a tight-fitting skirt, belt emphasising curves, décolletée, around her neck a scarf suggesting a studied but impoverished elegance and simultaneously her bondage in solidarity with her man. The eye make-up and the permed hair suggest allure – the necessary pose in her enforced role as prostitute – but also indicate that looking physically right for 'my man' is important to her. For *Gold Diggers of 1933*, she represents the ideal, Marcuse's permanent vision of gratification and fulfilment, as it mixes with the constraints of a specific sexual ideology. This is the women who responds sexually but caringly to men; the woman who is not ashamed to admit that once her man 'used to take care of me', reminding career girls that fulfilment need not always be sought behind a typewriter. As the masses kneel before her, they are the economically dispossessed saluting the coming New Deal through 'the spirit of the Depression'. They are also men kneeling before the goddess of their dreams.

The Merry Widow (1934) and Operetta

The contexts of film operetta

'I prefer Paris; Paris, Paramount' – Ernst Lubitsch

Operetta in the Hollywood musical means the tunes of Sigmund Romberg and Rudolf Friml, exotic Byzantine plots and chocolate-box settings, Kathryn Grayson, Ann Blyth, Jeannette MacDonald and Nelson Eddy as stars, and stiff dialogue that passes for English ('Follow the vulture and he will lead you always to death' – typical example from *The Desert Song*). As John Russell Taylor points out, film musicals grew out of stage romantic operetta and musical comedy, and should be distinguished from stage operetta of the Offenbach or Gilbert and Sullivan variety. The lushly romantic stage operettas of Romberg and Friml were translated to the screen in the thirties, and they initiated a tradition of sub-genre musical operettas that lasted well into the fifties with films like *The Desert Song* (1953), and *Rose Marie* (1954). *Deep in My Heart* (1954), the 'biopic' about Sigmund Romberg, featuring a galaxy of stars in choice clips from the shows, only proved that operetta was still box-office even then.

And yet, for all their undeniable charm, these films pay the price of taking their subject matter too seriously, and they are eclipsed by the brilliance of the ironical, quasi-satirical operettas made by Ernst Lubitsch and Rouben Mamoulian in the '30s, typically at Paramount studios. Both seized on the patterns of unreality, excess, uncomplicated heroism and spotless beauty, as inspiration for their own remarkably similar and unique blend of wit, elegance, shimmering beauty and what the movie trailers used to call 'Romance'. Paramount indulged their talents and the results were of course brilliant musicals like *Love Me Tonight, High, Wide and Handsome, The Love Parade* and *One Hour with You*.

If we concentrate on Lubitsch and *The Merry Widow* (made at MGM in 1934, but with characteristic Paramount feeling and style), it is primarily because of a conviction that this film manages more than the others to sustain an extraordinary balance between all the elements that typify the best work of these directors. *The Merry Widow,* in Lubitsch's hands, invites a mixed response: like the other Lubitsch–Mamoulian films, it is benignly iconoclastic where social pretension, loftiness or even love are concerned, but the film is not pure satire. It recognises the fatal allure of elegance, and therefore refuses to allow one the ambivalent comfort of a detached critical superiority. We note the folly of sophistication, but are made to feel that there is in glamour an unaccountable, almost mysterious power to exalt and vivify one's feelings. Jeannette MacDonald's gowns and lingerie are, from one point of view, worn in the service of irony, but, from another, they are designed to contribute to the film's atmosphere of chic eroticism: the film knows that love is for fools, an imprisonment of the heart and mind (as the prison scene makes visually clear at the end of the film), but we are rarely allowed to lose the feeling that life would be dull and meaningless without it, or, at any rate, without the illusion of its availability. As Jeannette MacDonald sings 'Vilia', scepticism and delight vie for our attention.

And although our own marginal preference for *The Merry Widow* over *Love Me Tonight,* its nearest rival, has meant favouring Lubitsch as the focus of our interest in this chapter, we are very conscious that Mamoulian is no stranger to the demands of the mixed response. Yet, if one reason had to be given for our choice, it might be that *Love Me Tonight* seems to lack, for all its matching wit and elegance, that touch of melancholy which makes its rival just a little closer to the elegiac reality of human existence, and therefore that much more irresistible to anyone not wholly addicted to frivolity. Like *Love Me Tonight,* it is a fairy tale. There are no fairy godmothers weaving tapestries about Prince Charming, as there are in *Love Me Tonight,* but the imaginative territory is identical.

Made and released the year after *Gold Diggers of 1933* and the same year as the brash Americana of *Dames, The Merry Widow* is the last of six musicals that form a group as coherent and quite as remarkable as either the Berkeley–Warners or the Rogers–Astaire–RKO series. The list runs: *The Love Parade* (Lubitsch, 1929), *Monte Carlo* (Lubitsch, 1930), *The Smiling Lieutenant* (Lubitsch, 1931), *One Hour with You* (worked on by both Cukor and Lubitsch, 1932), and *Love Me Tonight* (Mamoulian, 1932). All of these films were made at Paramount, but *The Merry Widow* is an MGM film, deliberately setting out to revive, imitate and outdo, with all the added resources and gloss of the wealthiest and least Depression-affected of the studios, the world of those earlier films. With that in mind, MGM brought together again many of the acting and production personnel who give those films something of the idiosyncrasy we associate with directors like Billy Wilder, Bergman, Buñuel in his last phase and Fassbinder, a sense of a mode that has found – whatever other pressures assail it – a perfect set of participants. Both Maurice Chevalier and Jeannette MacDonald appear for the fifth time, Lorenz Hart had already worked on *Love Me Tonight*, Ernst Vajda and Samson Raphaelson were old Lubitsch writers, with Vajda on his fourth musical, and Raphaelson on his third.

Franz Lehar's operetta, *Die Lustige Witwe*, first performed in 1905, has been a popular subject with American film makers: a two-reel film in 1912, von Stroheim's classic of 1925, then Lubitsch's version, and a later, un-impressive version directed by Curtis Bernhardt in 1952. Von Stroheim had already taken liberties with the narrative – in his hands the story concerns an American heroine who is widowed when her new but elderly foot-fetishist of a husband dies of over-excitement on his wedding night – but MGM probably had something less outrageous in mind when their later version was set up, although Mayer and Thalberg clearly believed that by signing Maurice Chevalier for the lead more of the wit and style for which the Paramount films were known could be brought across to MGM.

Like *One Hour with You* (1932) and *The Smiling Lieutenant* (1931), *The Merry Widow* was made simultaneously in English and French versions, with the supporting players different in each. The newly strengthened Censorship Code came into effect during the shooting of the film and caused changes in it at which Lubitsch publicly protested. While there is no doubt that alterations were enforced, it may be felt that Lubitsch's style of oblique innuendo was better equipped than many to survive, for the most part, the prudish activities of the censors. Lubitsch's wit tends to be rather hard to pin down, so when Queen Dolores (Una Merkel), compares Danilo with Gabrilovich and Cincovich, is she talking about their general allure or about their skill in bed? We know that the latter is more likely, but she and the film makers could plead the former.

In reworking *Die Lustige Witwe*, Lubitsch and his screen writers transform the slender narrative material of the operetta. Aside from the central situation in which a reluctant count is ordered to marry the widow to save the homeland's economy – in the film, unlike the original, Danilo and the widow are strangers – and Danilo's preference for the erotic world of the Maxim girls (the Grisettes of the operetta), almost every detail of the film is invented. Marshovia (Pontevedria), only mentioned in the original which is wholly set in Paris, becomes a major presence in the film, the real and unreal, satiric and romantic site of the narrative's beginning and end, with its gypsy orchestras, its ineffectual king and cheerfully adulterous chorus-girl queen, all new additions. The love story, initially complicated by Danilo wooing a mysterious masked widow, is further complicated when he is commanded to marry the widow in Paris, unaware that the two are the same. The further intricacies of Sonia's taking on the role of 'Fifi' at Maxim's and being propositioned by Danilo again, and of Danilo falling in love with 'Fifi' and therefore being unwilling to go through with his courting of the widow, are also innovations, enriching the central situation with the traditional role-playing and disguise resonances of classic stage comedy (such as in *Twelfth Night* and *As You Like It*).

When Sonia and Danilo finally confront each other without disguises, psychological complications on both sides, suspicion and hurt pride prevent them from moving easily to accept each other. In the last phase of the narrative, again wholly new, Danilo is sent back to Marshovia for trial because of revealing his secret to the girls when drunk. Sonia bitterly testifies in his favour that he did in fact do his duty – of betraying her. Later she visits him in his prison cell where the comically inept planning of the king and Popoff the Ambassador (Edward Everett Horton), eventually succeeds, and the reluctant lovers, moved by the gypsy orchestra's playing of the tune that symbolises their passion, the 'Merry widow waltz', are married. The conclusion is Danilo's statement (a revision of his earlier remark in court, where he claims that for falling in love he deserves to be hanged): 'any man who can dance through life with hundreds of women and walk through life with one, deserves to be . . . married', a statement which crystallises the film's attitude of affirmation qualified by irony to the romantic monogamy that is its closure.

Yet to consider these distinctive features of Lubitsch's version of *The Merry Widow* is not to take the naive auteurist approach of attributing every aspect and meaning to a single authorial source. Like other directors, Lubitsch worked within severe economic, mass audience and ideological constraints, and he worked, especially in the musical, in an intensely collaborative form. At the same time Lubitsch was exceptional in the Hollywood system. A figure both eccentric and central, at once an artist and an executive, he projected himself, before the age of the 'director as superstar', as a public presence, one of the few directors whose name was blazoned on publicity and constantly mentioned by reviewers. Rather like Hitchcock, he cultivated a look and a public personality that made him a name alongside the stars in film magazines. If Busby Berkeley is the type of the unconscious Hollywood artist, Lubitsch is the type of the conscious one, and to deny the significance of his ability to inflect and significantly modify the language of the cinema as he inherited it is as shortsighted as to see him outside the various systems that sustained and constrained him.

Lubitsch made musicals for only a brief period of five years, so that they form a relatively small part of his output in America where, of course, he moved after what was already a significant career in the German cinema. This later output was almost wholly in the comic genre, from *The Marriage Circle* (1923) and *Lady Windermere's Fan* (1924) to *Heaven Can Wait* (1943) and *Cluny Brown* (1946). The kind of musical that he was central in developing owed its difference largely to the fact that it is closer to his own non-musical comedies than to most other kinds of film prevalent in the developing genre around 1930, with its various types that held little interest for him – the back-stager, the revue (though he did work with ten other directors on *Paramount on Parade*), the exotic operetta, and such short-lived varieties as the campus musical. It is possible to imagine his non-musical comedies of the period, say *Trouble in Paradise* (1932), working with only a slight transformation as musicals, because the distinguishing feature of Lubitsch's development of the genre is his insistence that musical elements follow and delineate the complex narrative and pscychological values of his comedies.

At a deep level we propose that the success of Lubitsch's early comedies and musicals derives from their expression of two closely related themes both natural enough to a sophisticated emigré maker of comedies: the relationship between the American and the European, and questions of sexual identity, both of them clearly central not merely to his work but to the American cinema as a whole. The American–European antithesis is of course a constant tension in American culture, expressed in many different forms – engagement versus isolationism in the political sphere, the 'transatlantic' themes of Henry James and Mark Twain in the novel, with American innocence, openness, democracy and primitiveness placed against European style, knowledge, tradition and corruption; the physical movement of American artists to Paris in the years after the first world war, and so on. Within the popular Hollywood cinema America's feelings both of superiority and inferiority to the Old World are just as intensely played out, not just in narrative content and overt themes, but in the human material of the films as well. With the resources to buy up stars (and directors) from the European cinema, Hollywood has at all times complemented its ideas of ideal native types with European actors often felt to possess greater mystery, 'class' and sexual sensitivity than their American counterparts: a Pola Negri and a Valentino for a Mary Pickford and a Douglas Fairbanks, a Herbert Marshall for a Gary Cooper, a Marlene Dietrich for a Ginger Rogers and so on. In the early '30s this antithesis is particularly strong, with new, slightly tougher, Depression-resisting stars (particularly at Warners) such as James Cagney, Joan Blondell, Glenda Farrell and others, as against European stars such as Maurice Chevalier,

Herbert Marshall, Greta Garbo and Marlene Dietrich.

The need for such stars, even at a time when many dominant types proclaim a separate Americanness quite aggressively, suggests that though America might at the Armistice have inherited the world, there was the more than residual suspicion that the Old World knew how to live in ways the New did not. Looking at the three most significant groups of musicals in the thirties in this light proves to be particularly revealing. Unlike the Lubitsch films and the Astaire–Rogers films, the Berkeley–Warners films are wholly American in ethos and cast (in both senses). The Depression seems to turn them inwards, to render European values irrelevant in the parade of American types trying to get the 'long-lost dollar . . . back to the fold'. The major Astaire–Rogers films, made after the height of the Depression and the inauguration of the New Deal, use, at least in the early instances, European settings (London, Venice, Paris). Fred and Ginger as Americans enjoy the glamour and sophistication of Europe, the old world charms of bandstands in London and gondolas in Venice, but they are there as inheritors, superiors. Europeans are either too stuffy (like the recurrent Eric Blore Englishman), or too effete (like Erik Rhodes, actually an American but specialising in European gigolo types).

In the dance, as in life, Europe does have graces to offer (the waltz, the ballet, 'the Continental'), but it lays them at the feet of the American dancers and lovers. While the Berkeley films take nothing from Europe, and the Astaire–Rogers films take a great deal, the Lubitsch/Paramount films are, without exception set in Europe: 'Paris, Paramount', Monte Carlo, Sylvania or Marshovia, and feature without exception a European leading man (Chevalier and, in the exceptional case, in *Monte Carlo*, Jack Buchanan). And though some of them are made at the height of the Depression, they often invoke the hierarchical society of aristocratic privilege that Americans are supposed to have surpassed, sometimes satirically (as in the ludicrous business where Danilo and Popoff almost fight a duel over nothing in *The Merry Widow*), but sometimes nostalgically. This latter is not, one supposes, a literal yearning for those social forms, but for certain effects that they connote: grace, poise, a freedom from economic struggle, a life of style. Clearly in these films the European is in many ways to be admired, and the charm of Maurice Chevalier carries many connotations (in a comic mode) of the desirably European. But the process is not so simple as that; the benefits are not so uncomplicated or so one-sided.

The strategy that Lubitsch adopted in his comedies of placing the European male against American females produces a complex play between different sets of values, exhibiting nothing so simple as a straightforward

European superiority. Indeed there is a complexity built into the oppositions by the fact that Lubitsch's American actresses, Jeanette MacDonald, Miriam Hopkins and Kay Francis, are not, as the critics Carringer and Sabath claim, 'stereotypically American', 'incorrigibly American girl actresses', but American actresses who can play Europeans (at the same time we remember they are Americans), with great wit and dexterity. Jeanette MacDonald, of course, typically plays the European princess, a complicated sort of affair. More simply, American comic types such as Charles Ruggles, Edward Everett Horton, George Barbier and Una Merkel are used to poke fun at an idealised Europe. *The Merry Widow*, apart from such casting complications, is full of verbal reminders of an American perspective on the action. Thus the joke when the Madam of Maxim's, Marcelle, asks 'Fifi' if the Americans have arrived, with 'Fifi' later explaining to Danilo that it is a quiet night because there are 'no Americans', assumes a more than trifling significance. There is a similar resonance when King Achmed (played by the 'American' George Barbier) informs Queen Dolores (the equally 'American' Una Merkel) that Sonia is one of the richest widows in the world, only to have this assertion given its proper perspective when Dolores narrows it down to 'Europe'.

The other large, closely related motif that needs to be described before one can begin to understand the richness of connotation and implication in *The Merry Widow* concerns the patterns of sexual relationships. Once again, Lubitsch's interests need to be located within the larger context, the gradual evolution (brilliantly charted by Larry May in *Screening Out the Past*) of Hollywood cinema and its representation of the sexes from Victorianism and a moral 'progressivism' to a 'modern' ideology of fulfilment through consumption and leisure. Banal though they may now seem, those piquantly named De Mille comedies of the sexes, *Don't Change Your Husband* (1919), *Male and Female* (1919), *Why Change Your Wife?* (1920), reveal a sense of experimentation about male and female roles no longer as immutable as they seemed to the Victorian majority. However superficial the solutions they gave, however closely tied to the ideology of consumption, they are an important indicator of trends which von Stroheim and Lubitsch more probingly followed, often within a European setting and with an emphasis that playfully reflected doubts about 'His Majesty the American' (the name of the Fairbanks film of 1919). It is not only the European female who is used to signal a dimension missing from native experience, but the European male, in very different erotic-psychological manifestations von Stroheim himself, Valentino, Charles Boyer, Herbert Marshall and Maurice Chevalier. At one level, of course, a film like *The Merry Widow* might be accused of irresponsible escapism from the real world of the Depression. The economic crisis of Marshovia, for instance, can only be solved by the personalised action of marrying Danilo to the widow. By the upswing of 1934/5 the King can even indulge his own country's version of *The New Masses* in the dialogue with his valet (Donald Meek) about his East Side shepherds: 'Intellectuals: Let 'em talk.' Yet escapism, that term often used of the musical, must be escape not only from but to something, and while part of the appeal of these films obviously did lie in a flight to a happier realm, that realm is both complex and intriguing. Indeed, the most widely read and one of the best of feminist critics, Molly Haskell, sees the point that it is their very lack of interest in the material of the Depression that frees films like *The Merry Widow* to make images of great sexual consequence which frequently expose the folly of patriarchy and in so doing renegotiate, as the comedies of Shakespeare, Molière and Lope de Vega may be said to, within the limits of the consensus of their time, personal and social relationships between men and women.

The ambiguities of widowhood: aesthetics and ideology

'There's a limit to every widow' – Sonia

Despite the shortcomings of Rick Altman's argument in the BFI's published collection of essays on the Hollywood musical that all musicals are built on a dual-structured narrative (*Easter Parade* and *Gold Diggers of 1933* are clear examples of musicals which are not), *The Merry Widow* can usefully be considered as one that does seem to rely on a duality of focus. The plot of *The Merry Widow* is both elegantly convoluted, with its patterns of disguise and misapprehension, and at the same time in essence extremely simple, with its male and female principals overcoming external and internal stumbling blocks to the marriage at the end. The operetta's second love plot, which competes in interest with the main one between Danilo and Hanna (Sonia's original name), is now dropped, something which places greater weight upon the dual structure. The film's other characters – most of them invented for the screen – are not designed to compete as romantic lovers for the audience's attention and are, in fact, largely comic. Their contribution lies in their giving different perspectives on the value systems embodied in the central pair of characters.

Décor, lyrics, music, all play a crucial part in setting up these contrasts and potential interrelationships, and no element can really be treated in isolation, but the most important factor of all is the weight of significance that attends MacDonald and Chevalier. Chevalier was enormously popular in the early '30s, representing in the popular consciousness a kind of quintessence of Frenchness. Though the expression of this in advertising, interviews and reviews was often rather banal, with an almost obligatory imitation of his accent seeming necessary (*cf.* the Marx Brothers' imitation in *Monkey Business*), such shorthand should not – we have been at pains to suggest – be mistaken for mere emptiness, since it is crucially related to the complex image of the European. As Doctor Berthier, the character he plays in *One Hour with You* puts it, the Chevalier character 'can make love anywhere'. He represents a more direct expression of the pleasure principle than American audiences were used to, but because his was a persona modified by comedy, it could be accepted without seeming too threatening. MacDonald, on the other hand, constantly plays – though with an edge of comedy and self-parody that tends to be overlooked by critics remembering only her straighter, later MGM roles opposite Nelson Eddy – a character who seems aloof and aristocratic. In *Monte Carlo* she actually is a countess, whereas in *The Merry Widow* the joke is that Danilo is actually the aristocrat and she the commoner, but he is broke and she both lives and looks, as well as acts, like a princess.

Where he is pragmatic, she is romantic; where he is unconsciously humorous, she is self-consciously witty. Whereas he seeks for pleasure, she yearns for romantic love. Not just their manners but their voices too encapsulate the antithesis. MacDonald inclines (as does most of the music given to her or written for her) towards the operatic, whereas Chevalier's singing style is peripatetic, outgoing, casually humorous, full of chuckles and lack of pretension. If Danilo's voice and ethos dominate the beginning of *The Merry Widow*, his number 'Girls, girls, girls', sung in the streets in bright daylight, is soon followed by Sonia singing 'Vilia', high from her castle balcony, into the night, to an unknown object. She closely follows it with another song, 'Tonight will teach me to forget', also a soliloquy, full of secret interior reflections. As the film continues, these antithetical parallelisms proliferate. Sonia is alone, yearning for love; next we see Danilo about to enjoy sex with Queen Dolores; Sonia decides to go to Paris to live again, while Danilo is sent to Paris for other reasons; Sonia in Paris sings 'Melody of laughter' as she dresses, and her unwanted suitors wait for her as Danilo sings 'I'm going to Maxim's'. This pattern is complicated and eventually dominated by scenes where they cross or meet. At the most basic level the process of the narrative is the drawing together of the two principal characters and what they represent, and the modification of the initial positions of both of them in such a way that we feel there is gain on both sides rather than loss.

It is of course Danilo who first makes Sonia realise that her life as a widow

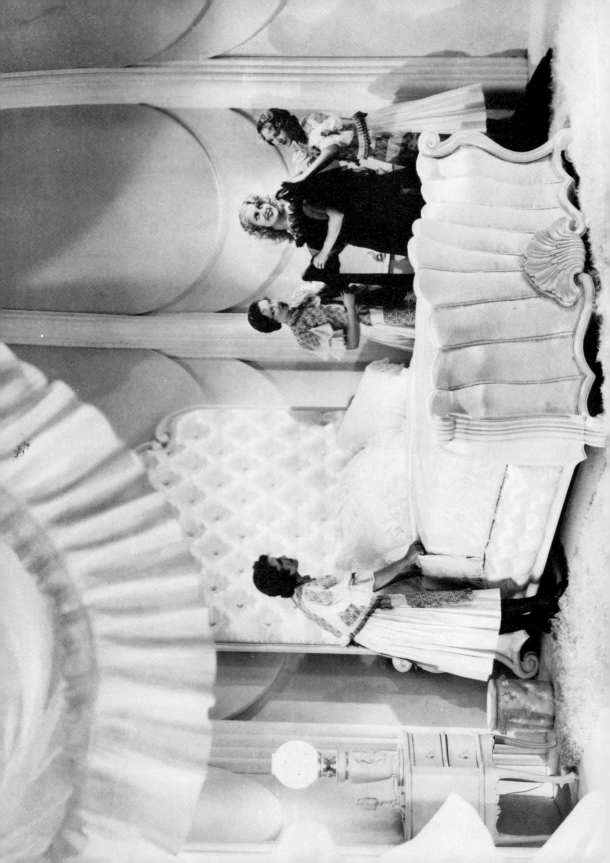

is more than a little preposterous. 'You're such a widow' (a minor revenge on the English as he brutalises the 'o' in 'widow'), he complains, thinking of her sexual reticence, but inadvertently drawing the attention of the viewer to Lubitsch's witty, complex and mature conception of the specific sexual and economic conditions of widowhood and, by extension, more generally, of womanhood.

There are two principal ways in which Sonia is allowed to function in the film: first, as a representation of a woman's legitimate ambitions and desires, and to that extent we see her, so to speak, from her own point of view; second, as the embodiment of male desires, expectations and assumptions. This second function is itself given a double perspective in so far as Sonia becomes at this level of significance both the portrayal of an individual man's dream (Danilo's), and a depiction of a woman's place in society (her value to Marshovia). Lubitsch's interest in her as a character in her own right entails a constant interplay between stereotype and individual. The stereotype is easy to spot, but Lubitsch is clearly determined to place it in an ironic context, for Sonia is not only imaged as a turn-of-the-century Olivia, infatuated with a narcissistic vision of herself in mourning, but given a lover and a social milieu as ludicrous in their posturing devotion to her as they are conceited in their own estimation of themselves. Lubitsch obviously delights in elaborating the joke to a point beyond excess: the funereal uniform is visually itemised so that not merely the exterior, such as hats and dresses, but the interior too, such as corsets and so on, are routinely and seductively black. Nor is the lapdog released from the sweet tyranny of her mourning, as its dyed black hair indicates. Only when she wearies of mourning and becomes exasperated with Danilo's neglect do the blacks, even the unfortunate dog's, magically become whites. Beneath this persona of frivolity, though, lies the film's most persuasive image of struggling integrity, for in contrast to Danilo's natural Don Juanism we are offered Sonia's capacity for true love.

Sonia's two most distinctive characteristics are her wit – a match for any man's – and her greater degree of self-awareness. Though initially out of place at Maxim's where she goes in pursuit of Danilo, she soon learns how to look after herself, at first by playing Danilo at his own game, and then by outwitting him through her own ingenious schemes. We have already been warned, before her arrival in Paris, that she is no stranger to witty sexual innuendo and experience since the overtly erotic music associated with

The Merry Widow: Sonia (Jeanette MacDonald) realises that there's a limit to every widow; Marshovia's chocolate-box heroine tires of funereal dress now she has seen Danilo.

Maxim's is, though first sung by Danilo, introduced to us orchestrally first via Sonia, at the very moment when she resolves to stop waiting for Danilo to turn up. Moreover, when she concludes that her relationship with him is, after all, doomed to fail, she melancholically sings a verse of the number as she leaves Maxim's by carriage convinced that Danilo cannot devote himself to one woman alone. Sonia is no fragile, vulnerable stage operetta heroine, helplessly victimised by unfeeling wooers or an unkind fate but, as the introduction of the Maxim music suggests, a woman who can learn how to outsmart a Danilo, even on his own territory, even at Maxim's: the visual signals to the Turk (later to be despatched by a jealous Danilo in the carriage of a bewildered Parisian cabbie to Constantinople!), the silent call to the fop with the impressive repertoire of eyebrow movements, the appropriation of Marcelle's language ('no Americans'), the teasing pretence that she must have been given, but cannot now recall the circumstances, the bracelet by Danilo, are all delightful and witty examples of Sonia's competence in a world where she might have been expected to be a clumsy novice. These incidents dent Danilo's pride and reveal Sonia's discovery of his more hollow and self-admiring attitudes and behaviour. When he pledges to love her 'forever' she asks for a definition of the word, which only prompts him to reply, amazed that she is ignorant of the codes by which Maxim's people lead their lives, 'What a question! At Maxim's!'. Without much prompting he exultantly reveals the secrets of his usual strategy with women, but before long recognises that his deceit has been exposed and, as if both in awe and in horror, asks, 'May I ask who you are?', Such is the measure of Sonia's superiority.

Danilo, in fact, is Lubitsch's portrayal of a man who, as yet, knows little of women, and as he asks the question we recall the irony, undetected by Danilo himself, of his own choice of the verb 'to know' when he first sets eyes on 'Fifi':

> Danilo: Don't you know me?
> Sonia: No.
> Danilo (to Marcelle): She doesn't know me!

Sonia/'Fifi' does, of course, 'know' him only too well, for there is little to know in one as yet so shallow, content hitherto to share out what little there is of his inner life with any woman, and now left with merely the husk of an identity. As we have already argued, Danilo, as played by Chevalier, retains from one perspective the charm, suavity and carefree sophistication of the civilised European. Even if one were tempted to explain the devotion of the Maxim's hostesses for Danilo as a cynical exploitation of his wealth, there would still be the evidence of the Marshovian peasant girls' infatuation which one could not explain so easily. So, there can be little doubt that the film is keen to draw attention to Danilo's appeal, but at a level which is perhaps ultimately transitory and, from the point of view of the more rewarding levels of human relationship, usually unsatisfactory. Until he meets Sonia, Danilo's notion of womanhood turns him into a sort of Busby Berkeley of turn-of-the-century suitors. A woman's real individuality escapes him as he contents himself with the suffocations through the frills, frou-frous, garters and lingerie of a bevy of faceless Lolos, Dodos, Joujous. As Sonia puts it, 'That's what every woman is to you: 'Fifi' . . . All your little tonights and not a tomorrow among them'. The only individuality the girls possess for Danilo is blatantly fetishistic: one is remembered for her tears of joy, another for her cushions (!), another for physical idiosyncrasies, all of them reminders of sexual gratification, and all of them indulged to boost an inflated but immature ego. Sonia, not 'Fifi', would neatly have slotted into this catalogue as the woman remembered only for her widowhood.

It is revealing that when Danilo first approaches Sonia, once he has climbed over her garden wall, he pretends initially to be the carrier of a message of love from one of her admirers. The scene not only marks Danilo's entry into Sonia's world under false pretences but also allows Lubitsch an opportunity to comment ironically on Danilo's hitherto fundamentally unsatisfactory pursuit of love. The device of the pretence to be carrying a letter for an imaginary suitor does of course provide Danilo with the practical means through which to reach Sonia, but the implications of the device within the whole framework of the film's interest in representation, make one conscious of the artificial, 'play-acting' and therefore insubstantial nature of his idea of love. When we hear that marvellous romantic tenor voice emerging from the comically unprepossessing Sterling Heywood, the eternal bellhop figure of countless films (including *Gold Diggers of 1933*), conventional expectations are for a moment wholly reversed. That such a voice should belong to such an exterior upsets the sense of a world divided into heroes and heroines who have grand romantic emotions, and the rest who do not. Danilo's commitment to Sonia – even though its depth may be unknown to him at this point – proves enduring, but the motives that draw him to her are fascinatingly complex and include dark elements that make the already worrying implications of a marriage set in a prison, in a film which is primarily a musical comedy, even more troubling and dissonant. Lubitsch's work in all his musicals is finely aware of the strengths and limitations of the affirmative qualities of the genre. He does not, as many later directors do, simply upgrade the musical by ridiculing and parodying the pathetic and

tragic concerns of some other kinds of art. He places them side by side and in these cases allows his audience's liking for one sort of answer over the other. That is not, on the other hand, to minimise the serious and problematic nature of his treatment of the films' chosen themes, and in *The Merry Widow* he is keen to see to what extent a mask of zest, charm and confidence can hide the imperfections of what is in some respects an immature personality bordering on fetishism.

Danilo's fetishism recalls satirical treatments of neo-Platonism in Renaissance literature. The fetishist, like the neo-Platonic lover, prefers not to know the reality of the ideal, as it is far better for him to imagine her and to mould her features and essence into the image of his own obsessions. All he needs is an elegant hand or a dainty foot and he is well on the way to picturing the rest. Sonia's face, fittingly for Danilo, is out of sight, curtained off from the rude gaze of the vulgar and revealed only to serfs, those doleful gypsies playing violins at her feet, or to her handmaidens, soon to mourn for their own futures now that a superior being, their mistress, has usurped them on Danilo's list. Not seeing Sonia's face, and imagining what it must be like, proves unendurably exciting for Danilo: idealised not only because unknown and therefore imagined, Sonia, of course, as a widow, also carries with her an aura of sexual experience.

But Lubitsch is not content to limit his interest in Danilo to the level of individual, idiosyncratic psychology. Danilo is made to function as a symbol of society's treatment of women. As Danilo is also conceived as a character riddled with fascinating contradictions it comes as no surprise to find that he should not feel inclined on some occasions to do his patriotic duty, and that he feels at times uncomfortable in the roles society casts him in; but, even so, it may be here, within the social parameters of his creation, rather than at the purely personal level of his functions, that the film's sharply satirical edge may be seen to lie.

Danilo is in the service of the state, an officer in the Royal Guard, the agent through whom the state hopes to retrieve a woman on whom every-thing in the state seems to depend. In consequence, there are many occasions on which love and politics are linked together in the film. That the king should be the character most anxious to marry Sonia off to Danilo should in itself indicate sufficiently the film's interest in sexual exploitation for socio-economic reasons but, should we fail to see the more complex pattern

---

The eyes, the eyelines, the expressions, the gestures all embody the complexities of Lubitsch's wit as Danilo (Maurice Chevalier) meets 'Fifi' at Maxim's, unaware that she is the Sonia he has already courted.

D

in this intricately designed tapestry, characters like Popoff are periodically there to point it out: 'Have you ever had diplomatic relations with a woman?', he asks Danilo with barely concealed sauciness, a devotee himself of carnal pleasures, keeping women's addresses in a well-stocked notebook. The film's *mise-en-scène* repeats this interdependence of themes, emphasising the comic tone of the film through its own varied touches of ribaldry, wit (Danilo lives, significantly, in Queen's Avenue – because he is the queen's lover – apartment B, second floor – presumably because the king lives in A on the first) and elegance. Sonia's castle is by turns awe-inspiring, because of its colossal size, forbidding, because of the empty and chilly vastness of the hall, and elegant, because of the frilly and luxurious bedroom, whereas, by contrast the king's palace is not merely colossal, as palaces must be, but characterised by huge and tasteless motifs on walls, beds and doors of rams' horns. The sets are extraordinarily opulent, and a great deal of detail has been put in to contrast the worlds of widow and monarchs.

As Marshovia is, after all, sheep and cow country, it is highly appropriate that the king should have ram motifs emblazoned all over his palace: the sign of his cuckoldry is there for all to see. Sex is there in abundance, symbolised not only by these animal motifs, but also by the live presence outside the king and queen's bedroom of Danilo, the king's personal bodyguard, standing to attention, holding his phallic symbol of a sword bolt upright. The metaphor of the sword as phallus is further elaborated when the king returns to his bedroom realising he has left his sword behind, and then puts on Danilo's by mistake: part of the joke's point is to make ideological associations between the two men as principal agents of a virile law.

By contrast, sex is wholly absent at the widow's castle, and its extinction in her life is symbolised by a huge statue in her hall of a soldier, also holding an erect sword. While the king's – actually, the queen's – soldier is the embodiment of live virility, the widow's is the sign of an immobilised sexuality. As these two symbols of sexuality are both male and military more links are made between sexual and socio-economic conditions of existence. The stiff, stony sword-bearer in the widow's castle is, on this reading, the king's and he is, consequently, a symbol of the far-reaching limits of the state's control and intervention in a woman's life. Once one notices this visual connection the ambivalent implications of the film's use of marching and dancing motifs in the numbers becomes increasingly clear. While Danilo, a man in the service of the state – however uncomfortably so – is primarily characterised by marching, Sonia, a woman threatened with state control, but seeking other than marching measures, is characterised primarily by dancing. Our first view of Danilo is as he marches in uniform down a crowded street in Marshovia, leading a squadron who concur that 'Though our country will never make war/We've a reason that's worth marching for./Not for battle our banner unfurls/But for girls, girls, girls!' Danilo marches with his soldiers through the bright sunlight, kisses raining on him all around, singing a song that glorifies male desire for a plurality of females in metaphors that see sexuality as a sort of warfare. From one point of view this is all affirmatively open, brazen, confident and sunny; from another, it is shallow and reductive, obsessed with appetite. Danilo's personality is Lubitsch's target for ridicule: so he allows a longhorn cow to enter the frame and disrupt the rhythm and pomp of a jaunty but ultimately silly set of ideals. Marching music also accompanies both the king's departure from his wife's bed and the arrival of Danilo to take his place. Images of marching, warfare ('I didn't fall in love; I was defending myself', Dolores explains to the king), duelling (the encounter between Danilo and Popoff in Paris), patriotism ('If you like her or not, you love her. This is patriotism', Popoff informs Danilo), are all linked together and form the basis of dominant beliefs and assumptions in Marshovian society, brilliantly satirised when Danilo is compared to Napoleon by Sonia at Maxim's. 'Girls, girls, girls' is a Napoleonic attitude to love because it is superficial, full of pomp and self-regardingly overbearing. And it is ultimately impotent: everyone knows the joke about Napoleon ('not tonight, Josephine'), so when Sonia ironically compares him to Napoleon through another of the film's military metaphors of love ('Great man. His mistake was he attacked too early'), not even a man as seriously crippled by self-love as Danilo can fail to see the insult.

But if marching is the metaphor linking shallowness and sexual exploitation, dancing is the unifying metaphor of potential fulfilment, creativity and feeling through harmony, sensitivity and shared experience. Not all devotees of the dance are able automatically, however, to benefit to the fullest extent from yielding the self to its power. The suitors, for instance, outside Sonia's bedroom at the hotel in Paris, waiting to escort her to the nightspots seem destined to gain only minimal insight into the truths of love, despite their desire to go dancing. When Sonia calls out from the other side of the door, 'Gentlemen, what are your plans tonight?', they reply that they will go to the Café de Paris, the Opera, and have supper at midnight; then 'we'll dance, if madam is willing'. She replies, 'How mad, how wild, how thrilling!', but we know better. Terpsichore would have a hard job making these preposterous, mannered, moustachioed clones in identical evening dress uniform bend to the laws of harmony (Danilo's infinite superiority over these suitors is signalled, among a variety of different ways, by the lack of a moustache). Killing time outside her door, they are made by Lubitsch to move in a fixed pattern:

their identical dress, their uniform moustaches, their drill movements all make of these wooers 'marchers' in the sense defined by the film. Neither these suitors, nor for a while even Danilo, are the true inheritors of Terpsichore's legacy. That is Sonia's destiny – eventually to be shared with an ultimately deserving Danilo – and the principal sign through which we know that she is in this sense divinely favoured is of course the 'Merry Widow Waltz'.

When Danilo does dance, it is to the Can Can, the music of which is adapted from vocal music in the operetta, and Lubitsch seems to want the audience to recall the extremely sexual basis of the dance's attraction with its promise of glimpses of the female sexual parts. Enclosed on the dancing floor by the Maxim girls he does a curious, almost hopping little dance from side to side. How different from Sonia. The force of the contrast is further underlined by looking at the way in which the film changes the source. Whereas in the film, when they go to the room of assignation, it is Sonia who invites Danilo to dance, and when the 'Merry widow waltz' begins to play, elegantly begins the circle of the waltz around him, in the source it is Danilo who dances round her and draws her to him. When he joins her in the waltz, though both are taken up in its emotional sweep, it is only Sonia who sings Lorenz Hart's adaptation of the operetta duet ('Lippen schweigen/'s flüstern Geigen,/Hab' mich lieb!'). This moment, the first of the three appearances of the great waltz which again brings them into a moment of harmony at the embassy ball and finally leads to their wedding in a prison cell, finds Danilo pulled for a moment into Sonia's sphere of values. When Sonia and Danilo waltz, it is she alone who sings the lyrics; the effect is that on the one hand Danilo's silence works to give greater status and weight to the 'Merry widow waltz' itself as the musical symbol of the lovers' real feelings for each other (a feeling suggested as beyond words in two of the instances, especially the finale of the film in the prison cell); and on the other, it contributes to a sense that Danilo and Sonia are still independent personalities, that their love is the meeting of two differences in a growing, creative relationship.

Here at last after the disappointments expressed in the 'Diary song', Sonia's heart is finally free to dance ('I thought that this day would be the day/ That my heart would learn to dance, dance again'); the woman characterised at once, as the number 'Melody of laughter' reveals, by an urge for gaiety and, as 'Vilia' indicates, by deeper longings as well, begins to show something of her true self to Danilo. Circumstances and a devotion to duty have hitherto meant the silencing of these other voices within her, and there is no more subtle scene in the film than 'Vilia' for Lubitsch's delicate and brilliant dramatisation of a woman's gentle imprisonment in the ambivalent comforts of those circumstances. As Sonia sings 'Vilia' Lubitsch reaches one of the peaks of his career as a director. The film is so full of stunning effects that to pick on one is inevitably to fail in evoking the richness and variety of his art. But as an example of his most lyrical composition the scene is unsurpassed in its haunting beauty.

The mood is set initially through the music, and as we consider its contribution it is worth recalling that the score of a musical does not just consist of the five or six or ten songs quoted in filmographies, and remembered by audiences, or even of the special arrangements such songs have in films, but the whole musical-dramatic effect, the product of the arrangers and musical directors, which deserves to be thought of in more than the rather slighting terms of 'background music'. It is rather easy to think of these little-known musicians as uncreative hacks bastardising their classical training and taking credit in the Academy Awards for music we all know was Irving Berlin's or Franz Lehar's. Hollywood film music comes in for a lot of unfair abuse, a good instance of which is Wilfrid Mellers' book, *Music in a New Found Land*, which continually uses the adjective 'Hollywooden' without any apparent understanding of the function music has in films, so closely attached to a specific image context that it is inseparable from it for anything like its full effect. It is salutary when considering film 'background music' to bear in mind the extraordinarily sensitive and intelligent comments of Dimitri Tiomkin who thought in terms of specific instrumentation complementing the speech characteristics of specific actors. Herbert Stothart's credit on *The Merry Widow* is a team rather than an individual one. On his score of *The Wizard of Oz* a few years later, which is much better documented, there were a number of other composer-arrangers, not all of them finally credited. It is not our intention here to research a difficult area of authorship, in which Richard Rodgers is also credited for 'additional music' and in which for some reason Gus Kahn wrote one lyric ('Tonight will teach me to forget' while Lorenz Hart wrote the rest), but rather to assert that under Stothart a score emerged that was outstanding in both of its primary functions: first, the adaptation of the operetta's songs into arrangements that fully integrated with audience expectations, with the film's thematic preoccupations and Lubitsch's visual imagery; second, the integration of the background score into the whole visual-narrative complexity of patterns, where it underlines, comments on, sometimes places in irony and even – such is music's privilege in the genre – dictates the action. The 'Vilia' scene is all the more hauntingly beautiful precisely because the score has been handled with an extraordinary sensitivity to the narrative and thematic demands of the scene. In the rescoring of 'Vilia' there is not only a heightening of the ethnic effects, subdued in the original, to match the significance of the gypsies – who do not appear in the operetta – as bearers of images of the wild and romantic heart, but also two other added elements: the plangent solo violin counterpoint that the gypsy player weaves into her vocal line as he steps forward into the courtyard, and the wordless chorus humming that accompanies parts of the song, surprising in its use of a bass part rather than just ethereal strains. This last is inseparable from the strange beauty of the last shot of the number where old men sit or stand in the foreground, facing away from Sonia who can be seen far away on her balcony, one of them quietly puffing a pipe, the other caught in a reverie. The image, so unexpected in the romantic context of the shots of Sonia on her Disney-like balcony, places desire in the context of time, shedding a gentle momentary melancholy over the proceedings. The melancholy tone drifts over more mundane considerations too. Sonia is society's goddess, but like any man-manufactured divinity she has an illusory status. Marshovians worship Sonia while exploiting her to the hilt in economic and sexual terms. On paper, on record, the music to these images might be less than remarkable, but in context it amalgamates with them perfectly, and draws one's attention even more firmly towards the film's delicate balances of outlook between the affirmations and compromises, between the self-revelations and masquerades, between the freedom and constraints that Lubitsch's comic vision of life usually allows.

Swing Time (1936) and the Astaire–Rogers Musical

'Night and Day'

'Only you beneath the moon
And under the sun'

Despite all his subsequent films with different partners, most people have an enduring feeling that Astaire goes best with Rogers. They made ten films together: *Flying Down to Rio* (1933), *The Gay Divorcee* (1934), *Roberta* (1935), *Top Hat* (1935), *Follow the Fleet* (1936), *Swing Time* (1936), *Shall We Dance?* (1937), *Carefree* (1938), *The Story of Vernon and Irene Castle* (1939), and *The Barkleys of Broadway* (1949). A significant number, but more films were made with other partners during a long and irrepressible career. Of these, Rita Hayworth was more transparently erotic, Betty Hutton more rumbustious, Eleanor Powell a better dancer, and many of the others had qualities that she lacked, but Ginger Rogers has remained in the public consciousness as the star who not only responded most naturally to the role demanded of her in the partnership but also drew out the best in Astaire.

Robin Wood has written about Rogers' contribution to their double act as a partnership of inequality, and while there is a sense in which this is obviously true – in so far as the narrative and ideology of the films presuppose a dominant role for Astaire – she was undoubtedly the partner who came closest to standing up to him, prepared as she was to exchange blow for blow, like a modern, sunnier Beatrice to his discreet Benedick, in a minor battle of wits and wills along the road to eventually submissive collaboration.

It took little for Astaire to adapt himself, after a Broadway career remembered now primarily for his association with his sister Adele, to the demands of film. As he said:

> Keeping the whole body always in action before the camera, there are certain
> obvious advantages that the screen has over the stage. You can concentrate your
> action on the dance; the audience can follow the intricate steps that were all but

lost behind the footlights, and each person in the audience sees the dance from the same perspective. In consequence, I think that the audience can get a bigger reaction watching a dance on the screen than behind a fixed proscenium arch – probably because they get a larger, clearer and better-focussed view, and so derive a larger emotional response.

As many have remarked, the visual style of the Astaire–Rogers numbers is characterised by long takes, medium or long shots during the numbers so that the full bodies of the dancers are on view, and a relatively static camera, features which contrast sharply for example with musicals made by Minnelli, Donen and Kelly – who were particularly interested in a dynamic camera to preserve some of the kinetic energy of theatrical dance – and others where the camera more or less keeps time with the rhythm of the music.

Astaire's strength of personality, clearly evident in offscreen decisions about production values, finds its mirror image in the narratives of the films themselves, since he is usually (though not invariably, as our reading of *Swing Time* argues), not only faultlessly elegant but also masterful. His eventual superiority is never in doubt even when circumstances temporarily conspire to deprive him during the middle part of the film (such as in *Top Hat*, to take only one example, where Ginger mistakes him for her friend Madge's husband, actually played by Edward Everett Horton, and is shocked by what she interprets as his unconcealed desire to commit an act of infidelity), of the chance to convince Ginger that she is the only woman he loves. Minor disasters do befall him but he always remains (even though in private he confesses to the heresy of having privately disliked top hat, white tie and tails), inwardly unruffled, the epitome of urbanity and chic.

Astaire's distinctive elegance is neatly summarised during an exchange with Eric Blore in a moment from *Swing Time*. When the manager of the Dance Studio, played by Blore, asks Astaire (who as Lucky Garnett is pretending that he needs dance lessons) what sort of instruction he requires – 'tap' or 'ballroom' or 'aesthetic' – Lucky's reply is significant in a way that transcends the purely comic level of his haste to reach Ginger Rogers: 'If it's all the same with you, I'll take a little of each'. The remark is also a definition of the various elements that comprise his dancing personality, and through that, of his overall persona: effortlessness, ease, a certain detachment, a modishness, without the slightest trace of dandyism, and shot through with a certain impishness. These are attached to a physical frame that is – if one could divorce it from the total style – almost grotesquely thin, with features that are hardly handsome in any conventional way, balding, meagre, lacking any sense of depth or ardour, and without the glamour of youth. There is not only the comic heroism of a Mickey Mouse (as Graham Green noticed), but also an absence of glamour emphasised in *Swing Time* through a series of visual jokes comparing him to Stan Laurel (as Arlene Croce observed) underneath the mask of ballroom convention. It is somehow of the essence of Astaire – both late and early – that such an unflattering comparison can be brought out into the open, since he is clearly not hurt by it and in fact triumphs over the lack of conventionally charismatic talents by wonders of style and self-possession. We are reminded of the apparently trite little homily on the wall of the Gordon Dance Studio that reads, 'To know how to dance is to know how to control oneself'. Some large part of the appeal of Astaire as a star resides in this contrast, the idea that it is style above all that counts, that those watching could also be transformed if only they could give expression to the true, elegant self within. That this triumph of manner, in the deepest sense of the term, over externals is, in the prevalent ideology of the sexes, both of the thirties and today, something that can be acted out in the male rather than the female, is shown by the fact that there is no female equivalent of Astaire, no such tension existing in the female star between interior and exterior. Instead, Ginger Rogers, like all Astaire's partners, is an icon of a certain kind of female beauty as well as of associated temperamental gifts.

This quality in Astaire is there with all of his later partners, but for nearly every moviegoer the others, despite their own extraordinary attributes, are mere substitutes for the true partner, Ginger Rogers. As has often been pointed out, this feeling does not rest upon the superiority of Rogers as a dancer, but rather upon the relationship produced between the two in their films. The distinctiveness of Rogers is that she brings together a number of characteristics thought desirable in the female, but difficult to mix in ideal proportions. She combines skill with grace, verve with tenacity and verbal wit. There is something in her of the tomboy, not afraid either, when necessary, to use fisticuffs playfully against the male, (*cf.* the mock boxing match in 'I'm putting all my eggs in one basket' from *Follow the Fleet*), and in this combination of wit and toughness one can see not only something of the gold digger she played in *Gold Diggers of 1933*, and on a greater scale in the cynical *Roxie Hart* (1942), but also of the managing executive she was to become in *Lady in the Dark* (1944), and the independent wife of *Monkey Business* (1952). That this aggression is an important constituent of the character is seen not just by the play that *Swing Time* makes on Penny's red hair (Ricardo sings at the end that 'The boys will cheer that guy and the redhead with him'), but by the obligatory tough-girl put-down of Astaire's advances which generically constitutes throughout the films the first phase of their encounter: in *Swing Time* she calls a cop, while in *Top Hat* she has already complained to the management about the Astaire character (Jerry) before they meet. The resolution of both narratives and dances finally places Rogers under Astaire's power – in the narratives of *Swing Time, Top Hat* and *Carefree* she is prevented from marrying the wrong man – but even so, when we say that the films, for all their assumptions of male superiority (Astaire as Svengali, Rogers as Trilby), feel as if they are making utopian statements about equality between the sexes, such a feeling is not wholly duplicitous; certainly, whatever ideological structuring of the Rogers character takes place, she is never merely Astaire's shadow in the narrative, but a humorous, trenchant partner, while in the world of the duet numbers, partly bracketed off as they are from the narrative as privileged moments, submissiveness is only one role among many and not in any way the full significance of their relationship.

It is, for instance, precisely in order to stress their various qualities of identity that Ginger dresses as a sailor in *Follow the Fleet* to sing 'Let yourself go'. We can appreciate that cross-dressing on this occasion is not entirely a jokey, sexy skit on gender definitions through clothes, nor just a way of emphasising her plebeian good looks, but perhaps too a visible sign of a woman's search for equality in a man's world. Ginger does succeed in looking extremely alluring as a woman in a sailor suit, but since she has already warned her dowdy sister in the film, in a remark choking with *double entendres*, that 'clothes make the man', we can be sure that her own choice of dress is a veiled unconscious comment on her refusal to be outdone by Fred.

This teasing, bantering, gentle rivalry is also noticeable in one of the early numbers in *Top Hat*. After shots of Ginger in unambiguously feminine clothes – in the scene where she is attempting to fall asleep while Fred dances 'No strings' in the room above – we are offered a view of Ginger in riding habit, looking once again more than a shade masculine in jodhpurs and jacket. When Fred begins to dance 'Isn't this a lovely day to be caught in the rain' in the gazebo, all out to impress her with his nifty steps, he is mildly shocked to notice that she can not only match his steps but also display a few tricky ones of her own. From that point on a touch of rivalry, complementing all the other conventional ingredients of the relationship between lead musical partners, is no longer in doubt.

It is perhaps within such a context that the so-called problem of the kiss in Astaire–Rogers films can best be understood. Like any other musical hero, of course, Astaire woos and loves his eventual partner in the narrative, but the curiously chaste, featherlight quality of this courtship bears some scrutiny. On the surface, Astaire's own explanation draws attention to the decorum he

Swing Time: the intimate rapport of the couple; from empathy to rivalry to submission.

felt was necessary, and in this respect seems to share the anxieties of actors like James Cagney about excessive 'mushiness' (to use Barney Hopkins' terminology) in films. Astaire writes: 'There was a legend going the rounds that I was not allowed to kiss my leading lady in pictures because my wife did not approve. This was ridiculous and untrue. It was my idea to refrain from mushy love scenes, partly because I hated doing them and also because it was somewhat novel not to have sticky clinches in a movie.' But in this prim sexuality there may just be a subtext of creative rivalry, a mutual recognition of contrasting as well as of complementary forces. The prohibition of the kiss is in fact broken in *Swing Time*, but it is interesting to see exactly how it is broken.

Mabel has goaded Penny by saying that she lacks the nerve to go and kiss Lucky. Angered, she announces that she has the nerve to do anything and rushes in a fury of resolve to Lucky's dressing room. Thus the context of the occasion is rather the response to a dare than a straighforward desire. Confronted with Lucky she suddenly loses her confidence and can only ask him how he likes her dress. At this he kisses her, but the moment is further converted into comedy, first by the fact that someone enters and does not see the embracing couple because they are covered by the opening door, and second by the camera's concentration on the ludicrous and slightly pathetic image of Astaire looking so very much like Stan Laurel, with a great lipstick kiss smeared on his face. The point is not that the Astaire character is seen to be inadequate with women, but rather that the moment seems to be dramatising the greater suitability of an image – at least from some points of view – where the erotic, by being totally subsumed into the larger metaphor of the dance, becomes ordered, lyricised, and perfected in an ideal way distinct from the difficult motivations and satisfactions of ordinary life.

There is too an almost mythic dimension in the exuberance and tension of their screen relationship, as if they themselves were conscious, as Robin Wood seems to hint, of representing unseen deities, like some modern Oberon and Titania, or in the terms of one of their most famous numbers, the representatives in *The Gay Divorcee* of the divinities of night and day.

Although Fred and Ginger are primarily associated with the fairy-tale world of genteel, expensive hotel-living society, there is a sense in which their roles carry with them a suspicion that they are not only touched with a kind of divine frenzy, through their skills in singing and dancing, but also with the spirit to find freedom from social restraint. The London club in *Top Hat*, psychiatry in *Carefree*, big business in *Swing Time*, the navy in *Follow the Fleet*, are all images of an enervating social sobriety that is finally exposed by the comic antics and the musical grace of Fred and Ginger. Their songs and dances are characterised as a kind of healthy danger, inspired by some pre-social memory of dimly recollected harmony, that places in jeopardy the dull certainties of the sensible society. Even Petrarch drew attention to the potential dangers of music – in the *De Remediis* while Pleasure constantly extols the virtues of music, Reason constantly draws attention to its negative effects which include delusion, luxury, and even death – and in the Astaire–Rogers musicals there is a dramatised recognition that these dangerous virtues, while no longer seen from a moralistic point of view, are no less potent and unsettling. While Petrarch and medieval theologians were troubled by the power of music over souls ready for debauchery, the Astaire–Rogers films seem to welcome the thought, if not of debauchery, then of elegant disruption in a world that has become far too fossilised in its conventionality.

Passing through the films Fred and Ginger draw attention to their graceful bodies, sing of stars and heaven in the settings of nature, not the real wilderness admittedly, but the furthest nature can reach in the urban world, in gazebos and parks, in snow, thunder and lightning. The dancing itself, for all its polish and sophistication and connections with urban life, is frequently mysterious and almost magical in the way it suddenly comes on like a fit (as Fred himself mischievously explains to Ginger in *Top Hat* following her complaint from the hotel room beneath his). The mood is of course always comic, but nonetheless profound for all that, and as Fred tries to explain away his attack of dancing fever to Ginger we can see that dancing is indeed a kind of fit, a memory, a pre-civilised and divine magic, 'bright as an evening star' (*Carefree*), perhaps even a kind of religion ('Sacrilege!' is, significantly, the word Edward Everett Horton uses when he hears Fred play popular rather than 'serious' music in *Shall We Dance?*), celebrated on the sun-patterned floors in the films' art deco cathedrals of the dance.

The gods and goddesses of the dance and of music are everywhere, but they recognise in Fred and Ginger the best of all mortal mediums for the expression of their sounds and rhythms, and call on them to provide some liberation from the restrictions of the social world. When Fred and Ginger meet, each inspired by their own deities, they not only expose the absurdity of the social world (such as in *Top Hat* through the satire, for instance of language: 'We are Bates' – Eric Blore; 'We are Jerry Travers' – Astaire), but seem to bridge the gap between heaven and a fallen, excessively social world. Music and dancing, their ideological implications notwithstanding, provide glimpses of different worlds, give us a scent of heaven when we are dancing cheek to cheek.

Fool of love

'This is a fine romance!'

Following Lucky's deliberate fall at the Dance Studio – part of the pretence to Penny that he knows nothing about dancing – Penny sings 'Start all over again', a suitable number in more than one sense since Lucky is also about to glide from one form of life to another. The song summarises Lucky's achievements up to the time he meets Penny, but there is more than a little irony to the words, 'Famous men/Who had to fall to rise again', for so far Lucky has little fame, beyond some of dubious value earned through appearances with a group of male dancers whose act is never picked out by the limelight. He had, however, been speeding towards fame in the form of social status, drawn inexorably by the snare of genteel ambition, too easily the victim of shallow attitudes and ideals. In passing, the film gently and self-consciously mocks Astaire's by now already established association with elegance, as he is made to be the dupe of his own fastidious concern for fashion. Whereas in other films – such as in *Top Hat*, through the caricature part of Bedini, the foppish, honour-obsessed narcissist, brilliantly played by Erik Rhodes – only minor characters are made to suffer for slavishly following the dictates of the vogue, *Swing Time* comically sharpens the focus of satire on Astaire himself.

When the other members of the dance troupe successfully prevent him from going to his own wedding, they do so through taunts that he has fallen behind fashion for failing to realise that this year's men of style are wearing 'cuffs' (turn-ups) on their morning-suit trousers. Surprisingly perhaps, Lucky is taken in by the ruse, and he cannot see that the cuffs on an advertisement in a men's fashion magazine have been mischievously pencilled in by one of his colleagues. While his trousers are despatched for alteration he begins to gamble with the other members of the group, and this second little vice of his is quickly established as a potential source of danger. Fashion-consciousness and gambling can both be exhilarating, psychologically uplifting and sheer fun but, taken to excess, are at best a time-wasting distraction from more fulfilling modes of life. The point is made when the tailor is asked to put cuffs on the trousers by Pop, Lucky's side-kick in the film, and the only other person not to be conscious of the deception, but refuses to commit such sartorial heresy. 'I'd rather be wrong than right', he exclaims, insisting 'No cuffs!'. But once Pop has asked, after a delay for thought, 'Why not?', perhaps he too, with the audience, begins to sense the fundamental absurdity and emptiness of all convention and fashion. What in the end does it matter to human happiness whether trousers do or do not have cuffs?

This simple question seems to cry out for a simple answer, but a straight negative is impossible since the pleasure of art itself rests largely on convention, and we have to admit that convention is a crucial part of the pleasure we get from watching Astaire's intricate dance steps, the razor-sharp cut of his clothes, or the impeccable timing and phrasing of his dialogue and singing. Without such adherence to convention – of elegance, rhythm, order – on which his own idiosyncrasies are based (his comic attitude, his bouncy walk, his unoperatic, airy way of singing), the effect would be sloppy, dishevelled and even bizarre. Conventions uphold standards, it would seem, even if in admitting as much we should not altogether distract our attention from the ephemerality and unavoidably labile quality of their agreed nature.

In this film then Astaire plays a character who, at the beginning at least, seems unfit for marriage precisely because he has not only picked out a wife on the grounds of social status (her father is a wealthy banker), but also preferred fashion and doing things *comme il faut* to getting to the church on time. As we later discover, however, this particular marriage would have been unsatisfactory, since his would-be bride and her father rage at Lucky for failing to turn up at the ceremony, less because this might be a sign of the true state of the bridegroom's attitude towards his bride than because of embarrassment at the thought of the guests' sneers. Their fury against Lucky is only diminished, such is their own intoxication with wealth and status, when he lies that the reason for his absence from the ceremony was due to a business transaction where he won $200. 'That makes it a little different', his would-be father-in-law concedes, and on Lucky's promise that he will try and earn $25,000 as a token of his eligibility for matrimony, father-in-law and daughter consent that the marriage could take place in the future after all.

As Robin Wood has pointed out, this is one of very few films where problems over money intrude in an Astaire–Rogers musical, but whereas Wood is inclined to gloss over the topic of wealth in the film we take the view that it forms an integral part of its narrative and figurative structure in a way that sharply contrasts with the treatment of opulence in films like *Top Hat, The Gay Divorcee* and *Shall We Dance?* Whereas these films do indeed offer Depression audiences a fairy-tale of wealth set in a land of expensive gowns, romantic music, suave socialites, and art deco, *Swing Time*, steeped no less profoundly in ideology, adopts at times an almost medieval attitude towards wealth. If wealth is scarce to the masses in Depression America, the studio might have thought it made sense to show a film that displayed the glamour of riches while at the same time exposing their snares and delusions. Wealth is increasingly associated with shady characters – the night club in New York keeps changing hands at the card table – and Lucky himself eventually sacrifices it for love. He refuses to go as far as winning $25,000 at cards for to do so entails giving Penny up and returning to his fiancée, by now no longer associated in Lucky's mind with love but with the shallow values he is at last trying to outlive.

At its crudest level the film traces the movement from the desire to earn fame and fortune to the recognition that true love grows without them. The wealthy are, by and large, the negative characters of the film – the gangsters, bride-to-be and father, and, up to a point, Ricky – while the film's positive values are associated with the poor: Pop, Penny and Lucky and Penny's friend, Mabel. Poverty here means, of course, having less than millionaires, for we never see Fred and Ginger threatened by starvation, not even, like Joan Blondell in *The Gold Diggers of 1933*, in a number. This is, after all, RKO, not Warner Brothers, and the definition of poverty is somewhat narrower; here audiences are expected to content themselves with a meta-phor of poverty rather than to see it realistically visualised on the screen. So Lucky moves from a woman who represents money and status, to another who is worthy of his attention for her intrinsic qualities. Fame and fortune may follow Lucky, since he has talent, but the film intends one to see that these are only compatible in private life with true love, the love that recoils from cupidity. Lucky's new beloved is named 'Penny', a word that high-lights her own and everyone else's inescapable association with materiality, but at the same time, is not 'Pearl' or some equivalent symbol of opulence, but the lowest coin of the Union. This woman struggling to make an honest dime in a somewhat shabby Dance Studio run by a prissy, obese, greedy little man – played with brilliant unctuousness by Eric Blore – draws the real Lucky out of the shallow pool of fame-seeking and fortune-hunting in which he had previously been floundering. The difference in the quality of Penny's love and in the sincerity of her attitude is noticeable towards the end of the film when, meeting his fiancée for the first time, she replies to the latter's enquiry about 'John' (the name by which he is known to her) that 'Lucky' is nowhere to be seen. Whereas Fred had merely been 'John' to his fiancée – a projection of her formality and stuffiness – he is now, as 'Lucky', more than fortunate in having met a woman who loves him for himself. Lucky's fortune is evaluated by a priceless Penny, and no longer exclusively by the standards of unalloyed materialism.

The key visual image that adds complexity to Lucky's progress from clown of fame and fortune to fool of love is, as we have argued, following Arlene Croce, the intriguing use made in the film of the felicitous facial resemblance between Fred Astaire and Stan Laurel, a coincidence that is emphasised most unambiguously and aptly in the number 'A fine romance', where in Lucky's clumsiness over love the word 'fine' is used by Ginger with the same irony that Hardy used to give it when addressing Laurel in the famous phrase, 'Here's another fine mess you've got me into!'.

But whereas Croce notes the resemblance between Astaire and Laurel, and passes over it, we take the view that there seems to be a deliberate effort to emphasise, in a film where Astaire is less dominant than in his other RKO vehicles, the comic potential, both ludicrous and witty, of this visual identity. In a film where the principal male character is frequently meant to be behaving ineptly it would have been natural for a director as sensitive as George Stevens to exploit the physical resemblances between his male star and a well-loved figure from early comedy. Laurel's persona was of course ineptitude combined with innocence of heart, his acts of absurdity as much the consequence of clumsiness in knowing how to cope with the ideological machinery of a materialistic age as of a native simplemindedness. What *Swing Time* does is to separate these twin strands of the persona and to add them, at separate stages, to Astaire's unquestionable qualities of 'class'. Moreover, whereas Laurel is always conscious, without ever feeling the need to articulate it, of the world's corruption and depravity beneath its chic and glittery exterior, Astaire as Lucky fails initially – and most particularly in his role as 'John' – to see beneath its surface.

The world is impressed by mere show – both in the theatrical and non-theatrical sense; as the policeman, representing the world, puts it to Penny, 'Does he look like a man who would steal a quarter?', when she accuses Lucky and Pop – justly, as it turns out, in the case of Pop – of stealing her coin; or, visually, as the very setting of the dance floors where Lucky makes his living repeatedly emphasises. It is particularly appropriate that the hard surfaces, the shimmering but impenetrable structures of the *mise-en-scène*, should be especially pronounced just before the 'Never gonna dance' number gets under way, for at this point Penny has forsaken Lucky after a series of misunderstandings, and is preparing for matrimony with Ricky, an inferior, snobbish substitute for whom in reality she cares very little.

Penny and Lucky are placed together, we see them reflected in a door mirror in an image that stresses the two-dimensionality of the way of the world to which Penny, seeing the hopelessness of marriage prospects to Lucky now that his fiancée has turned up, momentarily succumbs. The hopes of a carefree, largely world-free, perfectly swell romance have of course always been in jeopardy ever since 'A fine romance', where Lucky's courtship had too easily been victimised by Pop's unwitting interference, but when the real reasons for Margaret's reappearance are disclosed, the Stan Laurel-as-innocent-and-pure Lucky (we remember that 'A fine romance' is set in the symbolically pure and innocent setting of the snow) overcomes the Stan Laurel-as-simpleton 'John', the slave of fame and fortune, and the former role is passed on to Ricky, on whom the cuffs joke is now played as he prepares to marry Penny.

As the film ends, the true lovers look out from their skyscraper window and see the snow falling all over New York, a fitting reminder of their first snow-covered picnic in the park where there were still too many obstacles in the way of what was eventually to become a union of true hearts and minds.

Ideologically, the film is of course far from being radical: as Robin Wood argues, men are dominant, Latins are mocked for their smarminess, and the real social and economic problems of Depression America seem to be carefully masked. Even so, within the limits of its conditions of production *Swing Time* ranks not only as one of the very best of the Astaire–Rogers cycle for its visual and verbal marvels, but also as the film which most successfully interrogates its own values and attitudes, especially those attached to the whole business of sophistication and 'class'. In *Swing Time* fame and fortune are still courted by the principals, but within perspectives of irony. Another set of ironies is built into the film's plot structures. In this respect *Swing Time* follows the patterns of the other films in the series, by presenting a higher and a lower reality, the second of which tends to be a middle-aged couple, or even a single middle-aged character (in *Swing Time* played by Helen Broderick and Victor Moore). And whereas the rival lovers (like the effeminate macho Bedini in *Top Hat*, or the dreary bastion of dependability Stephen in *Carefree*), act unambiguously as foils to the principals, making Fred and Ginger seem all the more lustrous, the operation of these middle-aged characters is to sound a warning, which the audience will at first note but eventually ignore, that the difference between engagement and marriage, as Hattie the maid in *Carefree* puts it, is that the former is 'a lot better'. In *Swing Time* the middle-aged characters Pop and Mabel sometimes aid, sometimes hinder, parody or indirectly act as a commentary on Fred and Ginger's courtship. Above all, they shadow the principal lovers, at once portraying them as all that the middle-aged characters are not, but also pointing more realistically to what they will become. Yet even though we may be shocked into a vision of life's realities through the activities of these sub-plot characters, recalling for a moment that their clumsy antics and less than striking appearance are what is rationally true of life, we are left as usual with the overriding feeling that in the united image of Fred and Ginger a nobler, transcendent, emotionally thrilling life is at least a human possibility.

Terpsichore

'Never gonna dance, only gonna love you'

Important as the narrative is, *Swing Time,* like all the Astaire/Rogers films, is definitively a dance musical, the kind of film where, as Croce puts it, 'the dance values are more lucid and exciting to the mind than any other kind'. This is dance of a quite different order from the massive spectacles of the Berkeley films, for the most part based on the intimate rapport of the couple in modern but stylised dress, the *haut monde* uniform of ties, tails and gowns, all in reach of the common man and woman, an aristocracy assumed by dress rather than inherited by birth.

The film's central number, almost the purest of them all, is the 'Waltz in swing time', seemingly without narrative or metaphor, the nearest thing their work approaches to an abstract succession of movements, except that the movements relate to a whole nexus of ideas about the relation of men and women and the sublimation of sexual drive into romantic love. A waltz, but in swing time: the connotations of elegant refinement connected with the European ballroom but crossed with the American democratic social dance, swing; old world refinement and courtesy suborned by humour, brashness and go. It also represents a possible aspiration for which people handed over money at the growing number of dance studios in the '30s, to be trained to dance in the limited likeness of Vernon and Irene Castle, and eventually Fred Astaire and Ginger Rogers. In the great age of social ballroom dancing extra metaphor may not be needed; the dance does not have to have a subject or occasion beyond itself, the expression of male/female sublimated feeling, an elevated analogue to many of the audience's own experiences of dance-going.

Swing Time is the most self-consciously integrated of the Astaire–Rogers musicals, a fact of which it pleasantly boasts in its finale where two of its songs, 'The way you look tonight' and 'A fine romance' have been constructed in a way that allows them to be sung in counterpoint. In fact the whole score of *Swing Time* is highly developed, its background music – as distinct from the numbers on which the background music is based – playing a particularly complex role.

The only theoretical piece of writing on background music in the musical (by Alan Williams in the Altman collection) simplified the whole subject by taking a Berkeley film, *Footlight Parade,* where the disposition of background music is very simple (though not as simple as Williams makes out). *Swing Time* (music and lyrics by Jerome Kern and Dorothy Fields), would have been a better guide to the way in which musicals can sometimes be characterised by involved and skilfully deployed background music

which serves the narrative and ideational patterns. These are just a few of the ways in which such music counterpoints the film's underlying structures: the variations on 'Bojangles' (music later to be connected with style triumphing over Harlem's poverty, low life translated into the picturesque), as Lucky and Pop bum their way to New York on the freight train; or the sounding of a gloomy version of the musical phrase that carries the words, 'La belle, la perfectly swell romance' when Pop announces that Penny and Ricky are going to get married; or the set of equally sombre and creative variations on the score's numbers – 'Pick yourself up', 'The way you look tonight', and 'Never gonna dance' in the scene where Penny tells Lucky she is not going to marry him; or the way the music of 'The way you look tonight' is introduced into the dance sequence of the number 'Never gonna dance'.

Space prevents an equally intensive discussion of all the six major numbers and the finale, but before concentrating on two of them it is worth examining how, though linked in many ways with the narrative, the sequence of numbers acts out a particular version of the song-and-dance romance which is the centre of every Astaire–Rogers film. The first number, 'Pick yourself up', with its different levels of meaning (related both to love and the hard times of the Depression), reworks, as the audience ritually expects, the initial clash of temperaments between Fred and Ginger. This pattern stresses his insouciant nerve in pursuing her while playing too on her initially strong-willed rejection of him which eventually turns, under the spell of his dancing, into admiration and a kind of provisional submission. The entire progress of their relationship is played out in a short and primarily comic form here, though later elements deepen it and act out a near-tragic rupture in 'Never gonna dance'. If this first number dwells on rejection, deceit and acceptance, the second, 'The way you look tonight' (a number with no dancing, sung very simply by Lucky at the piano), is a statement of pure romance, or, rather romance apparently pure until Penny enters to listen and before long realises to her horror that she is a love goddess *déshabillée*, interrupted in the middle of a shampoo, a '30s Diana caught at her toiletries by an admittedly less prurient Actaeon. The number clearly has it both ways, at once affirming romantic love in the affecting movement of the tune and lyrics ('Some day when I'm awfully low/And the world is cold,/ I will feel a glow/Just thinking of you/And the way you look tonight'), and also setting up the situation ironically, emphasising the disparity between

---

A shot of the foursome rather than the twosome reminds us of the way the older couple (Helen Broderick and Victor Moore) represent a sort of reality principle. Will Fred and Ginger eventually become like them? Of course. And of course not.

ideal and actuality.

The third number, the 'Waltz in swing time', is both a performance number (Penny and Lucky on stage), and an expression of the stylish rapture of their relationship after the initial conflicts and before the plot interrupts it again. After this, 'A fine romance' (again a singing, not a dancing number), is a comic matter of complicatedly frustrated passion on both sides, with Penny at first courting a reluctantly reluctant Lucky (who hasn't yet told her about Margaret), and then, when Lucky has decided to respond, backing off from him because she has found out about Margaret. As the two of them begin to feel their way towards each other in the number, the forces of nature, in the snow setting of rural New York, are invoked beneath the characters' urbanity and the comedy of frustration.

All the numbers so far have expressed obviously positive facets of the Fred–Ginger relationship. The fifth and sixth are slightly different, in that the former, 'Bojangles of Harlem', involves Fred alone, while the latter, 'Never gonna dance' is the one place where the ruptures of the near tragic elements become part of the ritual of the dance romance. 'Bojangles' is the piece most detached from the central logic of the numbers, primarily existing to provide a solo spot for Astaire, comparable to those he had for instance in *Top Hat* ('No strings') or *Carefree* (the golfing sequence), or to Ginger's number in *Follow the Fleet* ('Let yourself go'). The number, a black-face homage to Bill 'Bojangles' Robinson, the black dancer, starts with a series of images as surreal as anything in the Berkeley films: a huge replica of a stylised black face, a body with enormous legs stretching all the way from back to front of stage, soon dismantled, in a way that faintly suggests mutilation, by the hands of the chorines who carry off the detached components of Fred's body. Eventually we see that, in spite of this surgery, Astaire has survived and he leads the chorines into patterns, commanding and enjoying the females without giving any one of them the favour of any special attention in what is, in fact, the first part of the number. This celebration of unfettered male sexuality leads into a second part, as the Bojangles figure dances alone, in circumstances that become slightly menacing when three giant shadows dance above him. Eventually these threats disappear and we are expected to enjoy through Fred the triumph of the individual over urban dangers, the power of the values and spirit of entertainment over the Depression. Harlem may be a slummy ghetto, but it buzzes with glamour and glitters with life. As we watch this number we realise the film is not, as we might have expected, exactly consistent in its attitudes, since it is sometimes moralistic about money and glamour, and sometimes, as here, indulgent towards them. As the lyrics make clear, people are more interested in Robinson and the glamour he represents than in questions of politics:

> Ask anyone from Harlem place
> Who dance like Bojangles did?
> They may not know who's President,
> But ask them who Bojangles is.

This, in 1936, is as we have argued a long way from the Berkeley–Warners films, even though there is again here a deliberate, witty play on contemporary social conditions, which in some senses recalls the moment when Lucky and Pop picket Penny's hotel room with the sign 'Penny Carroll unfair to John Garnett'. Yet these instances are of course largely apolitical. These related images show style triumphing over Depression circumstances, most notably in the spectacle of the top-hatted Lucky, an aristocratic hobo, as he rides the freight train to New York. Furthermore, the number is not so completely divorced from narrative considerations as might at first seem likely. A clever, devious link has Lucky, still in black-face, facing the double crisis of the unexpected arrival of Margaret and the angry gangsters now aware that they have been cheated. The continuing of Astaire as black man into the narrative wittily emphasises the antithesis between the native white American hero, Lucky, and the oleaginous Latin, Ricardo Romero. The contrast is also made, rather wonderfully, in the semiotics of song styles when, as we cut from Astaire singing 'The way you look tonight', we are introduced to Romero singing those same lyrics in a strangulated excess of gigoloesque insincerity.

The black-face worn by Lucky expresses – on a purely metaphorical level that does not compromise the hero's whiteness with anything but symbolic miscegenation – the feeling that if it is the world of symbolic blackness that Penny seeks, there is more of the black in Lucky than in the swarthy Ricardo Romero.

With 'Never gonna dance' the couple returns as focus, and obvious interaction with the narrative resumes with the dance following on Penny's declaration to Lucky that she is going to marry Ricardo. This dance is notably different from all of the others in this film and most of those in the series, and it is this difference that perhaps finally gives *Swing Time* a greater emotional depth – though no more grace and wit – than *Top Hat* and the others, since it introduces an element of near tragic dimensions, intensely played out in a number which complicates the spectrum of emotion at the centre of the film, even though the audience knows that the ritual nature of the Astaire–Rogers relationship ensures that there will be, as always, a successful resolution. Though the dance contains sections where the partners act in unison with each other, recalling the buoyant optimism of their earlier dances, this one is significantly different, full of pathos. Though Penny is swept up by Lucky into the orbit of his dance, her gestures and movements are less emotionally attached to him, tending to circle inwards, solipsistically on herself, making the elements that signify consent dubious. The previous number has appropriated the Depression to the triumph of entertainment and style; this one also raids it for an image, turning 'The big bad wolf' from a symbol of bad economic times to one of the ravages of love ('The wolf was discreet,/He left me my feet'). As Lucky sings, the line 'Left without a penny' changes surreptitiously into 'left without *my* Penny'. The effect is similar to Shakespeare's use of monetary conceits in the love sonnet (number 87) 'Farewell, thou art too dear for my possessing/And like enough thou know'st thy estimate', where the pain of forsaken love is, if not mitigated, seen as a superior reality to the economic world.

For ritual courtship to function most profoundly, to allow for maximum emotional satisfaction, the world of the lovers must be placed in danger, the possibilities of loss must be elegantly portrayed. So here the world of lost love is invoked, and so too the unthinkable: Fred Astaire declares he will be giving up dancing. The lyrics have him giving away his attributes in a mock will, turning away from the world of comedy by pointedly leaving his cravat to Groucho and his top hat to Harpo Marx – though he is significantly silent about Stan Laurel whose fine messes he has once again imitated in romance – in a song addressed to Penny, during a scene dominated by affecting subjective shots and stoical looks towards his seemingly lost beloved.

The number is an instance of how the slightest inflections can radically alter the meanings of the pair's familiar gestures. As Lucky blocks Penny's path his gestures are strikingly more diffident than usual, and the saunter that often preludes their dancing is here dejected and introverted. When they dance in unison, Ginger, as usual, looks at Fred, but her gaze is fixed, unmoving and expressionless. Eventually she turns away and simply wanders off. He grabs her arm dramatically, pulls her into the dance, but in the context of impending separation that has been established, her play with the panel of her dress that becomes a feature of the last part of the number, a trailing swirl of material, seems to connote interest centred on herself rather than on her partner, even though a brief waltz recalls the secure empathy of the 'Waltz in swing time'. (Part of the triumph of the Astaire–Rogers relationship is his overcoming – like Eve's Adam in Milton's version of the story – of an element of narcissism in the Ginger Rogers character.) The lovers are separate as they climb the stairs at the opposite sides of the stage. Meeting on the upper floor, they go into a final routine where she spins vertiginously into his guiding clasp and out again, then back again, seemingly into his orbit, only to exit, leaving him alone and bowed. Free of overt narrative and of all external metaphorical contexts – save for the images of the lyrics – the dance is exemplary in showing how meaning is made by reference to the courtship ritual of the dance alone, in keeping with the system of meanings inherent in the by now familiar, ever-same, but ever-varied romance of Fred and Ginger. At the end, of course, these patterns transpose themselves back into optimism in the finale's counterpoint when the lovers are viewed against a snow-pastoral Manhattan, into which the sunshine breaks.

PART III

Two from the forties

Jolson I and *II* (1946/9) and the musical 'biopic'

The Jolson Story/Jolson Sings Again

The Jolson Story (1946) traces the famous singer's rise from the child, Asa Yoelson, so obsessed with popular music that he secretly visits the burlesque theatre, to the man known as 'the world's greatest entertainer'. Discovered by the vaudevillian, Steve Martin, Asa is opposed in his ambitions by Cantor and Mrs Yoelson. But, after he has run away from home, his parents see there is no stopping him and put him in the care of the fatherly Steve Martin. Noticed by Lew Dockstader, he is offered a job with Dockstader's Minstrels. Loyal to Steve, he refuses, but Steve tricks him into going. However, work with the Minstrels does not satisfy him and he leaves. For a while he is jobless, but is eventually offered a part on Broadway. He becomes a star, making revolutionary changes in performance conditions, building a ramp from stage to auditorium and performing with the house lights up so that he can see his audiences. Rather than perform only on Broadway for a relative few, he tours all over America, and this desire to reach new audiences attracts him to the talking pictures. Just before leaving for Hollywood, he falls in love with Julie Benson (transparently Jolson's real-life third wife, Ruby Keeler), and they marry. However, his obsession with his art soon becomes a barrier between them. She is forced to go to California where, contrary to his promises, he makes film after film, and pushes her into a film career she does not really want. Eventually, rather than let his marriage break up, he retires with her to live in the country. But Julie and Steve Martin, now Jolson's manager, know that he is dissatisfied, however hard he tries to hide it. Visiting a night club, he is recognised and forced –

The Jolson Story: 'Rosie, you are my posy'. Jolson (Larry Parks) takes his chance when a fellow performer is indisposed. Talent and luck (the stuff of a million dreams) combine to give birth to the black-face star.

initially against his will – to perform. Falling again under the spell of his art, he fails to see Julie leaving. Out of love for him she has given him back to his first love, singing.

Jolson Sings Again (1949) – made in response to the great commercial success of its predecessor, and itself the top grossing film of 1949 – begins when Jolson realises that Julie has left him. He dedicates himself again to his career, but finds that it no longer satisfies him. Retiring again, he declines into hedonism until he is brought to his senses by the death of 'Mama' and the Cantor's disapproval of his lifestyle at a time when the Jews are being persecuted in Europe. When Steve suggests that Jolson should enlist to entertain the troops, at first he rejects the idea, but later begins his comeback at a base in Alaska where the officer in charge of entertainment, Colonel Bryant, turns out to be an old fan of his. While touring other bases, Jolson is taken ill and nursed by a young woman, Ellen Clark, with whom he falls in love. Their marriage succeeds because they both realise that Jolson needs not only personal love but also his career. In fact it is Ellen who pushes him into a full-scale comeback in spite of a serious lung operation which has made him feel he will never sing again. At this point, Colonel Bryant, who in civilian life is a film producer, reappears with the idea of making a film of Jolson's life. Jolson re-records his old songs and is portrayed on screen by a young actor named Larry Parks whose imitations of the star's performance mannerisms are uncannily accurate. The film is, of course, *The Jolson Story*. It is a huge success, reviving Jolson's fame and initiating a new career as a radio star.

The story – we propose to treat the two texts as a single double-text by analogy with such works as *Godfather I & II* – is both unique and very familiar. As one writer notes with amusing overstatement, 'It would seem that at one time or another, every composer, bandleader and entertainer who ever graced the stage or screen has had his or her life immortalized in a Hollywood biopic'. Its subject Jolson (so memorably embodied by Larry Parks) is, as we see and hear him, like no other performer. But, as anyone familiar with some of Hollywood's many musical biopics will know, this pleasurable recognition of the uniquely individual co-exists with a feeling that we are watching a familar ritual, that beneath the surface differences of the individual films are recurrent narrative structures, motifs, characters, problems and even the same scenes taking place in different guises. In other words, the musical biopic is an extremely conventionalised kind of film, with its own unspoken laws which belong not only to the musical proper but also to the non-musical biopic, that staple product of Hollywood. In order to understand the Jolson films we must see how they are formed within these unspoken laws.

Significant distortion: defining the musical biopic

'Let's agree about one thing at the start, boys. I don't think anybody cares about the facts of my life; about names and places. I'll give you a mess of them. You juggle them any way you like. What matters is the singing a man did and the difference that made' — Jolson, in *Jolson Sings Again*, addressing the screenwriters of *The Jolson Story*

The Jolson films, like other biographies, act on deep-seated needs. Accounts of other lives give vicarious entry into consciousnesses and circumstances outside our own, and, since all but a handful of biographies are of the famous, are also occasions for fantasies of power and glamour. More complicatedly, it has been suggested that biographies are so appealing because they present the lives of their subjects in terms of pattern and coherence, whereas our own, unfinished and in flux, seem formless in comparison. It has been further argued that although biography is by no means limited to the nineteenth and twentieth centuries, it has a special relationship with the later individualist bourgeois era. That is, while biography is a transhistorical phenomenon of at least relatively permanent appeal (embracing such various items as medieval lives of saints and kings, Boswell's *Life of Johnson* and ITV's *This is Your Life*), it has a particularly strong meaning in a culture which heavily emphasises personal uniqueness, competitiveness and success. Specifically musical biopics, the Jolson films are of course concerned with a very particular kind of personality and success, that of the musical star, in certain ways very different from, in others very similar to a queen, a general or a scientist.

Many commentators see the musical biopic, along with the Hollywood biopic in general, as a debased form of art. The perennial complaint is that the films do not tell the truth, purveying only stereotypes and panaceas. One critic complains that *Night and Day* (1946) has nothing to say about its subject Cole Porter's homosexuality, another that Buddy Holly's mother in *The Buddy Holly Story* (1978) is shown disapproving of his music when in fact she supported him. If we had ten pages to spare they would hardly contain all the reshapings of fact that go on in the two Jolson films. To restrict examples only to the matter of Jolson's marriage to Julie Benson in *The Jolson Story*, firstly 'Julie Benson' (Ruby Keeler refused to allow her name to be used in the film) was Jolson's third wife, not his first. Their marriage broke up not for the reasons given in the film, but because of the strains imposed on it by the success of her career when Jolson's was declining. The scene where Jolson attends Julie's Broadway premiere and rescues her from stage fright by singing 'Liza' to her from the stalls has – according to Freedland's biography – a much less exalted basis in fact, in Jolson's jealousy of her success which prompted this attempt to upstage her. And so on.

The watcher whose primary concern is the literal truth value of the accounts given by these films is going to find them unsatisfying, and perhaps even think of them as falsehoods fed to a wholly credulous audience. But such a simple view neglects how the traditional biopic, both by its extremely overt use of formula and by statements such as the one Jolson makes to his screenwriters, tends to signal its own fictionality, saying that 'what matters' is something other than literal fact. It is not just that the films signal this in various ways which, it might be argued, are only picked up by later minority audiences, but that the original audiences cannot reasonably be thought to have naively believed everything the films said to be the truth, since many of them knew about Jolson's troubled private life through newspapers and fan magazines. We may, in explaining the dualities involved, say that there was a kind of compact between makers and audience based upon shared ideological premises as to what should be represented in a biopic, but this is somewhat different from believing that what is stated is literally true. The biopic then may be said to gesture both to the real world and to extreme convention. It derives some sort of important authenticity from its relation to the factual that distinguishes it from the fictional backstage musical which it resembles, yet at the same time has much in common with the strategies of hagiography – lives of the saints – where reference to the real is controlled by the demands of an ideal pattern. Both of the Aristotelian categories of 'things as they are' and 'things as they ought to be' are invoked, though the balance between the two shifts historically. For instance, were we to imagine the unlikely circumstance of a contemporary remake of *Night and Day* or the Jolson films, Porter's homosexuality or Jolson's many marriages might well be represented.

The Jolson of the films is then a mythic invention founded on a substratum of factual reference (the many details in the film that are true, give or take a little). Whereas the contract between reader and writer of modern literary biography would lose all meaning if verifiable fact was altered (i.e. it is unthinkable that Ernest Jones should give us an invented date for the death of Freud's mother in his *The Life and Work of Sigmund Freud*), it is clearly not broken when Jolson's mother does not die in *The Jolson Story* as she really did when her son was ten. Since it is unsatisfactory to say that the films unequivocally identify the mythic with the real, a better definition is that the two are placed in an overlapping but not unproblematic relationship. The mythic figure operates with reference to a world of verifiable fact (Jolson did live as a child in Washington, his father was a Cantor, etc.) but within a conventionalised narrative designed above all to highlight certain values, conflicts and resolutions, and licensed to distort real world events so that they embody such elements to the highest power, like the more than realistic hyperboles of melodrama. For instance, 'Mama' dies in *Jolson Sings Again* in his early middle age during his period of cynical hedonism. His search for pleasure leads him to be away on a luxurious yacht trip and unable to be contacted when she is dying. The logic of the distortion is all towards heightened significance. Or, again, Jolson, after reading about Julie's divorce from him, has to go onstage to sing a number, a number that just happens to be, of all possible songs, 'For me and my gal'.

What, at the deepest level, do such stylised narratives act out for their audiences? Like other Hollywood genres they celebrate dominant societal values but also express tensions felt by the society from which they come. Musical biopics typically combine two general sorts of narrative: on the one hand, *success* stories, refined versions of what has a crude, stereotyped expression in the capitalist morality tales of Horatio Alger; on the other, *endurance* stories, chronicling the protagonist's ability to bear sufferings of various kinds. Musical biopics thus celebrate that confluence of talent, drive, industry and luck necessary for success in a competitive world, as well as the ability to withstand the operations of ill luck, bad fate and coming off worst in competition. The relevance of both to what the ordinary audience think about their own lives hardly needs a great deal of explanation. But the success stories do not work simply by celebrating success in the grossest terms. True success involves the protagonist in balancing the desire to succeed (the competitive ethos of the culture) with the preservation of emotional qualities (the liberal–humanist ethos of the culture). Without the second he or she would be a monster of egotism. Without the first there would be no dynamic movement to celebrate. The genre of the biopic, and the sub-genre of the musical biopic, are, at the most basic level, variants of the central opposition at work across the various Hollywood genres, the tension between individual assertion and societal values, between egotism and commitment to others. This opposition in the musical biopic is, however, complicated at its heart by the fact that the outlet for the star's egotism and narcissism is to provide his or her audience with images of ideal relationship – the sincerity and transparency, face to face and heart to heart communication popular music claims for itself – qualities which, in a constantly relayed irony, the star finds difficult to act out in private life.

E

A structural model of the musical biopic

So formulaic is the 'classical' musical biopic that we can construct a model of it – an ideal meta-text which generates the real instances – as follows.

MOVEMENT A (RISE)
 i The protagonist is marked out as exceptional.
 ii The protagonist risks all for success.
 iii The quest for success is shown to be more than materialistic.
 iv The protagonist endures a period of trial in which his or her talent is
    neglected.
  v The protagonist falls in love and marries.
 vi The protagonist achieves success.

MOVEMENT B (CONFLICT AND/OR AFFLICTION)
vii The protagonist experiences a conflict between the demands of art and
    the demands of life which endangers marriage and/or the family.
viii The protagonist is afflicted in some other way.

MOVEMENT C (RETIREMENT AND COMEBACK)
 ix The protagonist retires or falls from the height of fame.
  x The protagonist makes a comeback.

MOVEMENT D (SUCCESS AND RECONCILIATION)
 xi The protagonist re-achieves success.
xii Life and art are reconciled.

Such a model of 'an average legend' demonstrates, underneath the many differences of individual films, the presence of a constant narrative. A brief look at its structuring presence in two representative films, *Night and Day* (Curtiz, 1946), the life of Cole Porter, and *Rhapsody in Blue* (Rapper, 1945), the life of George Gershwin, provides a context in which to see the Jolson films.

In *Night and Day* the youthful Cole Porter (Cary Grant) is (i) marked out by his talent for writing university revues. He throws over a comfortable future as a lawyer (ii) and the shelter of his upper class position to strike out on his own. He refuses to write the most commercial kind of songs (iii), but, like other protagonists of the musical biopic, does something new – in this case writing songs that are witty and sophisticated. Publishers reject them for lacking the common touch (iv) and his first Broadway show is eclipsed by the sinking of the *Lusitania*. Success follows (vi), preceding (v) Porter's falling in love with and marriage to Linda, which occurs much later in *Night and Day* than in many biopics. Primarily this is because the force of function (vii) is very great, so that the claims of art make him deflect the claims of the women he will marry. When they are married, the function comes into its most obvious operation when his obsession with writing shows leads her to leave him, but in its preliminary manifestation it almost prevents him from marrying her at all. Movement B is specially intense in this film with (viii) being brought into play as well. Thus (viii) Porter is crippled by a riding accident that leaves him in constant pain so that his heroism in continuing to write songs is a major interest of the rest of the film. Since Porter never retires, Movement C is omitted and the narrative passes to Movement D (final success and reconciliation). Porter is so successful that in ordinary terms he cannot achieve greater recognition. What he can achieve, however, is (xi) the recognition of his old University, Yale, an honour that means more to him than any other. As he takes part in the ceremony (xii) his wife returns to him.

In *Rhapsody in Blue* (i) when Gershwin is a child his mother gets a piano for the home and George surprises his parents by playing it. He neglects the solid career his parents think best for him (ii) and is sacked by a music publisher for playing his own songs. Though in certain ways committed to wealth and hedonism, Gershwin (Robert Alda) has a higher moral purpose represented by his classical teacher, Professor Frank who urges 'George, you can give America a voice' (iii). For a short while Gershwin is unrecognised (iv), but (vi) one of his songs, 'Swanee', is performed by Al Jolson (played by himself) and soon he is well known. *Night and Day* is a little unusual in delaying function (v), love and marriage, but *Rhapsody in Blue* deviates even further from the norm in that its hero never marries and falls in love with two girls, the singer, Julie, and the painter, Christine. This leads to a particularly complex development of the important function (vii). First Christine leaves, then Julie refuses Gershwin even though both are in love with him. Both women nobly renounce their holds over him to free him for the artistic destiny they know domesticity would crush. It is typical of this film's interest in melodramatic excess (it was directed by Irving Rapper who made the great 'weepie' *Now Voyager*) that Gershwin becomes painfully obsessed with his failure to marry. (viii) He is further afflicted by the terrible headaches that signal the cerebral condition that will kill him. The narrative has no retirement and comeback in a literal sense, but (as happens in *The Glenn Miller Story* and also in the highly melodramatic *The Eddy Duchin Story*), musical biopics that end with the death of the protagonist could be said to enact a 'metaphysical' version of Movements C and D. So (ix) dying, he makes the ultimate retirement, but the essential Gershwin, his music, makes the ultimate comeback (x) and (xi), artistic immortality. As the announcer at the posthumous concert says, he 'will live as long as there is joy. As long as there is music in the world.' And in a trope of which there is a variation at the end of *The Eddy Duchin Story*, as Oscar Levant plays the piano, he dissolves into Gershwin. The drive that the traditional biopic has not only to affirm the protagonist's art and heroism, but also to solve the art versus life problems of function (vii), is very apparent in this film. Most of the narrative argues against any such resolution, but Julie decides to come back to Gershwin. He dies, however, before she arrives and the promise is never tested. The film cleverly has it both ways.

In these two instances it is clear how traditional musical biopics repeat and vary a basic pattern. But just as some contemporary musicals have complicated traditional generic conventions, so some recent musical biopics have differed from earlier ones. For instance, functions (i) and (iii), which establish the protagonist's difference and non-material motivation, can take a highly psychologised form in which they become a deflection of the star's feeling of inferiority. In *Funny Girl* (1968), Fanny Brice's urge to stardom is a compensation for her lack of beauty. In *Gypsy* (1962), the heroine's fierce project for stardom through stripping (!) stems from her childhood inferiority, while in *Lady Sings the Blues* (1972) for Billie Holliday music is an escape from racial oppression. The first two examples are particularly interesting in bringing to the foreground what is always lurking underneath the surface of the traditional films, the suspicion that the assertion of the performer's or composer's art as an uncomplicated extension of the ebullient self may be too simple. Here that art is overtly seen to have its source in a wish-fulfilling evasion of the rigours of reality and the replacing of love denied in the family with audience adoration. At certain levels the Jolson films – made well before the 'deconstructive' phase of the musical – work very hard to suppress or soften such dubiety; at others they will not or cannot. It is a marked feature of the three contemporary musical biopics mentioned above that in them function (xii), the healing of function (vii) with its art/life problematic, is denied (something that also happens in some contemporary non-musical biopics set in the entertainment world, e.g. *Mommie Dearest* (1981), the life of Joan Crawford, and *Frances* (1982), the life of Frances Farmer). So, at the end of *Funny Girl*, Fanny Brice belts out 'My man' to her audience, but she knows that in real life her marriage is over.

Turning to our double-text, *Jolson I & II*, we are now in a better position to appreciate the double action of sameness and difference the films display.

The Jolson Story

MOVEMENT A (RISE)

i The child Asa Yoelson is marked as exceptional in the 'discovery' scene when he sings at Kernan's Burlesque.

ii The young Yoelson first of all runs away from home and then is reluctantly allowed by his parents to leave their safe, old-fashioned Jewish world for the world of entertainment.

iii His desire to communicate with his audiences and his ear for the different black music of New Orleans show that his art has a higher end than just material success.

iv He endures a number of trials before his chance comes – first of all the minor calamity of his voice changing, then the seeming dead end of his job with Dockstader.

vi His success in the show *Vera Violetta* makes him a great Broadway star.

v After losing one girl, Ann Murray, through neglecting her for his art, Jolson meets and marries Julie Benson.

MOVEMENT B (CONFLICT AND/OR AFFLICTION)

vii In Hollywood the marriage is put under tremendous pressure from Jolson's obsession with his career.

MOVEMENT C (RETIREMENT AND COMEBACK)

ix When Julie seems about to leave him, Jolson retires to the country with her, but is unhappy away from his career.

x Eventually, accidentally, he sings again in public, both he and his audience falling under the spell of what he has denied for so long.

MOVEMENT D (SUCCESS AND RECONCILIATION)

xi The audience reaction as he sings shows that he is as great a star as ever.

xii However, very unusually for the traditional biopic, private and public cannot be rejoined. While Jolson sings, Julie walks away, surrendering him to his public.

In ending without function (xii) – which even *Rhapsody in Blue* gestures at, however unconvincingly – *The Jolson Story* is for its time unusual. The film, though, does not see this ending as simply pessimistic, since Julie's choice is presented as the right one. Jolson's love for the millions and their love for him has to take precedence over personal happiness, and Julie's denial of her own love on Jolson's behalf is itself an affirmation of the self-denying power of love. Also, the continued emphasis on the family in 'Mama' and 'Papa' Yoelson acts to affirm those traditional values. Nevertheless, the unusual rupture at the end of *The Jolson Story* is grave enough for many of the energies of *Jolson Sings Again* to be devoted to working to the point where function

(xii) can be fully asserted.

Because it is a sequel, taking up his life in mid-career, *Jolson Sings Again* omits the whole of Movement A, except for a replaying of (v) love and marriage. Instead of the relatively straight progression from A to D of the usual traditional biopic its structure is a series of repetitions and variations on Movements B, C and D which fill the narrative space left by the necessary omission of Movement A. So we have a series of different retirements (from disillusion, illness or audience disfavour) giving rise to a series of comebacks – the early ones of limited success – culminating in the final re-achievement of success with the film *The Jolson Story*. Until the final phase the emphasis is more that of an endurance story than a success one. The other main feature of the narrative structure is the replaying of function (v) which allows the full assertion in the later part of the film of function (xii).

> *Jolson Sings Again*
> MOVEMENT C (RETIREMENT AND *COMEBACK*)
> *x* Left by Julie, Jolson recommits himself to his art.
> MOVEMENT D (*SUCCESS* AND RECONCILIATION)
> *xi* Jolson reachieves success with his audiences.
> MOVEMENT B (*CONFLICT* AND/OR AFFLICTION)
> *vii* In a reversal of the usual, Jolson's lack of success in his marriage endangers his art and one night he walks off the stage after a single number.
> MOVEMENT C (RETIREMENT AND COMEBACK)
> *ix* Jolson retires from the stage and 'searches for a bluebird' through hedonism. His voluntary retirement at his peak means, however, that his place in the entertainment world is taken by other singers (e.g. Bing Crosby who is mentioned in the film).
> *x* Jolson, a largely forgotten man, makes a comeback entertaining the troops.
> MOVEMENT D (*SUCCESS* AND RECONCILIATION)
> *xi* Within this vitally important but limited sphere he is a great success.
> MOVEMENT B (CONFLICT AND/OR *AFFLICTION*)
> *viii* Jolson is struck down by a serious disease which enforces a lung operation and convinces him that his career is over.
> MOVEMENT A
> *v* Jolson falls in love with his young nurse, a girl from Arkansas named Ellen Clark. They marry.
> MOVEMENT C (RETIREMENT AND COMEBACK)
> *ix* The combination of an industry dominated by newer stars, entrepreneurs

unwilling to take risks, and Jolson's illness which prevents him from attacking songs in quite the old way, make a comeback seem impossible.

x Ellen pushes Jolson into making his comeback in the civilian music world. He is humiliated by being last on the bill for a charity concert, but sings a number that is heard by the producer Ralph Bryant.

MOVEMENT C (RETIREMENT AND *COMEBACK*)

x Jolson records the music for, and is the subject of, Ralph Bryant's film of his life, *The Jolson Story.*

MOVEMENT D (SUCCESS AND RECONCILIATION)

xi The film is a great success, reaching the widest audience and fully reviving Jolson's career.

xii Life and art are reconciled in a revived career and a happy marriage.

The Jazz Singer

In *Jolson Sings Again* Ralph Bryant watches an ageing Jolson sing his old hit 'Sonny boy', perhaps the most blatantly sentimental and dated of all his numbers (parodied memorably by the Andrews Sisters in 1941), and later discusses the performance with his wife. Mrs Bryant: 'Amazing how he can still get you with a corny old song like that'. Bryant: 'I think he can still get anybody singing anything'. Mrs Bryant, retracting a little, is doubtful: 'Singing styles change a little, Ralph'. But Bryant points to something within Jolson's style that survives changes of fashion, a complex of qualities he identifies in the rather banal shorthand of show business as 'heart'. The style – the films say – may seem old-fashioned, but it is a manifestation of the most essential values claimed by American popular music. Bing Crosby, who is identified several times in *Jolson Sings Again* as the star of the day who has replaced Jolson, stands for the ease and naturalness that are part of that tradition, for singing as an intimate conversation with the microphone, but Jolson stands for something more primary, for the 'heart' beating at the back of it and predating the naturalism of the microphone-created crooner.

Though every mimic can do a passable imitation of Jolson's dynamic stage act (Evelyn Keyes as Julie does one in *The Jolson Story*), Larry Parks' mimicry is something more, bordering on perfection. It only errs – but, it must be stressed, quite deliberately – in the direction of a pervasive refinement. Parks is slighter, more finely-featured, greying but ageless in the second film which manages to soften the potentially distasteful real age gap between Jolson and his last wife (60 to 21), less eccentrically slurred in speech. But in everything else the mimicry of Jolson's gestures is extraordinarily accurate,

bringing to life in the performance sequences the relentless kinetic quality which makes his the absolute antithesis of relaxed performing styles like those of Crosby and other crooners. As Jakie Rabinowitz turned Jack Robin in *The Jazz Singer* (a character who plainly signifies Jolson to the audience), even offstage he sways to a beat, syncopating even while he eats his breakfast. And coming on stage, he does not just enter – he runs on. In imitating Jolson so perfectly, Parks' body as he sings is seldom simply upright, but cants to the right, left or back. Characteristically he sways from one leg to the other, arms swinging up and down rhythmically, but with rather more vigour and energy than grace and elegance (though Parks adds to the latter qualities). In 'You made me love you' the hands clench and unclench, the arms swing up then crash down; during 'Ma blushin' Rosie' he clasps his hands together repeatedly, turns sideways to the audience, sticks his bottom out, delays one leg behind the other, dwells a little on it, sways and then jauntily moves off; in 'My mammy', kneeling down, arms outstretched, pleading face thrust forward, eyebrows tortured, every gesture is exaggerated past the point of parody; in 'For me and my gal' the constant energy highspiritedly spills over into a series of gestures with fingers and hands that redundantly parallel the lyrics' daydream production of infants ('A little home for two/Or three, or four, or more') with two handfuls and a roll of the eyes signifying comic shock accompanying the last. Movement means energy, linking the performer to the use of the body characterising primitive forms of black music (though with a repression of the sexual significations dominant with contemporary pop performers), as well as to the drive of the industrial present. Stasis means home, the past, old values; movement (as more sophisticated theorists of the national consciousness such as Gertrude Stein stated) means to be new, which is to be American. Where the sentiments of Jolson's songs hold on to the former, as they often do, particularly the myth of the South (e.g. 'My mammy', 'Swanee', 'Waiting for the Robert E. Lee') it is only through the medium of the latter.

Jolson's physical movements are the correlatives of an equally untramelled vocal style which pushes modes to the extreme, whether the sentimental ('When you were sweet sixteen'), the Southern nostalgic ('Swanee'), the buoyantly driving ('Toot toot tootsie'), or the piquant–comic ('Rosie'). Sometimes the message of the song is too urgent to be restricted by melodic convention. 'He was more an orator', writes Henry Pleasants, 'than a vocalist, a characteristic demonstrated again and again in his excursions into straight

Jolson Sings Again: Larry Parks, as himself, perfecting his mimicry: the unmistakable gestures of the Jolson persona's energy and studied vulnerability.

declamation.' So Jolson's numbers are typically 'dramatic' rather than 'lyric', in their large scale gesture, their insistence upon direct address (a great many of his songs address a person or a place, present or absent), their acting out of a present occasion rather than 'emotion recollected in tranquillity', and their recurrent tendency to declamation. The latter would seem to descend from the declamatory characteristics of black singing which mixes in with European modes in mainstream popular music (and in the case of Jolson's extremely florid style elements from his Hebraic cantoral background and the high emotionality of popular Italian opera – Puccini and the better known parts of Verdi – as popularised by singers with 'star' status like Caruso). Another important constituent of the style that also develops from black sources, though again in a toned-down form, is improvisation (perhaps more correctly quasi-improvisation or the interpolation of words or phrases, since in essence it is limited and fairly predictable). Mainstream popular music often gestures to this jazz value and appropriates it in small doses to give the impression of spontaneous, emotive utterance. Many moments in the films illustrate this; for instance in *The Jolson Story* when Jolson makes the aside 'Just for you, just for you' to Julie Benson in the audience between phrases of 'April showers', or in *Jolson Sings Again* when he performs 'Is it true what they say about Dixie?', first singing a phrase, then listening to the orchestra reply, then reacting with winks and smiles and the words 'Huh, that's pretty!'. In the middle, declamatory, section of 'April showers' in *The Jolson Story*, when he leaves the ramp from where he has been singing intimately to Julie and goes back on stage, the melodrama involves the pretence that his attention is suddenly caught by rain-clouds out front. In this and all its other manifestations, Jolson's act is robust, with little room for subtlety or innuendo. 'Singing with a tear' as Mary Dale describes it in *The Jazz Singer*, or exploding with energetic happiness, it is the act of the quintessential vaudeville performer. Its crudest elements of attack derive from the necessity to hold a difficult audience, its more than temporary appeal – the many records still re-issued, the various popular biographies, reshowings of the biopics – is based on its embodying so full–bloodedly (in ways not always open to more sophisticated performers) the values of the popular music tradition. How centrally Jolson as performer embodies these values – the reason for his prominence in the mythology of entertainment – may be seen by the comprehensiveness with which he is described by all five of the utopian categories Dyer defines in his essay on 'Entertainment', *energy, community, transparency, intensity* and *abundance*. The last is applicable in the case of the individual entertainer, working without glamorous décor and costume, if it is interpreted in terms of that characteristic outpouring of the self that the biopics dramatise. This spills over into the eupeptic excess of kinesic and vocal gesture that characterises his performances – vocally the vibrato, the nasality, the slides and slurs, the 'skidding, descending major third cadence' (Pleasants), the dips to a bass register, the ubiquitous *apoggiatura* and *portamento* and the manneristically contorted pronunciations that may have a double source in the crossing of the immigrant's fractured English shared by both audiences and entertainers with an imitation of operatic style in which pronunciation is distorted by musical and emotional values.

A brief look at what is perhaps Jolson's most typical song helps to pin down certain aspects of the meanings generated by his performances, enshrined in his legend as performer and celebrated in the biopics. 'My mammy', the song by Sam Lewis, Walter Young and Walter Donaldson, is perhaps the number most of all associated with Jolson. This centrality is asserted when the headline announcing Jolson's collapse in *Jolson Sings Again* reads '*Jolson Show Closes. Rest Ordered for Mammy Star*'. The importance of the number in Jolson's career is acknowledged also in *The Jazz Singer* where, after he has sung 'Kol Nidre' for his dying father, Jolson sings the popular song from the stage to his mother in the audience. The two biopics follow by giving it a significant place. In *The Jolson Story* 'My mammy' is the song sung by Jolson in his first big break as a solo singer in the show *Vera Violetta*, the moment of its delivery heightened by the management's attempt to cut him from a show that is running over time. Received enthusiastically, it sets him on the road to stardom. In *Jolson Sings Again* the performance of 'My mammy' is again a privileged moment as it is reprised in the preview of *The Jolson Story*. In fact it is when the song comes on to the screen that Jolson is drawn wholly into the cinema to watch.

'My mammy' is of course a 'black-face' song. Indeed it specifically depends (in ways that audiences used to it only through records or impersonations may have forgotten) upon the traditional outfit of the 'Ethiopian delineator' with his mask of black greasepaint, woolly wig, pouting lower lip and rolling eyes. In adopting this role from his time in the minstrels (something dramatised by the film) Jolson is a late participator in a dying tradition. Robert C. Toll in his history of nineteenth-century minstrel shows suggests some of the reasons for the great popularity of these acts in which white men imitated sentimental or comic stereotypes of blacks: that they satisfied white curiosity in non-slave states about blacks while, at the same time, through the grotesqueness of their representations, asserting white superiority, and that, through sentimental and pathetic songs they created an image of a distanced and idealised plantation life, an idealised family and home, from which the singer was cut off. (Mellers makes much the same point about the songs of Stephen Foster taking on a 'universalising' meaning from a white idealisation of black alienation.) Jolson's use of the black image depends heavily on this last and an idea of happy negroid extroversion. Though clearly such images carry an ideological charge, implying simplicity and dehistoricising actuality, they are thankfully clear of any of the viciousness of the 'coon songs' with their image of the black as faithless, violent, greedy, promiscuous, etc. But while part of the inherited meaning of the 'black-face' image is its status as a representation of the black, neither to Jolson nor to his audience was this the main effect. Rather 'black-face' by this time has become a traditional role, which is at the same time distinctively American, which allows the expression of emotions and attitudes which the urban white man wishes to project but with which he feels uncomfortable, perhaps because emotion is felt to be weak or un-utilitarian. For a Jewish entertainer like Jolson the role is further complicated by being the white outsider's use of the black outsider in order to project an image to appeal to the majority, a situation redolent with ironies, whether recognised or not.

'My mammy' then becomes a triple image of motherhood: the black 'Mammy' through whom the Jewish 'Momma' is evoked and through whom the Protestant and Catholic images of 'Mother' are called up. The full force of its meaning can best be approached by looking at its place and function in *The Jazz Singer*. In that film the myth of motherhood is placed at the centre of the narrative's thematic preoccupations. In a patriarchal culture, where men sternly discipline their children, room must be made for feelings, flexibility and softness, and this is traditionally the domain of the mother. The stereotyping pattern is in evidence even before the appearance of the unashamed subtitle *'God made her a woman and Love made her a Mother'*. The mother here, though conscious of her heritage and duties, is depicted as an intermediary between the old world of Jewish customs and the new one that demands accommodation with other cultures. So while Papa, until his death bed, turns his back on his modern son, Mama keeps in touch, understanding what her son is doing and trying to reconcile father and son. In the stereotype (which might also be looked at from a psychoanalytic perspective of the mother as origin and paradisal lost refuge), Mother is the encapsulation of feeling, forgiveness and, above all, home to the wandering hero who has left her behind. A remarkable series of intertitles in *The Jazz Singer* emphasises this: *'New York!/Home!/Mother!'*.

The song (intensified at every point by Jolson's remarkable delivery) manages to combine an extraordinary number of popular features. *The Jolson Story* emphasises its connections with black music, as the offshoot of his discovery of jazz in New Orleans, so that it acts out a tripartite union of

Christian, Jewish and black, only the first two of which can be shown socially in the film. It plays also on nostalgia for the agrarian South (like 'Swanee', 'Rockabye your baby' and 'Waiting for the Robert E. Lee'). It is an arche-typal narrative of journey and return, bathing in nostalgia but quickening to march-like rhythms in 'I'm a comin' . . . I'm a comin' ' and breaking out into the sheerest unabashed melodrama in its closing cries of 'Dontcha know me . . . I'm your little baby'. Down on his knees, hands wrung, Jolson invokes the sanctities of religion for his theme, the black-face both allowing the wholesale release of emotion and keeping a certain ironic distance from it.

'The melting pot'

Writing on 'The immigrant experience', Burchell and Homberger note the pattern of wish-fulfilment enacted in a popular play of the 1920s.

> The struggle between tradition and the American way of life was exceptionally difficult in real life, but on the stage reconciliation was not too difficult to bring about. In the third act of Anne Nichol's *Abie's Irish Rose* (1924), gentile Rose keeps a kosher kitchen for her husband Abie, but makes ham for her non-Jewish friends. They have two babies: Patrick Joseph and Rebecca. Relations between Christians and Jews may have been uneasy in the real world, but on Broadway the priest and the rabbi shake hands and agree that love conquers all . . . Socio-logists might remind us that intermarriage between Jews and Catholics was fairly uncommon. At the turn of the century the rate of Jewish 'in-marriage' was just under 99 per cent. By 1950 the figure was 96 per cent. How, then, can we explain the immense popularity of *Abie's Irish Rose?* Mainly in terms of the perfectly reasonable wish for some easing of ethnic tensions. The play symbolic-ally enacts not so much the end of Jewish apartness as the beginning of Jewish integration, as Jews, into the community. It evades the reality of racial and reli-gious tension, but not the underlying process, which was to bring Herbert Lehman to the governorship of New York.

These comments offer a useful perspective on a major concern of the Jolson biopics. Jolson, of course, was a Jew, actually born in Russia (as, among others, were Sophie Tucker and Irving Berlin), who became a legendary star of almost universal appeal to audiences far beyond his ethnic group. Among other things his life and career could be seen as a pattern of integration, a verification of the promise that any American, from any ethnic community has access to the rewards of talent, industry and imagination. Not just his career but his persona and style seem to bring together old and new, crossing the old ethnic virtues of expressiveness and 'heart' with the characteristics of forward-looking, de-ethnicised energy. The former are retained but only in as much as they are translated away from connotations of patriarchal severity and the customs of the ghetto. Oberfirst lists only one early Yiddish single (plus the English version) in his discography, 'Du Host a Liebes Punim' ('You have a lovely face') and the traditionally directed 'The Cantor' before four late releases, two Israeli nationalist numbers, 'Kol Nidre' (which he had performed memorably at the climax of *The Jazz Singer*), and 'Cantor on the Sabbath'. But when those four numbers are released on LP and 78 albums they are balanced by 'That wonderful girl of mine', 'I only have eyes for you', 'My mother's rosary' and 'Remember Mother's Day', which illustrates very well the point made above in talking about his great hit 'Mammy' – that the specifically ethnic is seen as part of a universalised emotionality, and here very carefully balanced by an appeal to the feminine and matriarchal. Descriptions of Jolson's stage act say that he sometimes went into Yiddish patter. This does not contradict our point, which is not that Jolson's persona completely abnegates his ethnicity, but rather that his Jewishness undergoes a complex resolution with elements that celebrate the American mainstream.

The myth of the melting pot was perhaps easier to believe when enacted in the specialised world of entertainment, since, for a variety of complex cultural reasons the Jewish contribution to show business (and especially to the Hollywood industry) was a dominating one. Seeing it at work in *Jolson I & II*, we are reminded that the Jewish leaders of the film industry (men like Harry Cohn, whose company produced the films, Mayer and the Warners), held enormous power and influence but, socially unsure, needed their own images of integration. So Goldfish became Goldwyn and Bernard Schwartz Tony Curtis. In both *The Jolson Story* and its fictional prototype *The Jazz Singer* the moment where the old name is exchanged for a new Americanised one – Jakie Rabinowitz for Jack Robin, Asa Yoelson for Al Jolson – is not a moment of shame or subterfuge, but of commitment to the new mobility, to America. Watching the Jolson biopics (and indeed the earlier film) we are struck by how much their subject's energy, ambition and sentimentality mirror primary aspects of the moguls' own psychology, and how his rise to success parallels theirs.

The Jazz Singer, made so much closer to the high tide of European immigration (nearly nine million in the decade 1901–10, nearly six in the decade 1911–20, and over four in the next, before dropping to one eighth of the last in the decade following), is supremely interested in the conflict between self-realisation in the American way and obligations to the past, to the family and to race. It prefigures the later biopic theme of finding a resolution between the two, but in the early film it is a struggle, something torn out of conflicting alternatives. In the later films the resolution is implicit from the very beginning. The ideal of the United States as 'the melting pot' is still there, but it is complacently seen as something already achieved. Neither makers nor audience wish to interrogate its doubtful realities.

Thus, at the very beginning of *The Jolson Story* ghetto opponents (Jews and Catholics) and the better positioned Protestants (represented by William Demarest as Steve Martin), in keeping with the optimism of the musical, are seen to live in harmony in a seemingly classless setting where music (and what it symbolises) is all that matters, riding as it does over racial and social tensions. (Blacks will similarly enter the picture, a little later, though very much on the fringes.) Whereas in *The Jazz Singer* certain aspects of life in the Cantor's home are seen as alien, as when the father throws his son out of the home and takes down his picture from the wall, here acceptably folksy aspects are stressed with little refinement – father as kindly patriarch; the parents apparently not minding Asa's friendship with Anne Murray, who is still having dinner at the Yoelsons' as a potential wife years later; 'Mama' as physical and emotional support for the men, endlessly making chicken soup and burning guests' tonsils with her horse-radish sauce, and pasting cuttings of Al in a scrapbook. But Christianity is also there too in other shapes than Anne Murray's. When Asa runs away from home he lands up, via an Irish policeman, at St Mary's School for Boys, run by the benign Father McGee. The Cantor is a little shocked when he and Mrs Yoelson arrive to find Asa in the choir singing the Bach–Gounod 'Ave Maria', but his initial unease at being in a Christian place gives way when he recognises the warmth and friendliness all around. Instead of protesting about his son singing to the Virgin, he merely grumbles that Asa is singing without his cap on. When the priest replies to the effect that it is what is in your head rather than what is on it that counts, he even smiles agreement. So, watched by the priest, Cantor and Mrs Yoelson hand over their son to the foster-fathership of Steve Martin (who, like Ralph Bryant in Part II is an invented character, part of whose significance lies in his non-ethnicity), and through him to the future and the democracy of entertainment.

The other racial dimension – significantly not embodied in any character important to the narrative – enters the story in two ways, first through Jolson's adoption of the role of black-face performer, and, second, when he is shown discovering jazz as he wanders round New Orleans. The integration of black and white is not shown in any extension beyond the fleeting rapport Jolson has with the black musicians he encounters, and obviously the film is uninterested in doing so, except for the vague utopian suggestion that an approvable miscegenation takes place in Jolson's singing. But at least as regards the white ethnic groups, the film proclaims that social harmony

prevails in the New World as it does not in the Old. The time is World War II and Europe is still rooted in antiquated racial and class feuding. In one of the few instances where a reminder of Jolson's Jewishness is given in terms other than those of family comedy, the Cantor rebukes his son in *Jolson Sings Again* for simply seeking pleasure in retirement at a time when the Jews are being persecuted in Europe. In joining up to entertain the troops, Jolson is loyal both to his past and his present, but he is seen as the representative of a new, more highly developed world protecting the old one from its ancient miseries. In *The Jazz Singer* the conflict between old and new comes to a head in the desperate choice Jack Robin has to make between his own opening night and singing 'Kol Nidre' for his dying father. He chooses the latter, apparently destroying his career. The narrative mends itself in two ways, first by an intertitle that simply asserts that time has healed the theatrical wounds caused by Jack's actions, followed by him performing on stage, and second by the film's motif of entertainment as a kind of secular religion, the stage as a site of ritual displacing the synagogue. Jolson does not literally sing Jewish hymns from the stage as does Cantor Rosenblatt ('sacred songs for popular prices') in a curious scene, but he carries over into his art Jewish feeling, in terms comprehensible to the gentile. The narrative of *The Jazz Singer* resolves Jack Robin's problems, but the fierceness of the conflict requires the symbolic death of the stern patriarch, adrift in a changing society where the extremes of his culture have no place. In the later biopics the patriarch is easily won over and comically becomes expert in translating the new *lingua franca* of *Variety* (Mama: 'What is "Sockeroo", Papa?' Papa: ' "Sockeroo" is double "Socko", Mama'). He can even crack a joke about excessive concern for Jewish customs when Mama worries how Al will get by entertaining the troops without Jewish food. 'Mama', replies the Cantor, 'Without Jewish meals year after year gentiles are surviving'. The removal of the cruder ethnic qualities of being Jewish (compare for instance the real-seeming ghetto world of *The Jazz Singer* with the idealised Washington of *The Jolson Story*), begun in *The Jazz Singer*, is completed in the 1940s biopics.

Art/life

'The intellect of man is forced to choose
Perfection of the life, or of the work — W. B. Yeats

'Mama' and 'Papa' (Cantor) Yoelson (Tamara Shayne and Ludwig Donath) watch their son, the great entertainer, unite the old and new, the ethnic and mainstream.

The long epigraph at the beginning of *Jolson Sings Again* contains the statement

> This is the rest of the story of Jolson – the man who loved to sing . . . who loved
> only that until he met and married a girl named Julie. But the love to sing
> remained stronger and so obscured his life with Julie that one day she told him a
> man with two loves can't keep both.

It is a theme traditionally expected of the 'artist' rather than the 'entertainer', of quasi-musicals that derive from the European art film such as Powell and Pressburger's *The Red Shoes* and *Tales of Hoffmann* with their artist figures tragically torn between the realms of fantasy and life. If we think this, the pervasiveness of what we have schematised as function (vii) shows us to be wrong. Its undoubted prominence in the musical biopic, which implies deep psychological appeal, resides in two overlapping factors, first that it represents with intensity the larger individual/social problematic already alluded to, with art as the area of individualist fulfilment and the family standing for the claims of the other end of society; and second, that it is a version of the theme of the lure of art (as the realm of fantasy, daydream, perfection) against the difficulties and frustrations of everyday life. Glamorous and gifted beyond their audience, the subjects of musical biopics at the same time play out exemplary symbolic versions of tensions felt by their audiences.

The star's relationship with the audience is profoundly ambiguous. Its positive side is, of course, constantly celebrated in images of rapt attention and energy and emotion passing between performer and audience, but it can also be destructive rather than creative, at least for the performer. When Fanny Brice, at the beginning of *Funny Girl*, stands alone on the stage of an empty theatre and guns down an imaginary audience, she expresses this underlying possibility openly.

The boy Jolson's first experience of an audience is given with great force. The slightly sordid surroundings of Kernan's Burlesque dissolve into an almost devotional *chiaroscuro* as the child stands in a pool of light singing 'On the banks of the Wabash' and the older audience surrounding him gazes at the *Wunderkind* with awe and love. Many musical biopics, beginning in the protagonist's young maturity rather than childhood as here, are consequently not so overt in suggesting the psychological basis for the protagonist's obsession with performing as the wish to recover the position of a child before an adoring parent, ever ready with praise and applause. Because musical biopics see stars as saying real things, making real connections with their audience by articulating their desires, the star's activity has a meaning and value beyond its genesis, but for the star it does have the danger that he or she may turn away from the rigours of personal relationships for the more ghostly mass one with the audience.

The Jolson Story sees the rift between public and private, between art and life, as insoluble. Its statement of this is not tragic because, whatever emotional deprivations Jolson suffers, his art is one that affirms the reality of feeling and emotional commitment. His private life is sacrificed, as it were, to nurture the emotions of others through his art. Part of him longs for wife, home, family, stability, but it seems that the only gifts he can give are the gifts of art, the present of the song 'April showers' to Julie when they first meet, his overcoming of her stage fright on opening night, the film career he gives her. But the home life that he gives her proves illusory. When the couple first retire to the country they play checkers by a huge open fire, incongruous in the Californian climate. They begin by ignoring Steve's remarks about the heat, but then start to feel it, shifting further and further away from it, eventually into another room. The fires of the domestic hearth prove too hot. The impossibility for Jolson of separating his private from his public life is symbolised by the fact that he even first meets and courts Julie in public, in performance.

When Julie leaves him, Jolson, turning back to his career, asserts the unreality of the private life. ' "Love", "a girl" – couple of words I must have picked up out of a song'. His true paternal role is to give birth to songs, not children, and his true child the script which he addresses with the words 'Come to Poppa'. But if his show life affects his private life, so failure in his private life destroys his drive to be in the theatre, fuelled as it is by his joy in living. After reading of Julie's divorce, he walks offstage after a single song. 'There just comes a night – how long can you go on knocking yourself out for? For what? Their four bucks and their applause?'

The Jolson Story ends with Jolson as a sacrificial figure, giving the world what he cannot have himself. One of the primary projects of *Jolson Sings Again* is to heal the rift. An older Jolson now understands the dangers of his egotism as he talks to his screenwriters. The moral enacted is that we can learn from rather than compulsively repeat our mistakes. Two figures prove the reality of both sides of his torn self. On the one hand Ellen brings him late love, while on the other Ralph Bryant – 'Duluth' – brings him proof of the reality of his audience's love, and the chance to make the film of his life. Ellen (based on Jolson's last wife Erle Galbraith), brings both worlds into harmony for Jolson, giving him a home but also pushing him into comebacks when he despairs of success. As if to drive away any remnants of the first film's dramatisation of the performer's narcissism, the second finds clear moral causes on which to attach Jolson's art. The endurance narrative predominates over the success one for most of the film as he fights illness, his lung operation and changes of audience taste, and his drive for personal glory is placed at the service of the war effort. While the first film emphasises the struggle between art and life, the second pervasively searches for reconciliation.

The glorification of cinema

Jolson: 'Wonderful. Who was that?'
Bryant: 'Young fellow named Larry Parks'

It is a paradox celebrated by *Jolson Sings Again* that the presence of Al Jolson is most fully embodied in the cinema in two films where he is absent.

Although Jolson's position in film history is a memorable one – as the star of *The Jazz Singer* (1927) – his film career was less substantial than that beginning promised, declining from stardom to a brief historical appearance as himself in *Rhapsody in Blue*. *The Jazz Singer* was the only one of his star vehicles to match the force of his performance style, but its unashamed sentiment and melodrama dated too quickly for it to provide a model for later films. In *Rose of Washington Square* (1939), where he is no longer the leading man but merely Alice Faye's faithful friend, his less than charismatic acting is unhappily clear, and the camera seems to respond to a feeling that his florid projection of numbers is antiquated among cooler styles, by backing off from a full encounter with him on stage. Maurice Chevalier, also from the musical theatre, by comparison found a style and place in the witty Paramount films, but his persona was more plastic, less blatantly rhetorical than Jolson's all-out assault on the audience, insinuating rather than imposing. It was also charming and sexy, two qualities Jolson, for all his dynamism, lacked.

Thus we have the claim of *Jolson Sings Again* that it and its predecessor have given their audience a Jolson in some ways more real than the real one. Cinema becomes a self-consciously stated theme as the second film builds into its narrative an account of how *The Jolson Story*, which so many of the audience would have seen, was made. In a populist version of something we associate with modern high literature (Joyce's *Ulysses* and Proust's *A la Recherche du Temps Perdu*) the narrative turns back on itself and celebrates itself as the final product of the events related.

More unreal, and yet more real. Jane Feuer's book on the Hollywood musical is built around the idea of the film musical's consciousness of a kind of original sin, its loss of the 'aura' of live theatrical performance, hence her demonstration of the way musicals build up an illusion of interaction by constructing audiences *within* the film whose response is a surrogate for the lost actuality. This is a just perception, but needs to be balanced by recognition of the unique compensation cinema offers for that vanished rapport – its ability to present the performer with an intimacy, a concentration, a closeness of detail which the theatrical view (distant and decentred in comparison) can never offer. Attempting, like all musicals, to heal the flaw of the performer's absence, but, more than this, announcing the cinema's ability to deliver that plenitude of presence which privileges it over other media, *Jolson Sings Again* proclaims itself as superior to the theatrical world it portrays.

Cinema as a self-consciously foregrounded theme is largely absent from *The Jolson Story*. His commitment to the new sound film is presented as an important stage in his career, as the ultimate extension of his search for larger audiences, but of necessity it is played down as spectacle. Because Larry Parks was not a Jolson look-alike, it was impossible – within the realistic conventions of Hollywood cinema – to display extracts from the old Jolson films. This means that when we watch Jolson watching the première of *The Jazz Singer*, the famous images are denied us. Such disappointing evasions are no longer necessary in *Jolson Sings Again* since the profilmic reality the film-within-the-film shapes is the narrative of *The Jolson Story* and its Jolson is Larry Parks' Jolson. This makes possible the vertiginous illusionism of a scene such as the one in the rushes theatre where Jolson (Larry Parks) watches an imitation of himself on screen (Larry Parks playing Larry Parks playing Jolson) and then meets Larry Parks (Larry Parks).

The emergence of *The Jolson Story* in *Jolson Sings Again* highlights various aspects of the film making process – rehearsals, Jolson re-recording his songs, Parks miming to a Jolson recording, montage of the film being edited, etc. In a way similar to the 'deconstruction' of the film-making process in *Singin' in the Rain*, this breaking down of filmic illusionism has its own magic (indeed depends on the extreme illusionism of two Larry Parks simultaneously on screen). It is a kind of romance of technology, suggesting not an industry working to economic determinants, but a technological vehicle for a spiritual tenor. Of course what we are not shown are heads of the industry discussing Jolson as a viable commodity. Jack Warner in fact turned down Sydney Skolsky's project for recycling his old star before Harry Cohn at Columbia took it on. Instead the film seems to issue straight from Ralph Bryant and his lifelong love for Jolson's art.

The preview, the culmination of the artistic and technological effort shown, generates a tension beyond the ordinary suspense of whether the film will succeed. There is a distinct suggestion that the protagonist is dying. (Jolson in fact died in 1950, the year after the film's release.) Too over-wrought to watch the film more than fleetingly, he collapses in the foyer with the ambiguous remark that he is 'just a little weary' (just tired, or ready to leave this life?). Resting in a room cut off from the showing, he knows exactly which point the film has reached – 'They're in the night-club now'. The images we see next are from his point of view, eliding the images of the film preview with those of his own memory, suggesting both that the film is the transparent rendering of Jolson's sense of his own life (at least of 'what matters') and that he is re-experiencing his life in its essence as in a flashback before dying.

In fact, of course he does not die and we see him newly famous – (Cantor Yoelson: 'Jolson records on the radio all day long. Mama would be happy') – with a comically screaming teenybopper audience that puts him on a par with Sinatra as well as Crosby. The point of the intimations of mortality is metaphorical, signalling the artist's shedding of his life into his filmic memorial. Jolson's inability to face his image on the screen at the preview also suggests not just anxiety or coyness, but awe. This too is what the film wishes its audience to feel at the power of the cinema, not least the ability it has, which is signalled in the title *Jolson Sings Again*, to defeat the transitoriness of theatrical performance.

Summer Holiday (1948) and the pastoral musical

Versions of pastoral

'Our town is a nice little town.' — Nat Miller.

Horace's *beatus vir* – the 'happy man' – withdrawing from the corruptions of urban life to seek the quieter pleasures of solitude, with his ancestors and relatives in the poetry of Theocritus, Hesiod and Virgil, is the ultimate prototype of families like the Millers and the Smiths in the musical's most appealing version of pastoral retreat, the small town world of films like *Meet Me in St Louis* (1944) and *Summer Holiday* (1948). Though a contrary tendency in the pastoral tradition recognises the possibility of rural (or suburban) imbecility, the mode has mainly a positive spirit, upholding moderate pleasures, serenities and 'the thousand decencies that daily flow' that Milton's Adam celebrated to his Eve. In these films, as much as in *The Georgics*, one is meant to approve both of the ordered, dust-free routines and securities of domesticity and of the underlying parlour philosophy that hard work reaps its own rewards of property, self-respect and esteem in other peoples' eyes. Sometimes urban musicals may mock 'the Stix', but more often, identified with the virtuous past of a new more complex and bewildering society, their virtues are nostalgically hymned.

The small-town world is never remotely wild. The vision of the wilderness as a domain of danger and evil, prevalent in western thought and art from St Paul to Hawthorne and Fenimore Cooper and the western, is replaced by a vision of nature as, if not quite a revelation of a divine order in the universe, at least a garden of tranquillity and, above all, of order. Even so, primitive natural forces, the true spirits of the wilderness, exist not too distantly beneath the surface in the anarchic Tootie in *Meet Me in St Louis* and Uncle Sid in *Summer Holiday*. Tootie, a child–savage, with an untutored mind, arouses primeval memories of existence before culture and the social order, while Sid is a Bacchic reveller with more authentic vine leaves in his hair than Richard has (we see him winning an astonishing *al fresco* beer drinking contest), and constantly tempted by the pleasures of transgression. Yet even these disruptive elements are well contained within an ethos in which a humanised nature is the handmaiden of moderation, stylised, harmonious and delightful, and a distinctive tone of reconciliation, understanding, and overriding but fragile content – every bit as compelling as that found in the classical prototypes – is established.

But if the pastoral musical is a modern reworking of an antique tradition, contemporary criticism demands that some account be given of the specific meanings, at a specific time, of its 'relatively permanent' themes. We cannot simply invoke the resonances of classical pastoral as pointers to a universalised cultural expression. We have also to look at the sub-genre within a set of more particular categories – e.g. the pastoral tradition in American literature and later in film; the long pro-pastoral, anti-urban tradition in American philosophical and political writing; the particular inflections such ideas have in the musical genre; and the question why it is in the '40s and early '50s, rather than at other times, that the small town pastoral musical flourishes.

The pastoral musical can be significantly illuminated by seeing it as a specific lyrical embodiment of the anti-urban tendency which is a major tendency in American thought from the late eighteenth century, in which (e.g. in the writing of Jefferson and Crèvecoeur) the idea of the uncontrolled city looms as the spectre of an undesired future. Morton and Lucia White's book, *The Intellectual Versus the City*, is a compendious handbook to the working through of this theme in American thought as it faces Jefferson's worst dreams of the exploding metropolis in the late nineteenth century, in which the ideal of a basically agrarian society declined from what had seemed a possible reality into an impossible, yet potent, dream. The situation leaves a profound mark on most of the major literary figures of the time – Poe, Hawthorne, Twain, Melville and others, but particularly striking are the reactions of those writers who find themselves face to face with the vast urban immigration of the later nineteenth century. Witness Henry James' striking description of 'that loud primary stage of alienism which New York offers to sight', and his conviction, while dreaming (in terms very relevant to the positives of the small town musical) 'of the luxury of some such close and sweet and *whole* national consciousness as that of the Switzer and the Scot', 'that there was no escape from the ubiquitous alien into the future, or even into the present; there was no escape but into the past'. James' 'let not the unwary . . . visit Ellis Island' turns in Henry Adams into the irrationalities of anti-semitism and the patrician's view of 'Our town' (New York) in turmoil.

A traveller in the highways of history looked out of the club window on the turmoil of the Avenue and felt himself in Rome, under Diocletian witnessing the anarchy, conscious of the compulsion, eager for the solution, but unable to conceive whence the next impulse was to come or how it was to act.

The most cursory contemplation of the values at the heart of such films as *Meet Me in St Louis* and *Summer Holiday* makes it clear how they are part of such a context – agrarianism versus industrialism, the past as repository of values threatened by the present, homogeneity endangered by heterogeneity, the human scale of life threatened by the inhuman. When the stage manager in Thornton Wilder's stage play *Our Town* (1939), a pervasive influence on this kind of musical, says to the audience, 'Nice town, y'know what I mean', and says of the small town afternoon, 'You all remember what it's like', he appeals, as these films pervasively do, to a mythology, an unarticulated network of values that is felt even by those cut off in most ways from any actual rural America. The larger urban cinema audience, addressed by these pastorals, must have read them obliquely, not just as offering them an irrecoverable past, but as a way of contemplating values that might, in some way, be brought into their lives in the 1940s, forty or fifty years on from the events depicted. Both John Dewey's educational theory (the 'progressive school') and the sociologist Jane Addams' famous Hull House settlement, an attempt to form an exemplary community in one of the poorer areas of Chicago (1899), may be instanced as theoretical and practical instances that in some way parallel what the small town musical offered its audiences, the recovery of older patterns of 'face to face' relations, of cohesiveness and community.

Thus far the city has been invoked in wholly pejorative terms. But an opposite tendency may be observed in many musicals – the celebration of the city. This is an undertext in perhaps the majority of musicals, since the dominant form of the backstage musical is almost always urban, caught up with the ethos of the big city, its glamour and its movement, its multiplicity and potentiality. In the very urban musical (quintessentially *On The Town*), time is dynamic as compared to the stasis of the pastoral musical where time seems unmoving, though the audience (both then and now) must have had a complex attitude towards their participation in this illusion since they know and knew very well that the moment crystallised within these films (c. 1900–13) is about to be savagely interrupted by history, to be shattered by the onslaught of technology, the first world war and its aftermath. Life in the small town musical is cyclical, repetitive, traditional. Indeed, in *Meet Me in St Louis* the change of seasons introduces each phase of the action, making the life that is shown seem a facet of nature rather than a social fact or fantasy.

The pastoral musical is also family-centred – 'Blessed be the tie that binds', to quote again from *Our Town* – reflecting conservative non-urban actualities in this, for, as the Lynds remark in their great sociological study, *Middletown in Transition*, 'Middletown is a marrying town'. Conversely, the urban musical often has its characters free of any ties but those of their own making, and this atomism is seen not as negative but as exhilarating, the individual free of tradition, responsible alone for her or his fate. In the title number of *New York, New York* (1977), when Francine Evans (Liza Minnelli) sings that she is taking leave of her 'Little town blues', she addresses 'The Big Apple' thus: 'I want to wake up in the city that never sleeps./I want to be King of the Hill and Top of the Heap.' These lyrics celebrate the harshness, the pressures, the glittering prizes given by the city, the ethos of the uncontrolled market (as distinct from the idyllic, limited, morally prescribed capitalism of the small town).

In setting things out in these terms we have displayed the opposition between the two worlds of city and small town. But many films (even those that seem to be the most extreme examples of the 'hot' and 'cold' societies, to borrow Lévi-Strauss' terms) in various ways soften the oppositions into a co-existence, stating that one set of values need not necessarily drive out the other. So in *On The Town*, relentlessly urban as it is, the Gene Kelly and Vera-Ellen characters discover each other to be really small town people; while in both *Summer Holiday* and *Meet Me in St Louis* (in the 'Stanley Steamer' and 'Trolley song' numbers) speed and technology co-exist with quietness and stasis the moment before technology irreversibly changes the world. The dazzling lights of the fair at the end of *Meet Me in St Louis* are the most extreme example of a metaphor that holds together both the past and progress in an impossible image, in spite of reason's claim that the world of the city, by entering the small town, must destroy it.

Our concentration on the small town musical as the most interesting type of the pastoral musical ignores certain other types – e.g. musical westerns partly set in an actual wilderness; the many musicals that evoke 'golden ages' of nostalgia or romanticism; those (coming closer to the small town films) which cast a glow over some exotic aspect of the American past; and the very interesting type of the black musical such as *Cabin in the Sky* (1943), *Hallelujah!* (1929), *Carmen Jones* (1954) and *Porgy and Bess* (1959). All these share the sophisticated pastoral characteristics of presenting complex themes in a location somehow simpler and less ravelled than that of their audience. In asserting the centrality over these of the small town musical, we are arguing that, though the type in its pure form is relatively rare, when it does occur it brings together in the most significant concentration the central concerns of the wider urban–anti-urban debate outlined above; it is no accident that *Meet Me in St Louis* is to so many viewers and critics such a pre-eminent musical. As relatively pure examples of the type we would list *Meet Me in St Louis* (1944), *State Fair* (1945), *The Harvey Girls* (1946), *Centennial Summer* (1946), *Summer Holiday* (1948), *Meet Me at The Fair* (1951), *Summer Stock* (1951), *On Moonlight Bay* (1951), *By The Light of the Silvery Moon* (1953), *Oklahoma!* (1955) and *Carousel* (1956), the last two films being re-workings of major stage musicals that belong (1943 and 1945 respectively) to the period of *Meet Me in St Louis*.

Of all these films it is *Meet Me in St Louis* which has had by far the most analytic attention, and it may be regarded as exemplary in a number of ways. First, in its loving evocation of a more stable family and wider community – though in all its details and assumptions it is a middle-class utopia – in the arcadia of the suburbs of St Louis, a city (or part of a city) that seems like a small town. This world is set back in the pre-first world war years of 1903/4, a time identified in the general mind as an era of a vanished grace and stability. Anti-urban feeling in this film is very pronounced since the plot hinges on the threat that for business reasons the father may have to move the family to the swarming chaos of New York. Lastly, the film exhibits at various levels (as Andrew Britton points out in the only really comprehensive piece of work written on an individual musical), a significant ambivalence about its richly presented world of positives or, at the least, sometimes exhibits with startling clarity some of the contradictions on which its world is based. (As for instance when Rose, one of the daughters, complains, 'I hate, loath and despise money' and her father replies, 'You also spend it'.) *Summer Holiday*, a less commercially successful and critically recognised film, but in our view equally fascinating and central, and the main subject of this chapter, shares these features with *Meet Me in St Louis*, as well as certain differences. Set at an almost identical time – 1901 – it is, however, placed in what really is a small town in Connecticut rather than what just feels like a small town to the Smiths in the leafy suburbs of St Louis.

Why should the small town musical have flourished precisely in the period it did, the late war years to the early fifties, though occasionally revived in films like *The Music Man* (1962) and *Hello Dolly* (1969)? Regionalism and small town nostalgia are common enough in '20s and '30s writing. *Ah, Wilderness!*, Eugene O'Neill's play which is the source for *Summer Holiday*, was performed in 1923, while Glynn Riggs' *Green Grow the Lilacs*, the source for *Oklahoma!*, was first performed in 1931. Thornton Wilder's *Our Town*, so dominant an influence upon the sub-genre, dates from 1939. There are also non-musical films of the 1930s that prefigure the later musicals

– obviously MGM's 'straight' version of *Ah, Wilderness!* (1935), but also John Ford's regional community films such as *Judge Priest* (1934) and *Doctor Bull* (1933) which portray, as Lindsay Anderson says, 'an ordered society . . . where the arts of living are still uncorrupt, unstandardized and spontaneous', and the values embodied in Frank Capra's comedies, especially *Mr Deeds Goes to Town* (1936) and *Mr Smith Goes to Washington* (1939). (Capra's later film, *It's a Wonderful Life* (1946), is also very close in many ways to the films considered in this chapter.)

Why the musical only fully takes up these prefigurings in *Meet Me in St Louis* is a puzzling question to which there is no simple answer. It may be that it was intuitively felt that in the immediate actuality and wake of the Depression such nostalgia – hyperbolised as it is in the musical – would have been unpopular, that its Claude-glass view would have collided too blatantly with immediate experience. It may be too that the film musical, which was very conservative in the late thirties (the era of Bing Crosby), could only slowly adapt itself to the new techniques (especially of the integrated musical) required for such films, and demonstrated in the hugely successful stage musical *Oklahoma!* (1943). It is, however, very interesting that the emergence of the small town musical as a product for audiences much greater than those on Broadway, or even for Ford's films, happened not at a time of extreme economic stress, but rather, first of all, during the war, with its separations and upheavals of the family, and then, later, during the period of uncertainty dominated by the Cold War, a time in which traditional hierarchies seemed threatened – American power by the Soviet Union, the force of traditional ideologies by shifting attitudes strongly, even hysterically resisted (e.g. in the witch hunts of the McCarthy persecutions). The role of the powerful, bad woman of *film noir,* is in some measure, it has been suggested, traceable to fears about the new independent power gained by millions of women who entered the world of extra-household work in wartime. It is suggestive that the small town ideal, a trans-cultural and trans-historical thematic present in many different ways in nineteenth- and twentieth-century American art, comes to have its most lavish and lyrical embodiment in the mass cinema at the same time that *film noir* flourishes, for its stable, ordered, inward-looking worlds are the absolute antithesis of the labyrinthine, shadowed, rootless worlds of *film noir* – the genre of submerged cultural angst – and its images of the harmonious family and woman in her traditionally sanctioned conservative role are an extreme contrast to the fears played out in the figure of the 'tiger lady' of that nihilistic and disruptive genre.

It is easy enough to type – from a 'progressive' viewpoint – these backward-looking, loving recreations of vanished societies as repressive and regressive, to accuse them of ignoring the difficulties of modern society and of suppressing, in particular, the problems of class, race and sexuality. As what we write specifically on *Summer Holiday* will show, this accusation, though clearly in many ways true, neglects the way that these films at certain levels criticise, or at least expose to view, the structuring principles of their worlds. But it is also not out of place to meditate on the pleasure that the serene happiness of these worlds gives audiences. Despite their limitations in analysis, these films link the powers that so many musicals have, of sensuous concrete rhythms, colours, melody and design, to an ideal of a better, more gentle, more cohesive life. Our position on such films is likely to be very double-edged, aware of their repressions as much as of their positive imagings; seeing the necessity of closely inspecting their process of myth-making, but not being content with a simple crude attack on the myth; being aware of the silences on which the films' affirmations are founded, but also that they speak about desires as universal as any found in art, and act out images of relationship and community denied to us in the more rigorous, but also more arid domains of 'progressive' art.

Summer Holiday

'I have it, this interest in ordinary middle class existence, in simple firm ordinary middle class traditions, in sordid material, unaspiring visions, in a repeating, common, decent enough kind of living, with no fine kind of fancy ways inside us, no excitements to surprise us, no new ways of being bad or good to win us.' — Gertrude Stein, *The Making of Americans*

A film which, shown in Reading (as reported in *The Daily Express*, 9 February 1949) provoked the audience into demanding its money back, can hardly be counted among the great successes of the time. Indeed – though its American reception was less dramatically unfavourable – its journalistic reception in England shows it attacked from almost every conceivable angle – as too conventional, as too unconventional in its mixing of modes, as disfigured by the performance of Mickey Rooney whose phenomenal popularity was just beginning to wane, and, most surprisingly, as over-explicit and even shocking in its presentation of Richard's meeting with the prostitute Belle. Thirty-five years later this hostility seems rather opaque and odd, the product of audience hostility to Rooney in an unaccustomed role in which he is slightly ironically situated, the audience's too conventional expectations of a musical (a constant problem for subtle and innovative makers throughout the history of the genre), and a feeling that sexual material of an un-idyllic kind should be taboo. Even after Tom Milne's positive auteurist view of the film as a Mamoulian musical (1969), a curious hostility sometimes surfaces in contemporary statements, as when *The New Yorker*, as recently as 1980, described it as 'this essentially ghastly musical version of *Ah, Wilderness!*', implicitly claiming, as the critics did in 1949, a knowledge of its source, Eugene O'Neill's one major comedy, that definitively places the film as worthless. The most interesting way of interpreting this hostility is as a tribute to the film's subtlety, its ambivalent mixture of affirmation and irony and its stylistic complexities. Certainly *Summer Holiday* is not the sentimentalised travesty of O'Neill that it has ignorantly been accused of being. Though the demands of the family audience musical in the late 1940s necessitated a toning down of the original's sexual realism, many of its subtleties remain, and a number of the film's own inventions are notable not only for their lyrical charm but for the way they articulate more problematical areas as well. That *Summer Holiday* is, despite its relative commercial failure, quite the equal of *Meet Me in St Louis* in interest, is a claim we shall substantiate below, but as a preface to such a demonstration it is worth reminding ourselves what a distinguished team transformed O'Neill's play, and indeed how much that team actually overlapped with the makers of *Meet Me in St Louis* (both from the Freed Unit at MGM, with Irving Brecher, Ralph Blane (the lyricist) and Charles Walters (the choreographer) working on both films). The scenarists, Hackett and Goodrich, though unconnected with *St. Louis*, had abilities well evidenced by their work on *The Pirate* and *Easter Parade* as well as the 1935 'straight' version of *Ah, Wilderness!*. And above all there was Rouben Mamoulian whose previous brilliant work in the genre (especially *Love Me Tonight* and *High, Wide and Handsome*) as well as his substantial connections with the worlds of 'high' drama and opera, argue the likelihood of a complex approach to the transformation of the original material, despite the film's trials in production and the brutal executive decisions which resulted in a final print shorn of as many as four of its highly integrated numbers, including a fantasy sequence in which Richard and Muriel are transported to the world of Omar Khayyám.

It is not accidental that *Summer Holiday* as a major pastoral musical, is – despite these disfigurements – among the most highly developed instances of the 'integrated' musical of the 1940s, which blurs the dividing line between the 'poetry' of spectacle and the 'prose' of narrative. What is a potentially utopic state of mind in the 'integrated' MGM musicals of the 1940s, becomes something much more pervasive in the small town musical where whole social worlds are presented as being what is fragmentarily and individualistically attained in other films, where the idea of utopia is not located in the vision of a protagonist trying to transform reality, but in a place, in a community and a set of concrete social and familial relationships. With such a setting these musicals are not, characteristically, about the individual's liberation from the oppressions of a constricting society, but rather about remaining within society. Utopia is what we have – or had – or, more complicatedly, imagine ourselves having had as a prelude to imagining what we might have again in the future. These films – especially *Summer Holiday* and *St Louis* – present worlds of great closeness and cohesiveness, and, set in what we are to see as a lost paradise, they develop strategies for lyricising the everyday. These include the casting of types (almost everyone in the film) who are idealisations of the ordinary; numbers that have the air of fragmentary epiphanies rather than staged spectacles; numbers that celebrate the social world as it is rather than the characters' individualism; and numbers that involve the community as singers and dancers. *Summer Holiday* is suffused with such tendencies, but they are perhaps most fully felt in the opening number which, though it also establishes Richard as a rebel, is (like its equivalent in *St Louis*) a statement of the priority of the community, delivered by numerous characters, involving the most ordinary happenings and gestures, and foregrounding a number of untrained voices (here Walter Huston, 'Butch' Jenkins, Agnes Moorehead and Frank Morgan). But in *Summer Holiday* the drifting together of narrative and number is even more developed in the 'Our town' opening by the constant movement between speech and song, with the poetry/prose distinction further blurred by the presence of rhymed dialogue as an extra mediation between narrative and number, all these held together in the casual *Sprechgesang* of Nat Miller (Walter Huston), newspaper proprietor, benign patriarch and *beatus vir* as he comes home from the office to lunch.

Summer Holiday deals with the rebellion of the seventeen-year-old Richard Miller (Mickey Rooney) against the *mores* of his home town in the summer before he goes to Yale. Far more faithful (both in detail and general spirit) to *Ah, Wilderness!* than its critics claim, its central action revolves around three points – Richard's ideological alienation from, and eventual reclamation into, the world of his father; Richard's courting of Muriel, the difficulties of which lead him into a sordid sexual adventure before he and Muriel are reconciled; and Richard's sympathy for and attraction to the genial but fecklessly alcoholic Uncle Sid (Frank Morgan), a thematic that resolves – without destroying the sympathies evoked for Sid – in Richard's learning the error of his ways.

Idealising small town America, the film presents perpetual summer.

There is no hint of bad weather and, by extension, little overt sign of moral or social turbulence. A feeling of pride, both in the innate goodness of the characters living freely in harmony with nature under the rule of a law which is fair and just, runs right the way through the film. The wilderness of O'Neill's play is therefore underplayed, though retained in the characters of Tommy (the unsocialised child) and Uncle Sid, and in a different way in the 'college tart', Belle. Even here, however, the qualities of wilderness are contained, allowed for and somehow defused, while the images of summer are allowed to surface from the text of O'Neill's play to create the moral and social as well as physical climate of the film.

The film's *mise-en-scène* reminds one of the ordered and sunny rural settings inhabited by the genteel lovers of Watteau's pictures. The characters in *Summer Holiday* are, naturally enough, sporting seasonal beige, white or pastel. Richard's beige linen suit, his white shoes and hat, create an impression of clarity, clean thoughts not seriously touched by the temporary insanity – in his mother's eyes – of his addiction to Wilde, Shaw, Ibsen, Swinburne and other subversive writers. Richard is the bright (in dress and mind) future for America. Although our introduction to the film is through the father, pointedly attending to a map of America on his office wall and their singing of a pedigree untainted, despite the accident of his name, by the sweat of manual labour, it is significant that our first view of nature is given us by Richard.

Our vision of it is carefully prepared. Richard and Muriel (Gloria De Haven) sit, opposite each other at first, sipping sodas through a straw, and without a hint that deep inside Richard's mind stir, though not very convincingly, the unsavoury thoughts of a socialist and a libertine. Like any other wholesome boy and girl they are set to re-enact yet again the rituals and ordeals of young love. Their setting – the drugstore – is safe and conventional and from that mundanity they proceed to the equally safe and ordered wilderness of their town: a park, complete with apple trees in blossom, neat flower beds and an artificial spring in a lake that holds no mystery. It is the equivalent of Watteau's *L'Escarpolette*, a domesticated nature in which everything is hazy and bright, all surfaces are iridescent, free of blemish and undertones of darkness. Nature here is as threatening as the daisy Lily picks for Sid's lapel. Moving to the *locus amoenus* of love Richard and Muriel find, instead of the mysteries of nature, a social landscape, a

Summer Holiday: 'Why should anybody be afraid?' In the garden of love Richard (Mickey Rooney) takes time off from classroom bombastics to give Muriel (Gloria De Haven) a love lesson.

well-ordered garden hardly different from the dwelling places of the community, and no real alternative to the gentle confinements of the parlours, studies, offices and other comfortable gaols (or 'goals' – remembering Richard's mispronunciation of Oscar Wilde's 'The Ballad of Reading Gaol') constructed by the adult world. The camera tracks and tilts back as Richard takes Muriel into a spirited dance through the park, an image of freedom, yet subtly prescribed. As the dance ends so the lovers' discovery of a superficial liberty dissolves into an image of Tommy dressed as a wild man, a Red Indian (as later he is a bandit and a sinister Fu Manchu-like Chinese) something that defines him as one of the two members of the family capable of genuine disruption. Tommy's transgressions are the license of childhood; Uncle Sid's of Dionysos himself.

Tommy (who must remind us of the disruptive Tootie in *St Louis*), or his independent Pan-like spirit, grows up into Uncle Sid. His is the voice of holiday and of topsy-turvy. It is of course 4 July, a day of release and revelry. When Miller exclaims after Sid's return from Waterbury, 'this makes it a real holiday', we feel that the words are double-edged: they incorporate Nat's genuine warmth and affection for Sid as a returning and fondly missed member of the family, but they also point to Sid as the film's incarnation of disruption, revelry and saturnalia. In the family the wilderness is vestigially alive in Sid. The 'Weary blues' have Belle 'upside down', but Sid's tipsy topsy-turvy is the child of drink and loose women. To a man intellectually convinced, as Sid is, that integration into society is to be desired, a temperament more suited to the pleasures of wine, women and song is, despite all the humour and wit of their expression, a nuisance. Sid knows his predestined choices are detrimental not only to his own but, by extension, to the community's, health. A society overrun with Uncle Sids would be as injurious as, on another level, a society of Tom Donophons shooting Liberty Valances. Yet everyone (with the exception of Lily) seems glad that Sid's serious moral values have failed to get the better of him. While the majority adhere to the improving sentiments that hard work, right reason, integrity and moderation lead to the good life, room can be made for a primitive voice, even if it struggles a little sadly in a man convinced that there is no durable joy in being degenerate. But while Sid himself laments his failure to integrate himself into society, the film's rhetoric, though aware of the pathos of the alcoholic, rejoices in his incompetence. Sid's loss through drink is, in some curious way, society's gain.

While all around him drink, or are in some way associated with, water, Sid is the embodiment, through alcohol, of fire. 'Water? What will they think of next?' Sid's *tour de force* of wit centres around an alcohol/water series of jokes, more or less faithfully retained from O'Neill's text and beautifully delivered in his bitter-sweet way by Frank Morgan at the family dinner that is the aftermath of his victory in the drinking contest. Sid's clever, upside-down remarks about drinking, where he becomes the innocent teetotaller and the prim Lily a dipsomaniac ('So fine a woman once and now a slave to rum'), are at once a self-conscious dramatisation of the sensible society's denunciation of excess and also a parody of good form, temperance and respectability. Water looms large as an image both verbally and visually in the film and, in Sid's eyes, aptly characterises the dull purity of the sober world: Waterbury, the tame water-jet in the park, the bluefish jokes, the kiss between Muriel and Richard to 'wash away' the stain of Belle, and so on. For in purity lies fear and restraint, and these are characteristics, to set alongside gentility, joviality and affection, prominent in the kind of family the film sets out to define.

We are offered opposing pairs of families. One (Muriel's) is portrayed as unsatisfactory, ruled by an ignorant boor of a father and husband, the spoil-sport Mr McComber. This other family is kept out of view for most of the film and exists only as a kind of yardstick by which to measure the success of the Millers. What we see of the McComber family is the patriarch's stuffy prudence (parsimoniously criticising his wife's budgeting), ignorance (the row with Nat over Richard's letters to Muriel), ungentlemanly, essentially trading-class values in threatening to remove his ad from Miller's paper, and his heavy-handed imposition of his will on his daughter. The Miller family seems to be the antithesis of all this, all the more potent an ideal to audiences dimly conscious, no doubt, of some kind of impoverishment of life in the decline from the older extended family to the smaller nuclear grouping, in that it has room for Essie's brother and Nat's sister (just as the Smiths in *St Louis* have Grandfather and even Katie the maid). Further, in this family, the traumas of 'family romances', the difficulties of family relationships, Oedipal struggles, the replacing of the old by the young, the struggle of the sexual instinct with the repressions demanded by civilisation, are softened and modified by love, affection and respect. Here people are as sensitive as Nat is when he welcomes Sid back to Dannville from his unsuccessful 'Waterbury whirl', pretending that the newspaper could not get by without him.

Even so, the Miller family is more than just a portrayal of a simple positive alternative to the McCombers. True, it has space – particularly in Richard's room, but also in his father's mind – for Beethoven, Whitman, Shaw and other unconventional thinkers. Late in the film, for instance, Nat chuckles over a volume of Shaw, calling him 'a comical cuss, even if some of

his ideas shouldn't be allowed'. But, like nature in this 'deadest burg' (Belle's bored epithet), the achievements of these great men are laundered to suit the ambiance of respectability that pervades the Miller home. In decent families an enlightened father allows his (male) children to become acquainted with radicalism not so that they can revolutionise society, but so that, being familiar with the radical's view of life, they can absorb a discreet dose of liberation precisely so that the wilder extremes of authoritarianism can be resisted, while the belief in a democratic conservatism shall not be in danger of serious challenge. So, of course, Richard's planned revolutionary speech at his graduation ceremony is meant to seem as ridiculous to us as it does to his father. His preposterous mannerisms and posture whenever he begins to recite or declaim reinforce this, and in case there is ever any doubt, someone is usually on screen to deflate him.

For all its benevolence, charity and fairmindedness, as defined from a certain – and the film's dominant – point of view, the Miller family is still committed to stereotype. The women are ignorant (Essie's comments), fussy (meal preparation scenes) and demure, and limited attitudes are ingrained in the children, particularly the anodyne Mildred and the pompous Yale man, Arthur. For all his revolutionary fervour, Richard can still advise Belle, 'You shouldn't inhale like that. Girls shouldn't inhale' and sing 'You ought to get yourself a husband; be a wife'. Richard is indeed, despite the irony in his name, no 'Gin Rickey'. Alcohol is one of the symbols of disruption, but as Richard fails to take his liquor like a man when he tries 'the pace that kills' with Belle, so he remains both eternally immature and, paradoxically, in the grip of the old world, not the old, precultural Dionysian world which surfaces in Sid and Tommy, but the old world of civilisation. This, after all, is really Nat's, not Richard's film. It is the film of a community, not smug, but perhaps all the same, well satisfied, content with its lot and what it sees as the unpromising post-lapsarian quality of the human condition.

Ruptures and resolutions: sexuality

To function as narratives films have to have a rupture, a problematic to solve and be re-ordered. In *Summer Holiday* this is Richard's threatened

---

An inept debauchee returning home with vine leaves in his hair, about to collapse into mother's arms. Richard gestures to Ibsen; his father Nat Miller (Walter Huston), brother Art, mother (Selena Royle) and Uncle Sid (Frank Morgan) confront the rebel, and the idyllic middle-class streets smile at the human comedy.

rejection of traditional values embodied in his reading of 'warm' literature, his encounter with Belle, and his threatened Marxist analysis of his society. By the film's end the political and sexual threats are nullified. They are only the product of Richard's idealistic naiveté and adolescent desire in the role of Ibsen's rebel cultural critic, Eilert Lovberg, to shock. Coming home, with vine leaves in his hair, his moment of rebellion collapses with the bathetic words, 'Mom, I feel rotten', and his attendant sexual adventuring has him fly in retreat from the castrating power that his fevered imagination gives to Belle. The power of the film's closure is very great indeed. The return to Muriel; the reconciliation of the generations in Richard's kissing of his father; the marvellous crane shot that moves above the peaceful moonlit streets of Dannville, Nat quoting lines from *The Rubáiyát* to Essie. The ending here produces feelings very similar to those evoked by Ford's cavalry trilogy, where benign power and judgement reside in the older characters, particularly John Wayne.

But, as we have seen, the text is not unaware of the costs of the idyll it enacts, and, just as (in a way brilliantly demonstrated by Andrew Britton in his work on *Meet Me in St Louis*) that film contains a subdominant undertext of contradiction and criticism of the *status quo* which centres around the anarchic child Tootie, whose grotesque death-centred words and actions have a subversive relation to the narrative's upper world of light and pleni- tude, so, in *Summer Holiday*, less dramatically, but also perhaps more subtly and pervasively, an undertext exists, some elements of which (centred especially on Sid) we have already considered, but which are also present elsewhere in multiple ambivalences throughout the film. Take, for instance, the happy number where the family ride, after the graduation ceremony, in the newfangled motorcar, the 'Stanley Steamer'. We have already briefly referred to this moment in the context of providing a reassuring image of the compatibility of technology with the pastoral, but it is also two other things, a moment of escape for the lovers (not 'the pace that kills', but still a speeding out of stasis), and also a family outing. If at one level the image softens inter- generational struggles by conflating the two, by saying that there is no con- tradiction between the individual's exogamous desires and family pressures (so that Richard ends up with the girl opposite as Esther Smith in *St Louis* ends up with 'the boy next door'), at another it provides an image of the family overpowering the freedom of the lovers as they sit, raised up like a collective super-ego, in the back of the speeding car, poised over the young pair.

Richard's transgressions in the narrative are both political and sexual. The combination of decadent poets and Marx makes a hot solvent for the bonds of small town living. Attempting to rouse Muriel to 'Life', he sends letters stuffed with Swinburne. When Muriel, under her father's influence, refuses to see him again, he goes out on a jaunt with Wint, who has picked up 'two swift babies', out-of-town showgirls, to the seedy environs of the Dannville Music Hall. This is the world of the only sexuality conceivable outside of Muriel's purity, and the parallelism between the two girls, Muriel and Belle, good and bad, is emphasised not only by the hyperbolising of the antithetical qualities of each, but by Richard and Belle in the bar mirroring the earlier scene between Richard and Muriel in the innocent drugstore. In both Richard is with a potential lover – though one stands for love without very much sex and the other for sex without love ('You'll never miss the things that love is not', Belle croons to him). In both he has drinks – with Muriel a shared soda, with Belle beer and a gin fizz. In the one he seeks the kisses of a reluctant girl (a struggle also dramatised in the song 'Why should anybody be afraid?'); in the other a woman of experience presses them upon him.

Although the verbal frankness of *Ah, Wilderness!* is diluted and any references to monetary transactions are dropped, there is a coded eroticism within the sequence that is rather startling; not only Belle's tumescent colour changes, but the extraordinary pose she adopts, sitting with one bared leg so arranged that her lower dress front looks split open, confronting Richard with too overwhelming a vision of 'the things that love is not'. In Marilyn Maxwell's marvellously overwrought performance the slightly staled carnality is oppressive and the close-ups emphasise her teeth as she bends over him, inciting nervous fantasies of *vagina dentata*. Also rather shocking (perhaps what so disturbed some critics in 1949) is the way in which the absolute dividing of female sexuality into good and bad in the world of the film (and of which the film seems aware), is played out, but also confused, in Belle, who becomes for Richard not simply the glamorous whore, but an uneasy amalgam of both forbidden sexuality and the mother. It is the unexpected yoking together in Belle of these two roles that gives the scene its edginess, suggesting in Richard an unresolved Oedipality that cannot envisage a mature sexuality, but swings between the pure image of the mother and the degraded object of the prostitute. Thus Richard finds himself with a temptress who also seems to be a mother-substitute, and, acting out the role of a 'Dapper Dan', he is also a child. This last is underlined both visually and verbally. Rooney's shortness, rather than being hidden, is exaggerated by shots so arranged that, whether sitting or standing, Marilyn Maxwell towers over him. Attempting to embrace her, his face nuzzles her bosom nervously as if his real end is the breast rather than the hard liquor his sexual pride makes him order. Addressing him, Belle constantly uses the term 'kid', and asks him sardonically, 'Tell me, does your mother know you're out'. The place of the mother in this scene is underlined by the drama of Richard's return home to Essie's sanctuary.

The last movement of the film is one of restoration and reconciliation, most importantly of Richard to his father and family, and of his sexuality to its proper channel, Muriel. 'We seem to be completely surrounded by love', Nat says to Essie before they go upstairs to bed, and the transformation of rebellion, antagonism and sexuality into love is the main movement of the film's last minutes. There is evidence that the Breen Office leaned heavily on the 'facts of life' interview between father and son, making it less open than in the play and pushing it more towards the traditional comedy of the innocent father who finds his son knows more than he does. Nevertheless, the main lines of Nat's embarrassed division of the sexual world into two kinds of girls remains, and the *mise–en–scène* adds irony by having two subversive literary figures surveying the scene from the walls of Richard's room; on the right Walt Whitman, the poet of polymorphous eroticism, and on the left Edgar Allan Poe, representative of the repressed psyche, alcoholism and the horror beneath the everyday. Clearly Nat's finding sex impossible to talk about within the family belongs not just to its benign local context, but to the wider context of sexual repression in the film, which is occasionally frightening, as when it is revealed that Lily has still not forgiven Sid for a sexual misdemeanour committed eighteen years ago! This is the scene in which Nat is so nervous that he unwittingly destroys one of the clay busts of Lincoln that his son has been modelling. That Richard should be making busts of the great president (who is dominatingly present in the graduation scene), rather than, say, of Marx or Shaw, is another significant subtlety of the film's *mise–en–scène*. The end of Richard's political rebellion is signified by this taking to himself of the native (rather than exogamous) father-figure at the same time that he becomes reconciled to his familial father, a father-figure who need not disturb the ideological *status quo* since he has been, like Washington and the Revolution, wholly appropriated into a mythology – Independence Day etc. – which largely excises the realities of history.

When Richard, having announced to his father's relief that he plans to marry Muriel, meets her it is again in the world of domesticated pastoral, by a brook in the moonlight, a moment that has a fairytale aura about it of conventional operatic assignations (Mamoulian of course worked extensively in opera in New York). Their meeting both releases their sexuality (it is where Muriel learns not to be afraid and where Richard gets his kiss), and contains it within conventional channels ('Gosh, but I love you'; 'Won't it be wonderful when we're married'). The violence of sexuality, Belle's emasculating threat, is echoed when an angry Muriel bites Richard, but softened too since it is proof of her feeling. When Muriel grants Richard his kiss, it cancels all others. 'Will it wipe off all her kisses? Wipe off all the memory for ever?' When Richard comes home, he enters dazed with emotion, just like Esther Smith in *St Louis* after she has been with John Truett. His entry parallels and reverses his return from Belle. His mother thinks he might be drunk again; Nat, however, declares, 'That's not liquor, that's love'.

The film's final moments resume the perspective of its opening, with Mr Miller as the presenter, the view from the balcony from which he and his wife look down on the town and 'Love's young dream' being that of benign wisdom and experience surveying the vicissitudes of the sublunary estate. After Richard has kissed his father and dissolved his problems into the unchanging human condition – 'You sort of forget the moon was the same way back then and everything' – the camera takes in Sid and Lily on the swing and Richard looking up at Muriel's window, with Arthur and Elsie Rand and Mildred and one of her beaux gestured to verbally. In Nat's lines from *The Rubáiyát* about spring and autumn, literature as social criticism gives way to literature as consolation. The film omits the play's conversation between the Miller parents which suggests that Sid and Lily will never marry and that Richard's and Muriel's relationship is temporary, obeying the unspoken laws of the traditional musical by giving what is, on the surface, a wholly affirmative closure, or at least one where it is left to the audience to supply the dimension of irony to the affirmations of image, music (the final nostalgic variations on the 'Our town' tune) and the camera rhetoric of the crane shot lifting high over the streets of Dannville. Yet at the same time the idyll is slightly punctured when Lily, offered lemonade by Sid, says 'I don't see how you could want anything better than this' and Sid, taking a sip, screws up his face before forcing a smile and saying 'Oh, you're right, Lily, you're darn right'.

Through a glass brightly: self-consciousness and 'distanciation' in *Summer Holiday*

Summer Holiday's primary impetus is towards affectionate affirmation. Disruption exists, but is largely contained within the film's celebratory ethos. We have at various points in our reading concentrated on such moments of disruption that question the ideology of Dannville life, but here we are interested in certain intimations that surround the film's dominant affirmations, suggestions produced by intense aesthetic workings such as Leo Marx refers to when he divides complex from simple pastoral:

> In one way or another, if only by virtue of the unmistakeable sophistication with which they are composed, these works – [i.e. certain American literary pastorals] – manage to qualify, or call into question, or bring irony to bear against the illusion of peace and harmony in a green pasture.

'Distanciation' is an ugly word that has been used of strategies within Hollywood films such as the melodramas of Douglas Sirk, indicating the presence of formal devices, not on the surface disruptive of traditional narrative, that render problematic what might not look at first glance to be so. One of the marks of *Summer Holiday's* sophistication – available to those who pick up the codes at work – is the creation of a mode of detachment that takes two specific forms. First, many images are presented in such a way as to draw attention to their ideal quality, as distinct from reality. Second, some of these, whether calculatedly or innocently, present through the medium of highly-wrought hyperbole rather extraordinary representations of the basic mechanisms of the culture they are observing.

The clearest case of the first is the Dannville High School graduation ceremony, the film's own invention. The point of particular interest is the sequence of shots placed within the narrative during the overwhelmingly nostalgic singing of the school song, 'All hail to Dannville High', with its emphasis on community, tradition and bonding. These shots occur within a context that has already emphasised the presence of icons (e.g. the large bust of Lincoln that presides over the entry of the students; the portraits of Lincoln and Washington). We move from a pan of the audience's reactions – Essie (proudly rapt), Lily (sadly nostalgic), Tommy (unimpressed) – to a series of patently unrealistic shots, seven in all, which pose characters outside the film's main narrative in *tableaux vivants:* for instance an elderly grandfather dandles a baby; two pretty waifs, a boy and a girl, appear mysteriously, as if from the riverbank, at the back of the hall; while outside a woman at a window and then a farmer with his horse and plough listen to the singing. Three of these *tableaux* are based on paintings by the well-known regional artist Grant Wood, 'Daughters of the American Revolution', 'Woman with plant' and 'American Gothic', and the first and last of these add a further complexity of effect since, although homogeneous with the others in that they are both denaturalised through the painterly effect and then half re-naturalised as they seem to respond to the singing, they differ in possessing marked satiric elements. In 'Daughters of the American Revolution' three grim, elderly bourgeois women, members of that august conservative body, stand before the heroic painting by Emanuel Gottlieb Lutz of 'Washington crossing the Delaware' (1851), an image that it is difficult to read in terms other than the grotesque, while in 'American Gothic' an equally grim rural couple, redolent of crabbed fundamentalism and spiritual poverty, are the subject. This placement of two satiric images – the former initiating the sequence – amongst others that present a Norman Rockwellish world of patriotic sentiment, argues a kind of double focus, suggesting that the images of apparently pure sentiment should not be read straightforwardly, but in the light of the others, as a projection of how the community wishes to picture itself. That all these images are constructed, that all of them are views of reality rather than objective transcriptions of it, is suggested when 'American Gothic' is not shown just as a finished image but in the process of construction, with its subjects actually stepping into the frame.

Another place in the film where the pervasive interest in icons (e.g. Daniel Webster on the wall of Nat's *Globe* office; the 'Athaneum' portrait of Washington by Gilbert Stuart (1796) that hangs above the Millers' bed) is given extreme expression is the Independence Day picnic. Here, twice, there are *tableaux* where characters are frozen, as if statues, into representative images, and then move back into the ordinary world of activity. First, three men in the costume of the Revolutionary war are immobilised in a well-known image, eventually coming to life to bow to the crowd's applause. Second, a little later, there is a shot of the matrons at their picnic in a composition that is all pastels and *fête-champêtre* which also begins as a frozen picture before the characters flow back into their game of croquet. What the reiteration of this effect produces is a distancing from reality, an announcement to the audience that what is being shown is reality through its most pleasing representations, a mythology by which the characters live rather than a simple statement of how it is. This interest in the relation of life to a mythology seems to us to run very self-consciously through *Summer Holiday*, even down to its most basic components (in the general audience's view), its characters, who are, without exception, played by actors who render so excessively the sense of the typical that to watch the film is to feel in the presence of a myth rather than reality. Walter Huston is so quintessentially the benign patriarch; Selena Royle as always so much the caring mother; Frank Morgan a national institution as the amiable middle-aged ne'er-do-well; Agnes Moorehead in her spinster role almost as much so; 'Butch' Jenkins the very image of the blond and freckled American male child; Gloria De Haven (in the palest pastel dresses and bows) the affecting stereotype of the innocent small town girl; and Mickey Rooney, even if more ironically placed than usual, with the associations of Andy Hardy to bring to the part. To say this is, we feel, to say something more than that the film is well cast along the stereotypical lines developed by Hollywood cinema. It follows such principles to an excess, underlining self-conscious stereotyping tendencies already very pronounced in O'Neill's play, furthering that sense elsewhere produced by the film that we are being given *images of images*. These are typically suffused with nostalgia but, because of their license to be constructed in hyperbole, they often go beyond the realistic and the unproblematically celebratory to produce extraordinary statements of the mechanisms of the culture they celebrate. For instance, the Independence Day picnic is actually divided into different segregated parties for the opposing sexes – for the men a Bacchic riot of drink and rebellion in which Independence Day signifies a sexual war ('Every day some treble/Joins the rebel/Band'), for the women the role of providing dainty foods ('We can't do our carving/Until Mrs Nicholls/Finds the dill pickles'). Only in the young people's picnic are the sexes together, as a fiddler, with girls circling round him, strikes up a tune to which the couples dance. But the images that precede it, chronologically displaced, seem to say that, as the rapture of courting passes, so the sexes tend to separate back into their prescribed worlds – the roles for the women being especially narrow. The cogency of this is seen by the way it parallels an analysis, made from quite a different angle of approach, in the Lynds' sociological study of American large small town society, *Middletown in Transition:*

> The worlds of the two sexes constitute something akin to separate subcultures. Each involves an elaborate assignment of roles to its members and the development of preferred personality types emphasising various ones of the more significant role attributes . . . But this culture says not only that men and women do different things; they *are* different kinds of people.

The difference between the film's perception of these things and 'post-feminist' analysis is that, for the former, such roles are not seen as wholly oppressive, but, rather more ambiguously, as simultaneously both gratifying and narrowing, not yet exhausted by cultural changes and criticism. Nevertheless, the film dramatises them with great clarity, as it does other sexual material, in a scene that is much less idyllic, Richard's encounter with Belle. The famous instance of Mamoulian's 'experimentalism' whereby Belle, dressed in pink, goes through colour changes, ending up literally as a 'scarlet woman', has often been remarked, but the changes have more than a formal brilliance, for what they articulate is Belle's status as image – the fevered vampiric unreality she has for Richard – the unreality of which is underlined by her prosaic behaviour at the beginning and the end of the sequence.

Part of the Dannville High sequence has already been examined in detail.

Other parts may be examined for distillations of societal meanings similar to the one given above. For instance, another focus of the Lynds' analysis is the role of the school in the small community and a growing tension felt between two different ideologies of education – the traditional one of the school as the transmitter of society's traditional values, and a newer one in which education is identified with the spirit of enquiry, 'of the culture, but also somewhat *over against* the culture'. Though the force of the clash is contained within nostalgia and comedy and all the connotations of sturdy, indulgent common sense pertaining to Walter Huston as the father, it is given exemplary representation in Richard's rebellion, based as it is on 'un-American' modes of thought. At the point in his class valedictory (which has an ironic double sense) where Richard is about to proceed to the words 'Lies! Lies! The world is run by dishonest *capitalists* who are sucking the very life blood from the poor *wage slaves*', Richard's father strides forward and brings the speech to an end by applauding and hustling Richard offstage, as if he believed Richard's speech to be finished. Much of the later action of the film inspects, and, generally speaking, finds ways of justifying this act of authority, yet the film does actually represent, rather than simply evade Mr Miller's forcible repression of his son.

PART IV

From the fifties to the present

It's Always Fair Weather (1955) and the Gene Kelly musical

'Hiya, Springtime! . . . You know you're gonna
wind up callin' me pet names' — *For Me and My Gal*

In the public mind Gene Kelly was to musicals of the '40s and '50s what
Astaire and Rogers had been to the middle '30s: the barometer of an era
which, in contrast to a previous time's climate of elegance, now showed that
the atmosphere was propitious for the encouragement of a breezy, brash,
unashamedly American urban hero, not sophisticated enough to refrain from
'taking a bow every time he heard a clap of thunder'. He came to Hollywood's
notice through his appearances as Joey Evans in the 1940 Broadway production of *Pal Joey*, an important milestone in his career for several reasons,
prominent among which were his meeting with Stanley Donen, a sixteen-
year-old chorus boy in the show, and his own playing of a part which in its
mixture of narcissism and vulgar city charm helped shape the persona that
was to become so familiar through his screen roles.

Donen, who collaborated with Kelly on the direction of such major films
as *On the Town, Singin' in the Rain*, and *It's Always Fair Weather* (but also, in
other ways, on films like *Cover Girl, Anchors Aweigh*, and *Take Me Out to the
Ball Game*), described his personality offscreen in a way that illuminates
much of the onscreen persona: 'He had a cockiness in himself, and a ruthless-
ness in the way he went about things that to someone as young and green as
myself, was astonishing. I also found him cold, egotistical and very rough.
And, of course, wildly talented. He was the only song and dance man to come
out of that period who had balls . . . it was the athlete in him that gave him
his uniqueness.' In parts the description could fit Harry Palmer, the role he
played in his first film, *For Me and My Gal* (1942), an opportunity that took a
long time to materialise. After one abortive attempt – largely of their own
making – MGM had finally given him this telling role of the song and dance
man, very reminiscent of Joey Evans, sliding from a life of unrestrained

ambition to chastened self-denial.

For Me and My Gal set him on his way to the parts with which he achieved universal fame. As he began to prove his value – both at the box office and on the sound stages (as early as *Cover Girl* when he would take over the choreography from the ailing and by now tamer Busby Berkeley) – Kelly gained correspondingly greater control over decision-making even though, of course, he was part of the musical-making unit accommodating a number of exceedingly talented writers (like Comden and Green), directors (like Sidney and Minnelli, with whom Kelly made *The Pirate, The Ziegfeld Follies, An American in Paris* and *Brigadoon*), actors and actresses (like Judy Garland, Kathryn Grayson, Cyd Charisse, Van Johnson) and other personnel (including Carol Haney and Jeannie Coyne, who as well as Donen, helped with the choreography), all brought together and supervised by Arthur Freed. Under Freed, Kelly was able not only to display the wide range of his talent on the screen but also to help shape offscreen the look of the new MGM musical which, in some ways to the chagrin of Mayer, could no longer reproduce the themes and forms of the Eddy–MacDonald films for which the studio had previously been known. Kelly's innovations in choreography, scriptwriting and experimental formal elements are evident in films as diverse in tone as *Cover Girl, Take Me Out to the Ball Game* and *On the Town*.

As MGM clocked up its Kelly successes and, as Clive Hirschorn puts it, his work as a choreographer in films like *An American in Paris, Summer Stock* and *On the Town* reached a level of virtuosity and originality as high as Agnes de Mille's or Jerome Robbins', the studio was even prepared to sanction his doomed but heartfelt project celebrating the history of dance in *Invitation to the Dance*. Even though Freed himself was opposed to the idea, Kelly – so exalted must his status have been at the studio by now – was allowed to proceed, but owing both to production difficulties in England, where the film was being made, and to the outside commitments of some of the personnel, the film dragged itself to a much retarded, much cut and doomed release in 1956. By this time Kelly was preparing to make his last film for the studio (*Les Girls*, 1957), the harmonious collaboration with Donen had been disintegrating, and cinema audiences were ready for a new kind of musical, signs of which, we shall argue, are already in evidence in the film that was in some senses more truly his swan-song for MGM: *It's Always Fair Weather*.

On a not so clear day you can see it's not always fair weather

It's Always Fair Weather may seem an odd choice among Kelly films

since it is generally thought less successful and is certainly less famous than
On The Town and *Singin' in the Rain,* those other Kelly–Donen collaborations that are almost synonymous with the genre. But there are good reasons
for investigating the lesser known work. The most important is its Janus-
faced position as a late MGM studio musical that also looks forward to the
more dissonant musicals of the post-studio period, illustrating, by the way,
Kelly's consistently adventurous approach to the genre. With some of the
major interests of the last third of this book being the tracing of themes of
growing interiority and the lyricising of material which would have been considered too intractable in earlier musicals, *It's Always Fair Weather* became
the obvious choice, built as it is on an intricate relationship of negation and
affirmation to the mainly joyous MGM musicals of the '40s and early '50s.
The film thus has a very real prognostic interest, and with *Carousel* and *On a
Clear Day You Can See Forever* (the subjects of the following chapters) forms
a triad of films through which some of the more interesting shifts in the genre
as it moves towards the present may be observed. We also see it – at least in
the context defined by this book – as a more interesting musical than the two
mentioned, whose greater status in the public mind perhaps owes most to
their typicality. This is especially the case with *Singin' in the Rain* which acts
out so attractively concerns which inhabit the majority of musicals – essential
self versus imposed role, popular art versus pretentious art, the self-referential
celebration of the values of entertainment – sets of meanings so bound into
many of the films already discussed that to pursue them again through
Singin' in the Rain would be repetitious. Though lesser known, *Fair Weather*
has had, nevertheless, a certain amount of critical attention, the result of its
being seen – correctly, but in too prejudicial a way – as a symptom of change
and decline in the musical towards the end of the studio era, beginning to die
the death in the mid-fifties. This view derives from Michael Wood's book
America in the Movies, where the film is rediscovered as the intrusion of
'darkness in the dance'. When compared with *On The Town* and *Singin' in the
Rain* it is seen to be filled with 'failing vision', 'decline and disintegration'
and 'disease of the spirit'. This 'decline and disintegration' are then related to
the decline of the musical as a genre in the fifties, the larger movement being
interpreted as the epiphenomena of subterranean changes in the self-
confidence of America and Americans in the Eisenhower era, qualities on
which the genre depended and, without them, failed. Later comments on the
film by Leo Braudy and John Russell Taylor look at it very much from this
perspective. But when, for example, Braudy writes, 'The sense of individual
style so celebrated in the 1930s and 1940s rings hollow in the Eisenhower
years. *It's Always Fair Weather* proclaims the collapse of the transforming

power of theatre and style . . .', the perspective is exceedingly limited, restricted to a model of the musical as the vehicle for the simplest kinds of affirmation, rather than a genre with affirmation at its base constantly shifting in response to exterior realities. The three critics mentioned all see *Fair Weather* as an ending, which in certain respects it is; but it can also be seen as a beginning, acting out (though many relatively old-fashioned musicals will continue to be made) premonitions of the new. Their argument is too apocalyptic for, after all, the musical did not die, and not only *The Sound of Music, Hello Dolly!* and *Grease*, but also *All That Jazz, Saturday Night Fever* and *One From the Heart* lie ahead.

Where we agree, though, is that *Fair Weather* is indeed a symptomatic work, registering important historical changes in the genre. But whereas Michael Wood insists on its interests being wholly the product of accident – 'I think they just wanted to make a musical' (he says of the writers and directors) 'and this is the way it turned out', we would stress, in what has always been the most self-conscious and intricately self-referential of the Hollywood genres, the element of conscious design in the film, particularly its parody (in the most serious sense) of previous MGM musicals, notably *On The Town*. We do not wish to conduct this whole argument simply at the level of statements of the makers' intentions, since clearly such statements have no absolute authority, but there is so much in the film that is systematically at a tangent from the usual that Kelly's remark that 'We wanted to make an experiment by treating a serious subject within the confines of musical comedy' must be given serious attention, supporting a positive view of the film not just as the inheritor of the brilliance and virtuosity of the MGM musical tradition, but also as the progenitor of the post-studio, contemporary and auteurist musicals described in the final chapter of this book.

This self-conscious relation to tradition is most obviously demonstrated as *Fair Weather* sets out to rewrite the optimistic *On The Town*. There the trio of sailors spent their twenty-four-hour leave in a hectic commitment to energy and romance in New York. Early on in the later film, Miss Leighton (Cyd Charisse), in deflecting Ted Riley's (Gene Kelly) crass advances, quotes to him from Shakespeare – 'Most friendship is feigning, most loving mere folly'. It is an epigraph that could not in any sense be attached to the earlier films, but looks ahead to *Sweet Charity, Cabaret, Nashville, All That Jazz* and *New York, New York*, with their very definite sense of playing the ideals of earlier musicals against more bitter experience. *It's Always Fair Weather* is, of course, still of the fifties, transitional rather than iconoclastic, so that these lines, however much they reverberate through the film, are finally disproved as the two cynical lovers discover reasons for dropping their defences, and the three army comrades find that their alienation from each other is the product of dissatisfaction with their own selves rather than with their friends. Nevertheless the lines do express problems in areas that most previous musicals have agreed not to find overtly problematic – such as that men and women might find it difficult to get and stay together; that previous experiences might leave one frightened of later opportunities; that beneath the veneer of sophistication one might not really be enamoured of the self one carries around; that the bonds of friendship and the sense of meaning forged in earlier life might not prove durable against change and disappointment. Things *will* work out, the film affirms eventually, in a way reminiscent of that earlier venture in post-war mixing of social realism and sentiment in the treatment of the adjustment problems of ex-servicemen, *The Best Years of Our Lives* (1946). But it is a close-run thing as greater reality invades the utopian genre. This does not mean that we find the optimism of earlier musicals childish in the light of the later. Such optimism was part of the generic compact between makers and watchers that the musical would deliver a utopian world. *It's Always Fair Weather* is a film that stretches the terms of the compact almost to breaking point at times. In comparison *On The Town* is a work of dazzling (unpejorative) shallowness, inviting few feelings of disjunction between thought and action, desire and fulfilment. Though we know that only one of the film's three sexual relationships will last (between Kelly and Vera-Ellen) the greater part is still exhilaration, the release of energy rather than the expense of spirit. This positive shallowness, emphasising surface over interiority, is encapsulated in the film's last moments as a new trio of sailors runs off the boat, replacing Kelly, Sinatra and Munshin. In contrast, the later trio of Kelly, Dan Dailey and Michael Kidd, the pristine white uniforms of the sailors changed to the emblematic flannel suits of fifties' city man, carry with them a certain gravity of individuality too complex to resolve wholly into types. On the edge of middle age, experienced in disillusion, they have too much weight of being simply to dissolve into the cyclical. Of the analysts in the air at the time – a thought prompted by the film's interest in psychoanalysis discussed below – it is, one feels, Jung with his interest in the later phases of life who would have most to say to them.

In *On The Town* each of the three sailors finds a partner, though the minimal plot spends most time with the more complicated search Kelly, as the most soulful of the three, has for 'Miss Turnstiles', as Sinatra and Munshin are grabbed by the cheerful sexpots played by Ann Miller and Betty Garrett. The only problem is that Kelly and Vera-Ellen should lose their poses of sophistication and accept each other for what they are. Whereas time in

On The Town is a dynamic forward thrust (with the hours and minutes sometimes ticking away at the bottom of the screen), it is immediately more complicated in *Fair Weather*. The film begins as if it is going to parallel the adventures of the three sailors with the straightforward chronology of the adventures of the three discharged army buddies also arriving in New York. But the opening turns out to be only a prelude which sends them off separately to the greater world with its promise of ambitions to be fulfilled (Ted/Kelly to be 'just a great man'; Douglas/Dailey to follow Kelly's role in *An American in Paris* as a painter; and Angie/Kidd to learn *haute cuisine*). The disillusionment of the next ten years is wittily expressed in a montage that follows newsreel clips compressing the passage from the Truman to the Eisenhower years. Douglas and his paintings are obliterated by a plethora of consumer goods; Angie almost vanishes beneath his offspring; while Kelly is surrounded by chippies. The degenerating heroes form what amounts to a symbolic triptych of *Homo Americanus* in the fifties, at least from the lower middle class up – the organisation man, the smalltime capitalist and the hustler. When the three meet, *bonhomie* turns to dislike and the only thing that keeps them together for the finale of the narrative is the plan hatched by Miss Leighton on behalf of the 'Midnight with Madeleine' TV show to use the trio's reunion as an ersatz human interest item.

Ted Riley makes a pass at Miss Leighton and is rebuffed, but her plan causes them to be thrown together and a relationship develops. His compliance in the 'fix' he finds has been arranged for his fighter, Kid Mariacci, eventually disgusts him, and to prevent the fight going ahead, he knocks out the boxer, causing the contest to be abandoned but also putting himself on the run from the gangsters he has crossed. Meanwhile, Douglas has also become disgusted with himself and causes a drunken scene at an advertising party. When the trio are gathered together in the TV studio and the 'This is your life' surprise is sprung on them, the gangsters invade the place looking for Ted. However he and Miss Leighton combine to trick the gang boss into confessing the 'fix' live to the nationwide audience. In the brawl that follows, the new rapport between the old companions is given an embodiment reminiscent of wartime action as they combine against the mob. The film ends back in Tim's Bar, where the comrades originally made their pledge to remain friends and later reunited, with another farewell as each goes back into the ordinary world – Ted with Miss Leighton, Douglas with the chance of reviving a marriage dulled by his compromises in the world of advertising, and Angie, accepting his limitations, to his home, family and job.

Thus the film traces the journey to a bitter but ultimately creative self-recognition by its heroes – Douglas to his outburst of previously stifled rage at the world of 'Miss Klenzrite' into which he has sunk his talent, and his statement to his wife over the air that the horribly factitious TV show 'is truly a fitting climax to ten years of self-degradation', and Ted to his cleansing definition of himself as 'a bum, a smalltime operator'. It is hard to know if intention or forced narrative economy (the omission of Angie's/Michael Kidd's balancing number) is responsible for the sense that Angie, though giving up the pretension of his 'Cordon *Blue*' restaurant for 'Angie and Connie's Roadside Diner', has changed less from his aggressively-defensive posturing than the others. Whereas both Ted and Douglas react to the questions of the chat show hostess Madeleine by defining their inadequacies, Angie (admittedly in response to her condescending reference to the 'army of little grey men') defines himself aggressively and self-righteously in terms of the classic small-time capitalist, very much seeing his adequacy bound up with his own unaided power to support his wife and children. Whatever the cause, Angie emerges as the most superficial of the three characters, the one most trapped by convention, his resistance to change playing as a sort of reality principle against the difficult new perceptions that the more mature characters arrive at. Quite where the more thoughtful Ted and Douglas will go and what they will do the film leaves unclear. Do we take it that Douglas is through with the banalities of advertising? That Ted will find a steady and fulfilling job now that he has found Jackie Leighton? But if so, where? How can one escape the rat race? The film can give no answer to these questions, caught as it is between feelings that on the one hand it is one's inner attitude that matters, that if one can, unegotistically, come to 'like' oneself, as Ted declares he does and Douglas is determined he will, then what one does will not matter because one will be protected against the world; and, alternatively, the contrary feeling that the structure of the world portrayed in the film, epitomised by the factitiousness of television, advertising and boxing matches that are rigged, is responsible for the way the characters feel. A further ambivalence is acted out in the ending which manages an affirmation in the singing of 'We'll be friends until we die' etc, but is also suffused with sadness and loneliness. The final big crane shot surveys the trio (though Ted is now with Miss Leighton) setting off in their separate directions without, rather pointedly, any arrangements being made for a future reunion. This omission is quite significant. To put in some statement about meeting again in five or ten years would have been the obvious thing, but here, as in many other places, the film is interested in fugitive and rather delicate feelings and effects. If friendship survives it will be a friendship carried in the mind, in memory, rather than acted out in the present, and this version of togetherness in separateness looks forward interestingly to other instances in the following two chapters – the reconciliation between the living daughter and dead father in *Carousel*, and the love without consummation at the end of *On A Clear Day You Can See Forever*.

Of course, there has always been a sub-text of the problematic in the musical, even in the sunniest MGM films. The difference is a matter of centring, the contrast, to use a Shakespearean analogy, between a comedy like *As You Like It* and a 'problem' comedy like *All's Well That Ends Well* (which shares with *It's Always Fair Weather* a similar balance of affirmation and irony in its title). In *It's Always Fair Weather* things pushed to the margins in other musicals begin to leak into the centre. An overt sign of this is the way that, although no psychiatrist figure appears, the topic of analysis (with its emphasis on troubled and ambivalent states of being) invades the film. For instance, when Miss Leighton complains about Ted's 'two-bit snap analysis' of her defensiveness and delivers one back, it causes him to admit, 'That was no snap analysis, lady, that was my life' (a remark that plays against the superficiality of the 'This is your life'-type TV programme). And, leaving the Grove Costume Company he has visited with Miss Leighton (a location that suggests disguises and role playing), Ted, wryly commenting on these concerns, hands the attendant a tip and advises him, 'Go get yourself analysed'.

As we might expect, such narrative dissonances are reflected in the numbers. Michael Wood makes the significant point that in two of these (the ballet with the trashcans and Douglas' drunken interruption of the cocktail party) it is *alcohol*, an artificial stimulant, rather than traditional euphoria that is the instigator of the number's release. Jane Feuer also notes how Douglas's 'Situationwise' number 'assumes an inner compulsion to destruction and chaos, qualities buried in the classical musical's affirmation of liberation and personal energy'. Further, the number set in 'The Turquoise Room' restaurant plays against the upfront explosion of communal energy in the title number of *On the Town* and 'You can count on me' from the same film. Here the number is completely interiorised into soliloquising over-voices, and based on the hidden grumbles rather than the open ecstasies of the characters. Meaning is hidden from the other characters rather than celebrated with them. Tensions developing through the meal take form to the rhythm and melody of 'The Blue Danube' which is being played by the dining-room orchestra, and each of the principals is in turn isolated by a frame within the frame as he soliloquises his thoughts ('I shouldn't have come . . . This guy is a slob and that one's a hick' sings Ted, Angie's equally sour version includes 'This guy's a cheap punk and that one's a heel', while Douglas laments having flown in from 'Chi' to drink Scotch at noon with a

hick and a goon'). 'Hick', 'slob', 'punk', 'heel', 'goon', 'schlemiel', the catalogue of vulgar abuse plays against the graceful connotations of the waltz (The Blue Danube/The Danube Blues). A second number also acts against the rapport that is so marked in *On The Town*, by presenting the trio together on the Cinemascope screen, together in time, but apart in location, a device with an effect quite opposite to its beautiful use in *Love Me Tonight* where Maurice Chevalier and Jeanette MacDonald, apart in reality, are brought together by the split screen. Here the characters' solitude is signalled even though their dances are synchronised and again the number is sung by interiorised overvoices, again expressing disenchantment ('Once upon a time I had two friends' etc). 'The Blue Danube' number is exceedingly inventive in combining the traditional and the vulgar, and also in making, through André Previn's clever score, a number out of scraps of background music, as in other places numbers are ingeniously fashioned out of pastiche material – e.g. 'Now the time has come for parting' with its echoes of 'The Whiffenpoof song', the Stillman's gym parody of the generic Ivy League college song, and Douglas' manic outburst with its scraps of 'Jeannie with the light brown hair', 'Be my love', *The William Tell* Overture, etc. This one is equally inventive in making its dances not just out of casual everyday movements, which would be true of many a soft-shoe shuffle, but specifically out of ruminative, introspective gestures. For instance, a hunched-forwards shuffle with hands in pockets, a scuffing kick at some object on the ground, tap dancing while puffing at a cigarette, banging a knee with a hat in a gesture of frustration, walking rather aimlessly, turning and walking again, as distinct from the more extrovert gestures that usually make up such dances. Such gestures, expressing thought rather than dynamism, become almost correlatives for the *temps mort* that we will soon become used to in the European cinema of the 1960s. If there were such an unlikely thing as an *avant garde* tradition of the Italian musical, we might fancifully imagine that Antonioni's characters would dance so. What keeps it within the bounds of the musical's traditional ethos of affirmation is the wit of the piece, the relaxed understatement of the dance which has the traditional magic of a few props (hats, cigarettes that provide the clinching image 'Gone are my dreams/Up in smoke') made to suggest much, and, in the end, an anti-tragic, quotidian ethos of making do, getting by.

It's Always Fair Weather: 'community' and 'transparency' break down – 'This guy is a slob/And that one's a hick.' Angie (Michael Kidd), Douglas (Dan Dailey) and Ted (Gene Kelly) soliloquise their dislike for each other while the lunch-time orchestra plays 'The Blue Danube'.

Taking 'the male initiative': Cyd Charisse, the fifties female, and 'You knock me out'

Very much concerned with the bonds of friendship, the film a little demotes the usual central love interest of the musical. With two of the female partners only existing as already-married offscreen presences, the traditional discovery of new love is restricted to the meeting between Ted and Miss Leighton. And even here a certain odd understatement exists in the way the film deals with the pair's progress through initial misunderstanding and self-imposed barriers to mutual dependence. For some reason the film does not contain the expected song and dance duets between them. The logic of the distribution of numbers surprisingly gives precedence first of all to a series of trios asserting either the unity or fragmentation of the comrades, then to a number by each of the main male characters (though Angie's was cut from the final print) as well as Miss Leighton, and thirdly to the two numbers performed by Madeleine (Dolores Gray) the TV hostess, which can be considered as parodic inversions of the values of some of the other numbers. Kelly's song and dance number on rollerskates 'I like myself', is, of course, linked to his feelings for Jackie Leighton, or, more correctly and subtly, to what his feelings of her perception of him make him feel, but Cyd Charisse is given no moment of romantic interiority as, say, she is given in *Silk Stockings* when she dances solo the drama of her changing feelings. She is in fact given only a single – though memorable – number, 'Baby, you knock me out', which is pointedly not even performed to Kelly; he is actually out of the room when she gets together with the fighters from Stillman's gym. Some readings of the film would see this as confusion, but we would suggest a systematic emphasis on relationships and interior states not subsumable under the traditional uncomplicated affirmation of the couple, with several of the numbers built around frustration and disappointment and those that are more obviously affirmative built out of less conventional material than usual. The film tries very hard to avoid the expected with its couple, partly by eschewing conventional numbers and partly by a play with character and persona that moves away from ideas of an easy transparency in relationships. If Ted Riley is a subtle variation (perhaps the most refined of all) on the brash but ultimately vulnerable character typically played by Kelly, with, in this case, his aggressiveness emerging from a damaged idealism in both love and a career where he expected to be a mixture of 'Babe Ruth, Dick Tracy and Justice Holmes', Jackie Leighton is an equally interesting use of a primary part of the Cyd Charisse persona in MGM musicals. In several of her major appearances (with the softer romantic character in *Brigadoon* an exception), certain possibilities of her persona are very much heightened to produce variations on the dominant female. This may, in the fantasy world of some numbers ('The Girl Hunt' ballet in *The Band Wagon* and the 'Broadway Melody' ballet in *Singin' in the Rain*), actually take the form of a criminal woman, a terpsichorising of the *film noir femme fatale*, quintessentially expressed in the much reproduced still from the latter ballet where she sits, arms akimbo, in one hand a long cigarette holder, removing with the foot of an outstretched leg the hat from the head of an anxious Kelly, an image of the predatory vamp, castrator and destroyer. This is an extreme (and even slightly comic) version of elements more complicatedly treated as problematic but legitimate in Charisse characters like Ninotchka in *Silk Stockings* and Gaby in the narrative of *The Band Wagon*, 'strong' characters, capable of intimidating the male protagonists, who, however, eventually come within their dominance. Both these 'legitimate' and 'criminal' variations highlight that contrast between the rather cool, expressionless facial features of Charisse and the power, authority and dominance of her body. These bodily qualities seem to demand to be used in a dance style that highlights her height and authority to the full and often displays swift scissor-like movements of her legs which are, to say the least, formidable. Like Ninotchka and Gaby, Jackie Leighton (or, as she is severely called throughout the whole film, 'Miss Leighton') finally softens and moves into the ambiance of her lover. It is, however, too simple to see *It's Always Fair Weather* (or indeed the other two films) as constructing its narrative for the sole purpose of punishing the threatening 'career girl' (as she describes herself). For one thing, she is seen to teach Ted a thing or two. For another, the depiction of her can be seen less as the product of a crude wish to do her down than as a bringing within the boundaries of accepted views on the matter of a character who encapsulates, in a more than half positive way, stirrings of dissatisfaction with the largely passive–erotic–domestic combinations of female roles in films of the early fifties (a matter dealt with by Marjorie Rosen and Molly Haskell in their books). Like other (male) characters in the film Miss Leighton may be mixed up and neurotic to a degree, but there is clearly much in her to be admired, some of which seems to be directly connected with her independence – for instance her competence, wit and knowledge, besides, of course, the splendid female power of her dancing, so that within the romantic relationship of two rather defensive and cynical characters moving out of the straitjacket of their belief that 'Most friendship is feigning, most loving mere folly', there is another level at which are imaged changes in the balance of sexual relationships that may be seen as precursors of attitudes becoming more prominent in the sixties and seventies – another sign of the way *It's Always Fair Weather* faces forward as well

UNUSUAL and RARE
ARTICLES and REMEDIES
MEDICINAL HERBS • 1000
ELD PHARMACY
MUrray Hill 3-7599 • 485 WEST 26th

as back.

The buoyant and boisterous 'Baby, you knock me out' is in some respects the traditional affirmative musical number *par excellence*, comparable in some ways to Jane Russell's muscle-flexing parody 'Is there anyone here for love?' in *Gentlemen Prefer Blondes,* a show-case for the dancing of Cyd Charisse, laced with the Runyonesque wit of its setting in the prizefighters' *Alma Mater.* Indeed, comparing it to the various downbeat qualities of the other numbers, Michael Wood sees it as briefly returning the unsatisfactory film 'to the old musical vein . . . where some of that willingness to face all futures still seems alive'. What is very much worth pursuing further is the question of what exactly the number is being optimistic about.

Fighting in various forms – literal and metaphorical – is a pervasive preoccupation in the narrative. The film begins with and constantly looks back to the wartime experience of the three ex-comrades. The tense luncheon between the buddies at the swanky Turquoise Room almost turns into a brawl. The 'Midnight With Madeleine' TV show ends in a battle between the trio and the gangsters in which the three see a kind of 'action' again. Ted, of course, belongs to the fight game, owning the promising middleweight Kid Mariacci who is to fight Rocky Heldon. When Ted becomes ashamed of taking advantage of the 'fix' that has been arranged behind his back by changing his own bets, he knocks the Kid out, thus setting the gangsters against him. A remark of Miss Leighton's draws our attention to the parallel between the fight world and business and career worlds of the rest of the film when she says to Ted that she herself has been mixed up in some 'fixes'.

Fighting as it runs through the narrative has an ambivalent status. At one level it signifies a time of past rapport and selfless comradeship. At another it is a manifestation of criminality, some taint of which leaks over into the competitive business worlds of TV and advertising, as much a 'fix' themselves as the Mariacci–Heldon fight. At a third level it is used to resolve issues as simply as convention allows; the comrades knock out the gangsters. But specifically as the sport of boxing it also signifies a ritualised and very masculine ethos which in the 'Baby, you knock me out' number Miss Leighton very interestingly enters. It also mixes itself with the old metaphor of 'the war of the sexes' which is another area presented ambivalently in the film. All of the sexual relationships we see or hear about are distinguished by bickering and aggression. Douglas' Dorothy is consulting her lawyer about a divorce; the relationship between Angie and Connie is marked by his resentful dependence

---

K.O. courtship: Cyd Charisse a cute contender for Kelly.

and her jealousy; while that between Ted and Jackie Leighton is one of verbal skirmishing and low blows from the beginning. Miss Leighton even uses a pugilistic metaphor when she says that Ted's analysis of her has hit her 'square on the nose'. If we are encouraged to see his aggression towards her and her aggressive defensiveness towards him (such as when she takes the initiative from him by kissing him in the back of the taxi in order to put an end to his advances) as dictated by a cynicism that reduces sexuality to a contest of aggressions, at the same time disapproval is not unalloyed. The encounter appeals in its anti-romantic romanticism, in its street-wisdom about power struggles in relationships, as in some measure exhilarating and energetic. This is the creative, as distinct from the negative side of the contest – creative because it does not reflect merely a comfortable stasis in ideas of male-female relationships but admits of adjustments in the balance of power and distribution of roles. It is this delicate balance – a self-sufficiency and witty transgressiveness that are admirable, combined with defensiveness and self-protectiveness that are less so – that is acted out by Jackie Leighton.

'Baby, you knock me out' is staged near and inside the ring at Stillman's after Ted has introduced Miss Leighton to the fighters and left the room to discuss business. On the personal level their relationship is worked out elsewhere in the film, but this extravagantly witty number in which Charisse performs with the rather battered assembly of prizefighters and veteran trainers is based on matters relevant to it (the fighting metaphor with its extension into the 'war of the sexes', the question of her appropriation of his 'male initiative', something he twice complains of), while the material of the number has already been broached in the scene between the pair in the taxi where, in answer to his facetious supposition that she will know as much about Kid Mariacci as everything else, she astounds Ted by reeling off the boxer's vital statistics. This response is even more surprising than her knowledge of Planck and Maxwell, since 'the sweet science' (to use the sportswriter A. J. Liebling's phrase) is even more obviously the man's world than science proper. Her entry into the gym rehearses various ambivalences that pervade the number. The male/female differences, outraged anyway by her incursion into this all-male sanctum in which women can only be regarded as a danger to a fighter's stamina, are comically stressed by the dialogue: 'Riley! Someone to see you'. 'Someone about 6′4″, with a broken nose and an i.o.u. in his hand?' 'No, 5′5″, neat little nose, and an "I love you" in her eyes.' And when Ted facetiously compliments her for being on time, she replies, 'I'm just a machine', an exchange that sparks on a series of suppositions and counter-suppositions about male and female characteristics. Her remark that she has come to experience the ambiance of 'the colourful world of fisticuffs', though readable as asserting a rather insensitive superiority, makes better sense as an ironic statement that mockingly aligns itself with Ted's assumption of her motives.

The number gains various levels of piquancy from various elements – for instance from its beauty and the beast format and from its mixing of Miss Leighton's 'class' with the proletarian look of the boxers, but most of all from its placing of the female in a wholly male world where she is allowed (within the license of comedy) to triumph. In a similar and memorable moment in *Broadway Melody of 1940*, Eleanor Powell descends with breathtaking agility from the mast of a ship to a waiting and enraptured male crew to sing, 'I am the captain of this boat/From stem to stern/She's my concern'. What, like that number (though the earlier example is much less integrated into the thematics of the film) 'Baby, you knock me out' does, is celebrate both the beauty and intelligence of Miss Leighton/Cyd Charisse, in terms that hold together both power and vulnerability, stressing the unusual former but moderating it with reminders of the latter. In short, it redefines to some degree what was permissible for the times in female attractiveness by highlighting her intelligence as well as her impressive physical manifestations, her activity more than her passivity. Wolf-whistles greet her as she enters the ring and many aspects of the number concentrate on the display of Charisse's body, but equally it is the play of her intellect that is applauded, since what most of all prompts the boxers to admiration is her ability to recite the list of world heavyweight champions from John L. Sullivan to Rocky Marciano, as well as more arcane information such as the round in which Dempsey knocked out Firpo and where ('Round two', 'The Polo Grounds'), etc. That is what specifically gives rise to their eulogy: 'What a Dame! What a Dame! She belongs in the Hall of Fame!' The lyrics that follow join celebration of her body with praise of her intellect: 'You're the dame with the brain in the picture hat!'. As she moves about the ring, the boxers' fighting crouches draw extra attention to her height, accentuating the domineering aspects of her presence while the lyrics also acclaim comically her mock-destructive powers as she enacts the referee's countdown to her victims – '1,2,3,4,5,6,7, 8,9,10 *Bong!*' But in this battle there is always another round, the fight is joined voluntarily and both sides, ideally, win, hence her invitation for more ('Come on!'). If these lyrics genially enact her power, others suggest a complementary vulnerability as well, though equally comically self-aware. The words 'You got me hangin' on the rope' are twice repeated, and, as she passes by one of the boxers, she murmurs, in appreciation of his male power, 'How strong!'. It is not just that she possesses knowledge, but knowledge of a masculine activity, a male preserve. This breakdown of order, this transgression of barriers is, though, not seen as a threat, but as something that can be accommodated and might even be a welcome relief from the stultifying tedium of roles that are too fixed. Significantly, however, though the number has many erotic connotations, it ends with a tableau that fades them into the background. When Ted re-enters the gym at the end of the number, he finds Miss Leighton seated with the boxers engaged in a discussion (presumably of other details of boxiana). Seeing this, we do not believe that her knowledge is, as she has said elsewhere, just 'a trick'. As a boxing aficionado it is clear from this tableau of relaxed camaraderie that she is quite unlike the usual film portrait of the woman interested in boxing – the floozie attached to money and fame, or the vamp drawn to sado-masochism. When Mr Fielding, Douglas' overweight boss, introduces Ted to Miss Leighton, he jokes that she is 'one of our best ideas men, or should I say, women'. His heavy wit and the tension that Ted expresses twice on the subject of his 'male initiative' are explored in this number where a female invades a male preserve without losing her traditional femininity; where, though seen as a sexual object, the definition of sexuality includes her intellectual powers and where, finally, in the image of camaraderie at the end, the sexual difference, though not laid aside, is, where it might be oppressive, suspended.

'I like myself': a coda on self love

Traditionally the musical sings that the true self is found through relationship, most obviously with the love object. We think of Nellie Forbush singing 'I'm in love with a wonderful guy' in *South Pacific;* of Don Lockwood singing 'You are my lucky star' to Cathy in *Singin' in the Rain'*; the examples could be listed endlessly. There has always been an aspect of the musical that parodied such optimism. Think, for instance of the part Luther Billis (Ray Walston) plays in *South Pacific* or the half-approving presentation of many of the toughly anti-romantic gold digging figures in the Berkeley films. But it is only in the later musical, of which *Fair Weather* is the true progenitor, that the love object begins to take second place to the self in an emphasis on interiority that may finally end with the self as sole love object, as with many of the characters in Altman's *Nashville* or the hero, Joe Gideon, of Fosse's *All That Jazz*. However, it is not with such narcissistic dangers that we are concerned now, but rather more positive images of self-concern, particularly those centred around Ted Riley's discovery through a mixture of the influence of Miss Leighton and his own introspection of his degeneration, and, through that realisation, of his own potential in a world which tags the suffix 'wise' ('sales-wise', 'resistance-wise', 'saturation-wise', etc.) to almost every phenomenon, but in which real wisdom is a scarce commodity. Notably, though, the process is expressed in terms of a number called 'I like myself' which establishes a sense of positive self-love as the precondition for the love of another. Ted Riley falls in love with Jackie Leighton, but he can only like her because she teaches him to like himself. In exploring this (which is paralleled by Douglas' progress as well) the film sets up an opposition between two types of self-love.

On the one hand there is the flamboyant egocentricity of Madeleine (Dolores Gray) the TV Queen, and her representation of what the cinema – by now very conscious of the inroads TV has made into its audiences – sees as the worst of TV values. On the other, there is the superior and essentially unegotistical type of self-love which from Plato, through the New Testament to Meister Eckhart, Montaigne and St Teresa of Avila, to the wholly secular instruction of the psychoanalytic movement and its popular offshoots, people have been taught to cultivate. The two types are nicely juxtaposed in *Fair Weather* as first of all Kelly sings (under the influence of Cyd Charisse's interest in him) 'I like myself', and then, almost immediately afterwards, Dolores Gray, on the TV, sings to her mass audience, 'Thanks a lot, but no thanks', a riotously profane hymn to herself.

Kelly's song of self-approval is, over and above its place in the film, a witty meta-textual satire of his own recurring persona. As many people have remarked, Kelly does give the sense of liking himself as a performer a little too much, and though this is an element that is cleverly built into many of the characters he plays, whose brashness undergoes some degree of chastening, even at his most likeable (perhaps exactly when he most attempts to project an intense likeableness), he exudes smugness and full-chested self-regard. With hat cocked back as far as it will go, 'crocodile' smile stretched into place, he has few pretensions to modesty and he acts, sings and dances like a man who believes he is doing everyone a favour by sharing his voluminous talents with all around him. Although he creates a generic character who does in the end achieve heroism – on a comic scale of course – he can come perilously close, however brilliant his skill as a performer, to straying into an offensive banality in his search for approval of his undoubted genius. The contrast with the detachment of Astaire is extreme. But here, in *Fair Weather*, Kelly at last seems to recognise and satirise this aspect of his egregious manner. More substantially, however, the number marks the character Ted Riley's return to peace with himself after wasted years.

On the run from the mob, he has found temporary shelter in a roller-skating rink. Exiting hurriedly, he forgets that he is still wearing the skates,

and rolls down a busy New York pavement incongruously dressed in a suit
and trilby. Using a mode of transport associated very much with the young at
play, Kelly (the casualness of his demeanour at the beginning of the number
very much recalling and thus, in part, cancelling the pessimism of 'Once I
had a friend'), explains his state of mind:

> Why am I feeling so good?
> Why am I feeling so strong?
> Why am I feeling when things could look black
> That nothing could possibly go wrong?
> This has been a most unusual day.
> Love has made me see things in a different way.

Love makes him feel in a different way, but the statement comes out a little
more introvertedly than 'the world-famous feeling' felt by Nellie Forbush
('I'm as corny as Kansas in August, High as a flag on the 4th of July'):

> Feeling so unlike myself;
> Always used to dislike myself.
> But now my love has got me ridin' high.
> She likes me, so so do I.

> Can it be I like myself?
> She likes me, so I like myself.
> If someone wonderful as she is
> Can think I'm wonderful,
> I must be quite a guy.

The film juxtaposes this spectacle of restored personal harmony, applauded
by the crowd of urban onlookers, with the ostentatious, minatory nature of
Madeleine's projection of self-love, the confection of emptiness and glitter of
the single-eyed monster, Television. On the set, where a sort of 'This is Your
Life' programme is about to go on the air, Madeleine tells the audience she
will sing for them, but assures them that if the song fails to move them she
won't mind, as long as she can still depend on their love. In the number itself
acrobatic suitors in evening suits (whose athleticism reminds us of the 'Baby
you knock me out' number) somersault backwards and otherwise throw
themselves around the singing hostess. Although she acknowledges these
slaves of love by name ('Hello, Bill', 'Hello, Jasper'), it is only to reject their
material and physical gifts which she does not need since she has both in the
improbable conjunction of 'Clifton Webb and Marlon Brando combined'
(with Clifton Webb suggesting a rich older figure). Thus the refrain, 'Thanks
a lot, but no thanks'. Either dynamiting or otherwise sending into oblivion
the last of these suitors, she provides another link with the boxing number
(knocking out/blowing up), though clearly most of the positive connotations

are with the boxers and Cyd Charisse.

That TV advertising is the context of all this is, as we have noted, an indication of the way film was waging war on its belatedly discovered enemy in the mid-fifties. Yet even though we see television condemned as factitious, corny and mind-deadening, the film interestingly comes round to dramatising its role – or its possible role – in a more positive way. There is finally a recognition of something of the proper role and function in social life TV could play, though this might seem naively optimistic in the context of the wasteland of the major networks. TV need not simply mean adverts – soap and cleansers peddled by camp sirens. Neither need it be, as it often is in the film, something that panders to the narcissist in everyone. When she triumphantly exclaims to the trio, 'Yes, boys, you're on Television!', Madeleine stresses 'Television' as if it were paradise, and her exaggerated manner encapsulates the film's feeling that TV is in danger of usurping life itself, of drawing out the worst impulses in everyone, of trivialising everything, of becoming merely a mirror for crassness and vanity. (When Rocky Heldon is knocked out in the final brawl he looks up at himself on the screen and clasps his hands above his head in a victory gesture, before losing consciousness.) But the positive side is that it is actually through TV that the villains are revealed and apprehended. As the gang boss accuses Kelly of subverting his plans to 'fix' the fight, and reels off the names of all involved, the entire nation is his witness. Documentary, not self-advertisement, is what the role of TV should be, as it was in the Kefauver Senate Special Committee crime hearings of 1951 and in the CBS 'See it now' broadcasts on matters touching McCarthyism in 1953 and 1954, culminating in the April 1954 ABC coverage of the McCarthy army hearings which, as Erik Barnouw in his history of American television, *Tube of Plenty*, noted, 'proved the decisive blow to the senator's career. A whole nation watched him in murderous close-up and recoiled.' The moment where the gang boss, Charlie Culleran, betrays himself nationwide, obliquely but unmistakably alludes to the senator's downfall, over which the largely liberal creative personnel of the film – Kelly himself having been under serious attack – would have shed few tears.

In private life – and certainly at the outset of his career, largely through the influence of his wife, Betsy Blair – Kelly had aligned himself with liberal causes. Liberalism, however, is not the first thought that comes to mind when we think of Don Lockwood or Ted Riley. Kelly's on-screen politics are more all-embracing, and though he might have thought of himself as a Marlon Brando of the dance (to Astaire's Cary Grant), the comparison only holds true for cinema audiences on the level of the proletarian, athletic, star-hungry qualities of his persona.

No radical, then, and despite the ambitious Europeanism of *An American in Paris* and *Invitation to the Dance*, Kelly is essentially the all-American boy using his talents as actor, singer and dancer to articulate the primary feelings and unlimited ambitions of the ordinary person in city streets. When the New Yorkers in *It's Always Fair Weather* gather round to applaud Kelly after his display of virtuosity on roller-skates it is as though they are showing not only their amazement at his skill but also their approval of his ostentatious representation of downtown, uptown or boulevard Americana. That is predominantly what Kelly signified on the screen, and it was an image – primarily positive but, as we have argued, not without its more problematical side – which was duplicated, regardless of setting (the Highlands of Scotland or the streets of New York), or of role (vaudevillian or sailor boy), in all the films. Even in those films not co-directed by Kelly himself, he achieved through his onscreen versatility and his offscreen imagination (both through choreography and his sometimes uncredited scripting) a range of coherence, power and vision which rivalled Astaire's recognised claims to authorship.

Carousel (1956) and the Rodgers & Hammerstein musical

Rodgers and Hammerstein

'Sentiment has never been unpopular except with a few sick persons who are made sick by the sight of a child, a glimpse of a wedding, or the thought of a happy home.' — Oscar Hammerstein II

It is probably fair to say that *Carousel, Oklahoma!, South Pacific, The King and I, The Sound of Music, The Flower Drum Song* and *State Fair* are remembered by the great majority of their admirers primarily as Rodgers and Hammerstein musicals and only secondly, by a long way, as the work of the directors Henry King, Fred Zinnemann, Joshua Logan, Walter Lang, Robert Wise and Henry Koster. There is what at first seems like an elusive yet recognisable tone and quality to these musicals, unkindly termed 'goo' by some, which seems to spread over the films no matter who directs. The sentiment, whimsy and folksiness of numbers like 'When the children are asleep' in *Carousel*, 'People will say we're in love' in *Oklahoma!*, or 'Getting to know you' in *The King and I* positively triumph in their lavish Todd AO or Cinemascope 55 exposure on the screen. The ethos of disingenuous emotional display, of disarming simplicity, and sometimes of an excess of schmaltz is nonetheless usually very finely balanced by a set of narrative and other formal elements which ensure that the tensions of form, content and ideology create a fascinating, compulsive and distinctive mixture of interdependent patterns.

Even in his days with Lorenz Hart, Rodgers could be relied on to compose a tune of rare lyricism, such as 'Bewitched, bothered and bewildered'. But the alliance with Hammerstein, after the traumatic, brilliant but perhaps predestined unhappiness of his collaboration with Hart, characterised by the latter's controlling wit and cerebral playfulness in shows like *Pal Joey* and *The Boys from Syracuse*, meant not only a happier union of hearts and minds but also the beginnings of a partnership that would break all commercial records on both stage and screen. It was to be a harmonious complicity between a composer who was capable of writing exceedingly romantic tunes and a lyricist who had a strong taste for the moods and narrative forms of operetta. Hammerstein had worked with Vincent Youmans (*Wildflower* and *Mary Jane McKane*), Sigmund Romberg (*The Desert Song*), Rudolf Friml (*Rose Marie*), and Jerome Kern (*Showboat*). Here in these collaborations on stage operetta – the last three of which were made into very successful films – with four of the most brilliant composers in the mode, Hammerstein had learnt how to integrate number and narrative. This enthusiasm for operetta, both in the quality of the music and in the interdependence of lyrics, music and narrative became a hallmark of the Rodgers and Hammerstein musical.

Circumstances dictated that instead of being filmed immediately, the most successful Rodgers and Hammerstein shows became films of the mid- and late '50s rather than the '40s. This delay – enforced so that film versions would not compete with the tremendously popular stage versions – had certain repercussions on the films that are often interpreted in a negative way. The tendency is to see them as encrusted by reverence for the popular classic status of the originals, bowed down by respectful fidelity, vast budgets that encouraged conservative treatment and ponderous commitment to the new wide screens, and given to 'safe' directors without track records in the musical. There is some evidence of considerable conservative interference by Rodgers and Hammerstein in the making of *Oklahoma!*, and even where this was not present in the later films, pressures of a generally cautious nature persisted. The partners had from their earliest days striven in an efficient and commercial way to promote their carefully cultivated image. So protective over it did they become that they were less than generous in publicly crediting the contribution of others, such as Joshua Logan in *South Pacific*, for fear that any element, however trivial, that was allowed to diminish the aura of the Rodgers and Hammerstein label would tarnish their reputation and shorten queues at the box office.

Even so, we by no means share the tendency to denigrate these enormously and deservedly popular films, negative criticism of which is often extremely impressionistic: such as dislike of Logan's use of colour filters in *South Pacific*, or claims – for which we can see no justification – that many images in *Oklahoma!* are poorly composed, or, as far as we are concerned, the quite misguided notion that Fred Zinnemann and Henry King knew little about making musicals. In our view the background presence of the authors, the conditions of production, the lavish treatment and an ethos borrowed and modulated from the stage originals, the unexpected choice of directors, actually succeeded in creating a musical with a new look. To assert, as some contemporary reviewers did, that these films signalled the decadence of the musical is to ignore the natural processes of development in any art form and to remain blind to new complexities of form and content.

The films derived from the most popular Rodgers and Hammerstein musical plays of the 1940s arrange themselves into two distinct groups: on the one hand stories that turn inwardly to native America (*Oklahoma!*, *State Fair*, *Carousel*) and on the other, stories that place Americans in exotic environments (*South Pacific* and *The King and I*). *The King and I* admittedly has an Englishwoman as its heroine, but she is quite clearly, even so, a symbol of American values as her championship of Lincoln (rather than, say, William Wilberforce), and her admiration for *Uncle Tom's Cabin* confirm. The recurrence of the theme of cultural integration in the work of the Rodgers and Hammerstein musical is marked, playing a large part in *The Flower Drum Song* (overseas Chinese integration into American society), and even some part in *The Sound of Music*, since the well-known real-life end of the Trapp family story is their arrival and renewed success in America. The two tendencies are, then, not contradictory, but related. The inward-looking films – whatever else they do – celebrate homogeneous America, an America which is not just new but has its history, traditions and 'folk' truths. The outward-looking ones place in a more complex way Americans and American values alongside other cultures, and create a rather larger spectrum of attitudes, ranging from self-assertion to self-doubt. What make the celebrations of *Oklahoma!* possible are the unspoken repression of the Indian who plays no part in the musical (although the 'territory' in 'Territory Folks should stick together' was specifically *Indian* territory), and the expulsion of the 'bullet-coloured' alien Jud, the 'hired hand' (foreign, proletarian, a reading much enforced by the casting of Rod Steiger in the role). But, on the other hand, the doubts and complexities of *South Pacific* in particular emerge from the denial of self-sufficient isolationism that accompanies the assertion of American supremacy in the war and ensuing Cold War.

South Pacific, of course, is set during the conflict with Japan, which – as regards the stage version – is very recent history indeed, part of the experience of many returning veterans and their families, while *The King and I*, though historically distanced, plays, consciously or otherwise, on America's past and present sense of a natural hegemony in south-east Asia ('Getting to know you'). While in one way these plays and films assert the naturalness of American influence and power, they also – much more radically in the case of *South Pacific* – suggest limitations and difficulties, on the level particularly of the inter-racial and inter-cultural love plots of the latter. The songs 'My girl back home' and 'You've got to be carefully taught' are fascinating from this point of view. There is moreover an enactment through the characterisation of Bloody Mary of the repulsive side of the Americanisation of alien cultures. Some aspects of the racial debate at the heart of these narratives may also have had a meaning as much directed towards home as overseas: Nellie Forbush is, after all, a native of Little Rock, so America's own colour problem may not lie too far away from the thoughts of the authors.

It would be foolish to try and settle on a restricted number of historical determinants for the complex phenomena of works of entertainment, and in stressing the wartime and Cold War genesis of the original stage shows (which are faithfully translated into film) we do not mean to be reductive, rather to emphasise one interesting set of circumstances. And even though *Carousel's* thematic concerns are more interior, without the same nationalistic appeal, a good deal of the show's original popularity must have come from its incidental but powerful concern with the American past. *Carousel* the film, in our view, is not merely a footnote to a '40s play, but one of the key '50s films not just in the musical genre, but in the whole sphere of sexual relationships, that complacent Eden ripe for the serpents of dissent.

Romantic love and marriage

'It's possible, dear, for someone to hit you . . . hit you hard . . . and it not hurt at all' — Julie.

Whatever other meanings it has contained, the Hollywood musical has always highlighted the love story. From Dick Powell and Ruby Keeler to John Travolta and Olivia Newton–John, successive couples have paired off before the final credits, and happiness has been promised as a concrete reality in romantic monogamy. Such is the strength of the convention that when it is broken in contemporary musicals like *Cabaret,* we do not feel merely that the lovers' inability to relate to each other is a piece of realism, a reflection of the way we know the world to be. This is because the genre has traditionally rejected the broken promise, offering romantic monogamy as the one Utopia possible, to sustain us even in its absence.

In embodying so blatantly the promises of the ideology of romantic love, the musical tells us how much of ourselves is entangled, for better or worse, with variants of this ideology. Even the post-studio musical, attacking its conventions directly, does so from the position of the disillusioned believer, no more wholly free of its influence than George Meredith was when he wrote his sonnet sequence *Modern Love* (1862), which is the key statement of that inextricable mixture of assault upon and mourning for lost illusions which seems the fate of the erotic in the modern western psyche. The musical of course did not invent this mythology, though it gave it a unique version, nor can it ask how it was arrived at, a question that would have to consider a complex course of interacting effects.

Of all Hollywood musicals *Carousel* perhaps gives the ideology its most heightened as well as its most ambiguous expression. That the two should be combined is not surprising since the more extreme the assertion, the more likely its contradictions are likely to reveal themselves. A resumé of the plot suggests something of this. The story begins in a kind of purgatory where the recently deceased Billy Bigelow (Gordon MacRae) is employed cleaning stars. Interviewed by the Starkeeper, he recounts in a flashback his life on earth in a small New England fishing village in the late nineteenth century. There Billy, a handsome but shiftless carousel barker, meets and marries Julie Jordan (Shirley Jones), a mill girl. But the marriage is not happy. Frustrated and restless, Billy beats her. As he is on the point of agreeing to commit a robbery with his criminal friend Jigger (Cameron Mitchell), Julie tells him that she is about to have a child. The news transforms him (despite the scepticism of Jigger and Billy's old mistress Mrs Mullin), and he welcomes the idea of fatherhood in the song 'My boy Bill'. But during the song his mind moves to the more troubling idea that his child might be a daughter. His desperation for money now even greater, Billy goes through with the robbery, in which he is accidentally killed. Back in the afterworld, the Starkeeper tells him that he is allowed one day back on earth to attend to any unfinished business. At this point Billy returns to earth in the present time, sixteen years after his death. Here he watches his posthumously-born daughter Louise daydreaming unhappily. Later he approaches her, posing as a friend of her father's, and learns at first hand the way in which her fierce identification with him and equally fierce resentment towards him have troubled her life. When he offers her the gift of a star from the afterworld, she refuses to take a present from a stranger and he loses his temper and hits her, thereby repeating the old cycle of his mortal behaviour. It seems that his trip to earth is doomed to failure, but he goes unseen to Louise's graduation ceremony where he speaks to both Louise and Julie. The old country doctor (the same actor who plays the part of the Starkeeper) delivers a homily to the new generation and tells them not to be defined by the actions of their parents. 'Believe him', Billy whispers to Louise, and 'I loved you' to Julie (who has picked up the star in such a way as to show she has recognised his presence), and both optimistically join in the singing of 'You'll never walk alone', while Billy returns to eternity.

What is immediately interesting here is both the rhetoric of the narrative and the combination of extreme affirmation with the extremely problematic.

From the point of view of its rhetoric, the film is not only marked by a beautiful symmetry – since it begins and ends with the machinations of the character with a dual function and status, first seen as the Starkeeper and subsequently as the doctor at the graduation ceremony – but also by a display of an intriguing complexity created by the partial flashback structure of the narrative. As he narrates the events of his life to the Starkeeper, the 'truth versus lies' issue of all art is raised with a considerable degree of subtlety. The film resists a crude interest in the simple question of the veracity of his narrative. That particular issue is raised and dismissed as soon as the Starkeeper lets Billy realise that he knows Billy is lying when he refers to himself as the former owner of the carousel. From that point on what Billy relates has to be factually true, so the enthralling aspect of his narrative is the extent to which he selects, compresses and distorts the events of his life. As Billy describes his life so, since the narrative is confessional in form, the image of a man defeated by circumstances is very clearly painted. Billy admits his errors but is careful to suggest through his rhetoric that he could scarcely have avoided his fate. 'What are we? Just a couple of specks of nothin' ', he observes with some resignation and bitterness to Julie. It is appropriate that our first view of a man conscious of his limited power over his own destiny should be in the star setting of eternity, for stars are not only by tradition signs of constancy, lucidity and divinity ('the guides to ev'ry wandering bark'), but also, of course, of fate (as the revellers in *High Society* remind us: 'Have you heard it's in the stars. Next July we collide with Mars').

What else could we have expected, the film seems to ask, of Billy's life, given the odds, both economic and ideological, that were against him? What room is there for love on terms such as these? The film's answers are necessarily opaque and ambiguous. Love is both immortal and also an essence independent of the acts which constitute it, unmarred by the fact that in this case it was unsuccessful, that in most senses the partners seemed completely at odds. This love – though it culminates in Billy's being able to say 'I loved you' to Julie from beyond the grave – is practically seen as the domain of the female. On earth, Billy's inclinations and frustrations lead him away from it, whereas in Julie the principle is constant and undimmed. For Julie, love becomes a force that conquers all moral and reasonable distinctions. When Billy remarks, 'Well, you wouldn't marry a feller like me (i.e. a criminal), would you?', Julie replies 'Yes I would, if I loved you. It wouldn't make any difference what you . . . even if I died for it'. She also tells Billy that she has remained with him on the night they meet 'So you won't be alone'. Her only motive seems to be to give. Reason or 'wondrin' ' has nothing to do with love, which is a kind of secular act of faith. When her friend Carrie Pipperidge is in trouble with her fiancé, she turns to Julie with the words, 'God, it makes you wonder, don't it?'. Julie's reply is first, 'Yes it does, Carrie', and then a song that places love again totally beyond mundane considerations of judgement:

> What's the use of wondrin' if he's good or if he's bad,
> Or if you like the way he wears his hat?
> What's the use of wondrin' if he's good or if he's bad?
> He's your feller and you love him, that's all there is to that.

That, as expressed here, the power of love has become a female power, can be shown by the experiment of imagining Billy, the male lover singing them, and the shock at the excess of self-abnegation we would feel if he did. Not even flinching at the blow he has once dealt her, Julie harbours a love that is a kind of redemption, reaching out to save the male. The double movement of contradiction and affirmation of this secular faith is made by allowing the male to resist it until the end, when he posthumously accepts it (thus acting out our sense of its improbabilities), while almost all of its actual practice falls on the female.

In *Carousel* the love of Julie and Billy is contrasted in two ways: with the attitudes of cynicism and experience associated with Mrs Mullin and with Jigger, and also with the alternative loving couple, Carrie and Mr Snow. Jigger, whose name has a certain sexual connotation, actually parodies the idea of the sanctity of the family, so powerful in the film, when he reminds Billy, who is ecstatic at the prospect of fatherhood, that 'my (i.e. Jigger's) mother had a baby once'.

More complex though than Jigger's contribution to these preoccupations is the film's placing of Mrs Mullin, Billy's employer and older former mistress. *Carousel's* interest in the relationship between Billy and Mrs Mullin is part of a larger pattern in Rodgers and Hammerstein musicals relating the topic of innocence and experience to the love between two people of unequal ages: Anna, the King of Siam and Emile de Becque are all characters who are no longer 'younger than springtime', though the innocence and spring-like qualities of Liat in *South Pacific* are precisely those which attract the American naval officer to her. The vulnerability of relationships between lovers of different ages surfaces with as much complexity in *Carousel* as it does in *South Pacific*, and perhaps the best way of examining it is by comparing it with the delicate way in which the incongruities and incompatibilities of the conventional pairing between Billy and Julie are depicted.

It may be that the origins of Billy's inability to treasure his relationship with Julie lie partly in his memories of experiences with a mature woman. In the scene – later mirrored in *South Pacific* where in the 'Some enchanted evening' number Leon Shamroy's magisterial photography catches the

mutability of passion in the lovers' reflected images in the water – where Julie
and Billy hesitantly declare their feelings for each other, constructing hypo-
theses of love as they sing 'If I loved you', we are made to feel that here not
racial complications as in *South Pacific*, but the innocence of maidenhood
may lead to love's demise. For, by comparison with Mrs Mullin, Julie is a
novice of love, devotedly attending to her husband's needs, fatally ignorant
of her self-inflicted ruin through subservience. Julie's love, extreme enough
to be servile, encourages the tedium of domesticity; Mrs Mullin, more self-
indulgent, knows through experience the rewards to be earned from feeding
a man's narcissistic dreams of heroism. While Julie satisfies a desire to
destroy the rootless nature of his existence, Mrs Mullin indulges his desire to
shine, to cut a dash. The humiliations of a poor and neglected childhood
anchor Billy forever in immaturity, and Mrs Mullin, not his match in age,
and despite the tawdry aspects of her profession, is able with warmth and
care after her own fashion to cosset him. She is at once a portrayal of the
woman on the threshold of late middle age, conscious of losing yet more of
her sex appeal to handsome young men and, also, of the mistress grown
accustomed through experience to the deeper needs of a youthful and volatile
infant of a lover. Each of her appearances gives us this nicely-drawn duality
of function: preliminary menace is followed by the revelation of finer
feelings. It is the measure of Julie's recognition of the fundamentally caring
and maternal nature of Mrs Mullin's relationship with Billy that she allows
her a few moments of privacy with his corpse after he has been knifed. The
scene delicately expresses the victory over jealousy of the finer feelings of
someone who knows her husband has retained a part of his heart for another
woman.

Naturally enough the association between Billy and Mrs Mullin is not
envisaged as a positive alternative to the marriage of Billy and Julie. After all,
Billy does in a sense leave Mrs Mullin for Julie, so even though the marriage
is defective it remains quite obviously the film's ideal. Yet through its
portrayal one is able to notice the film's preoccupation with the sentimental
and contractual duties and commitments of all marriages. Billy's liaison with
Mrs Mullin is unsatisfactory, on the grounds of age if on no other. But
marriage to Julie, while eminently suitable on the grounds of age, proves to
be nonetheless mainly (and paradoxically) through innocence no more satisfactory. Julie, in Billy's immature eyes, has no spirit, no essence of her own
to meet the demands of a man taught by culture to pursue virginal brides, but
through intimacy with older women to cherish the palpable rewards and con-
solations of sexual maturity. Billy fails to realise until he is in purgatory that
Julie is inadequate in his eyes not principally through any shortcomings of

her own but through his own confused notions of what a wife should be. Billy refuses until it is too late to re-learn his own role as a man, now that he has chosen to be a husband, and this failure prevents him from seeing that re-adjustment and improvement through love and hope are possible in marriage.

How sad is life, the film seems to say, when even relationships as full of promise as that between Julie and Billy are ultimately prey to disaster; what hope is there if only marriages between the Carrie Pipperidges and Enoch Snows of this world alone survive. The Snows are the most important parellels to the Bigelows and are the film's target of ridicule. As Julie meets Billy, Carrie almost simultaneously has fallen in love with Enoch Snow (whose name suggests a certain antithesis to the springtime/summertime setting of 'June is bustin' out all over', a fertility-rite number reminiscent in function of 'Spring, spring, spring' in *Seven Brides for Seven Brothers*). When Carrie sings about her commitment to Mr Snow in 'When I Marry Mr Snow', the context suggests romantic love, but the love is orientated, almost paradoxically, not towards present happiness but a vision of the happiness to come through entry into marriage, 'that wonderful day of days/When I marry Mr Snow'. A second song, a lulling melody as the couples scud across to the clambake in Mr Snow's boat, is also oddly fixated on a future from which vantage point the present will appear beautiful, rather than the moment itself. It projects the lovers years ahead to a point after the formation of the family and has them sitting reminiscing about the past:

> When the children are asleep we'll sit and dream
> The things that every other dad and mother dream . . .
> . . . When the children are asleep I'll dream with you,
> We'll think what fun we had and be glad that it all came true.

The view of the Snows that we are given sixteen years later is depressing. Their differences have not proved mutually beneficial; instead they seem wholly apart, comically symbolised in the separate entertainment memories they report from their New York trip: Carrie's night at the variety theatre and Mr Snow's at *Julius Caesar* (men in nightgowns who drove Carrie to sleep). If Billy has too little virtue (though more than Jigger), Mr Snow has too much, and the children take after him, marching mechanically behind their father in the ballet and chastising Billy's daughter Louise when she strays from social decorum: 'Shame on you! Shame on you!'. Less unpalatable than Mr Baskham – a caricature of the worst excesses of puritanical capitalism – Mr Snow is only slightly less preposterous in attitude. Not a flicker of sensuality can be seen in his whole being and, though a fisherman, none of the suggestive sexual connotations of fish apply to his way of life. Fish may now be Carrie's 'fav'rite perfume', but what appeals to her is not its erotic potential, rather its tacky whiff of domesticity. Where animal imagery is used in connection with Billy, sexual implications are prominent: the carousel horses are used here, as they are by Hitchcock in *Strangers on a Train*, to emphasise a character's burning passion. So while Mr Snow is sexually inept, Billy is passionate; while Mr Snow lacks spontaneity, Billy is highly and attractively unpredictable; while Mr Snow is a rigid conformist, Billy is a rebel given to impulsiveness and insubordination (even in purgatory he is not unnecessarily obedient, and steals a star on his way down to earth); while Mr Snow has off-putting personal mannerisms – like his asinine giggling – Billy has none; where Mr Snow is unprepossessing to look at, Billy is endowed with boyish, rugged and confident good looks. Moreover, Mr Snow's virtue is mocked when Jigger leads the clambakers into the 'Stonecutters' number: 'I never see it yet to fail/I never see it fail/A girl who's in love with a virtuous man/Is doomed to weep and wail'. During the song the participants divide into two camps, half of whom agree with the sentiment, half of whom oppose it until the surprise ending where the female chorus declares, 'There's nothing so bad . . . As a man who's bad or good'.

All these different attitudes – Jigger's, Billy's, Julie's, Carrie's, and Enoch's – are built on the amoral world of sexual nature celebrated in 'June is bustin' out all over' where even Carrie can sing 'And the ewe sheep aren't even keepin' score'. The weighting of the film, its design to place the audience in one position rather than another, could be summarised as admitting the reality of all sorts of other attitudes towards sexuality, most less elevated than Julie's and (eventually) Billy's, while still exalting the meaning the two principal lovers act out. Nevertheless the structuring, like all parallel or multiple plot functions, is intrinsically ambiguous. Do the lower plots act as a foil (that is, do they, in their inferiority, elevate the higher)? Or do they criticise the higher, arguing that its pretensions are less true than their basics? Or are they to be seen as a way (this is an effect Empson describes in *Some Versions of Pastoral*), of forestalling criticism of the higher by a small admission of the reality principle? We may feel that a combination of the first and the last describe the intentions of the writers of *Carousel*, but once the second is admitted as a possible effect of the structuring, its implications may resonate through the text more extensively and profoundly than intended.

Such a view can be more persuasively taken if one concentrates for a moment on the way in which the lyrics of *Carousel* often play a slight dissonance against the affirmations through their stress on the doubtful and the hypothetical. For instance, Julie's and Billy's duet, reprised at various points musically and vocally in the film begins and ends, '*If* I loved you', and its lyrics circle around the idea of a meaning (love) that is grasped in an unutterable intuition by the subject but cannot be conveyed to the object:

If I loved you,
Time and again I would try to say
All I'd want you to know,
Tryin' to tell you but afraid and shy,
I'd let my golden moment pass me by.
Soon you'd leave me,
Off you would go in the mist of day
Never never to know
How I loved you – if I loved you.

We have already noted how 'When the children are asleep' and 'When I marry Mr Snow' share something of this in their inability to conceive of the present except from some future imagined point which gives it meaning. In the former, Carrie and Enoch seem (presumably unconsciously, since they would not believe it could be true) to share this doubtfulness as they each sing flirtatiously of their future state: 'If I still love you the way,/I love you today . . .'. Such verbal dissonances are softened by the drowsy, innocent cadences of the kind of music Rodgers wrote for Hammerstein, but there are enough of them to make this musical a problem film in a deeper sense than the overtly problematic racial and cultural interaction of a musical like *South Pacific*.

The fantasy ballet

'Beautiful dreamer, come unto me.'

The fantasy or dream ballet is one of the great innovations of the stage and film musical in the late '30s and '40s. Potentially, and in a few cases actually, it relates to the rest of the narrative as night to day, the latent to the manifest, a third state underlying the familiar bifurcation of narrative and number. It is nowhere more finely wrought than in the '50s films of *Oklahoma!* and *Carousel* in which the original stage ballets are reworked, with the greater surrealist possibilities of the cinema used to their fullest advantage. In *Carousel* the stage show's original choreography for Agnes de Mille is reworked by Rod Alexander. The fantasy ballet differs from other film ballets which have dreamlike qualities in that it represents the unmediated experiences of a character in the film's narrative world, distinguishing it from the more common examples that are stage numbers, part of a show. If the ordinary transforms reality according to the singer's or dancer's conscious emotion, the fantasy ballet transforms according to an imitation of

the workings of the unconscious. Whereas in the ordinary number the subject is shown as knowing what he or she is doing, here the subject is shown as unaware (Laurey in *Oklahoma!* is dozing, Louise in *Carousel* is daydreaming, Manuela in *The Pirate* is hypnotised, and so on). The proliferation of dream sequences in American films of the late '30s and '40s (such as *The Wizard of Oz, Dr Jekyll and Mr Hyde, Spellbound, Lady in the Dark, The Woman in the Window*), testifies to the popularisation of psychoanalysis, especially a simplified version of Freud's dream theory.

The cinema, with its dream-like ambiance, is particularly suited to reproduce the phantasmagoria of dreams – the unconscious as a spectacle and therefore the obvious subject for cinema – and its processes of condensation, displacement, distortion, symbolism and so on. These reproductions, it should be stressed, are not dreams *per se* but imitations of the narrative and symbolic procedures of dreams, delineated with the artificial clarity and surface coherence demanded in works of art. Part of their effect is to convey feelings of opaqueness, but at the same time they must present relatively intelligible meanings to the audience. If we accept Freud's analytical procedures with dreams, very little meaning is available at the manifest level, which means that only analyst and patient in combination can decipher the latent meanings. But the film dream is addressed to an audience of crude 'wild' analysts who have to be able to make instantaneous sense of its relationship to the everyday narrative world of the film. Thus the fictional dream differs from the real dream in making its latent meanings manifest and therefore decodable by the audience.

The comparison between dream sequences in musicals and Freud's theory of 'dream work' is made by Jane Feuer in *The Hollywood Musical*. Where we find her argument unsatisfactory is in her model of the workings of these sequences which, though it may be adequate to the very simplest instances (for instance the completely unmysterious 'Miss Turnstiles' sequence in *On the Town*), or the simplest moments of the more complex instances, is incapable of comprehending the dream ballets in *Oklahoma!* and *Carousel*. Basically her argument is that these sequences, unlike real dreams, have a direct issue in a narrative resolution, that is, dreams in a musical 'come true' in the 'real world', and take four different forms: simple statements of the dreamer's amorous desires; a tentative working out of the narrative's problems; a road-testing of possible mates by the dreamer; a sort of psychic cleansing process for the dreamer. While each of these is able to describe some part of the works of the *Oklahoma!* and *Carousel* sequences,

---

Carousel: The fragility and immortality of love; 'If I loved you' in the setting of the imaginary.

neither singly nor in combination can they deal with the way the ballets dredge up meanings which cannot be identified with the overt desires of the protagonist, or that expose the problematic issues as distinct from being part of a problem-solving action. In other words, the material expressed in these dream ballets is both more subtle and often more anarchic than Feuer's view admits.

The *Carousel* ballet, equally haunting and almost as central as *Oklahoma!*'s, is also given, like *Oklahoma!*'s, through the subjectivity of a woman, as if to stress the more extreme social repressions demanded of the female. The vision is Louise's, though we are to understand that Billy apprehends it, an ability made doubly possible, first by his love for her, and second by her psychic similarity to him rather than to Julie. At its simplest level Louise's daydream has two parts. The first is a fantasy of aggression against her social world. The second is that reality's replacement by the visiting carousel which for her symbolises the worlds of art and of her father, as well as romantic sexual fulfilment with the boy who controls the carousel, but which the film has already taught us to associate with the removal from her father's life of responsibility and control. Billy had been as if branded, cursed, controlled by the carousel wheel, eternally driven by it in a circular motion that offers a false notion of progress, because of course however long the wheel's journey may seem you always end where you began. The carousel wheel is the Rodgers and Hammerstein equivalent of the wheel of fortune of earlier literary traditions: Billy is on a diabolical carousel wheel of fortune that brings transient pleasures, irresponsibility, petty thieving (he is well-known to the police for luring girls to the carousel so he can swindle them of their money), and in these circumstances it is not without significance, though it may be a case of the pot calling the kettle black, that Mrs Mullen refers to him early on as the devil. In fact she hugely overstates the case. Billy is by no stretch of the imagination diabolical, only through carousel life susceptible to the wiles of the devil, here personified, in a secular context of course, by Jigger. Where the devil's messenger, Jud, fails in *Oklahoma!* to triumph over Curly, in *Carousel*, played with more cunning and menace by Jigger, he succeeds. Like her father, Louise is now also associated with the carousel wheel as she spins round on a discarded carriage wheel on the sea-shore – in the identical setting where her father had sung to his unborn child – prior to her absorption in complex and troubled feelings about her life which are expressed through the fantasy ballet. Like her father, too, she is in danger of being trapped by show, superficiality and their attendant mutabilities. An inner need to rise above her impoverished (economically, but also emotionally through the loss of a father) family circumstances risks loss of control over her own life, of forfeiting it to the powerful will of the fortune wheel, in other words, to be eternally at the mercy of chance and other people's whims. Billy's Achilles heel had been his inability to control his life, a failure which had grown from his difficulty in finding a self through respectable work. His work at the carousel – though exciting from one point of view – had been inescapably linked with seediness; as he remarks to Mrs Mullin shortly after being sacked by her, 'The day you bought the carousel it got a bad name'.

As Louise's fantasy develops, obvious wish-fulfilment gives way to something like the operation of a reality principle. The boy abandons her, the carousel leaves, and she suffers social condemnation for her unorthodoxies, the cries of 'Shame on you!', uttered by the Snow children. This precipitates her into an extreme of antipathy towards her peers. Shouting 'I hate you! I hate you all!', she throws herself weeping on the wheel, where at the beginning of the sequence, she had stood gesturing optimistically.

Again, while there are details of Louise's reverie interpretable in the light of simple wish-fulfilment and of a playing out of overt narrative problems, much of the ballet must be understood in terms of less obvious, more subterranean material. While Louise's status as asexual queen of the band of Tom Sawyerish boys with whom she rompingly dances, and her triumph over the oldest Snow girl, who has insulted her, are fairly straightforward, reality intervenes as she is thrown out of the children's dance. The same pattern is present in her relations with the young barker. She dances with him ecstatically, but then is left by him, abandoning her to the mockery of her peers. Once again, though simple wishfulfilment explains part of the sequence, it cannot, in the simple form Feuer gives it, explain why her wishes should be blocked. We shall not here pursue a possible Freudian reading – which would make perfectly good sense of the narrative figure of Louise – of the disruptions actually being the fulfilment of her masochistic wishes, but concentrate rather on two other elements dramatised in the ballet: Louise's attempt to find authenticity through and beyond the role models given her by her mother and absent father; and the dramatisation, in the episode with the carousel barker, of Louise's Oedipal fantasies, presented as both creative and dangerous.

Louise's search for a femininity beyond that handed down to her reaches out further than the stereotyping (however positive, however much validated by the earth-angel qualities of Shirley Jones) of the female that at the primary level dominates the film. Rejecting her mother's extreme passivity, at the opening of the ballet she is first seen playing and leap-frogging with a gang of boys who accept her without sexual differentiation. Positive though this is in

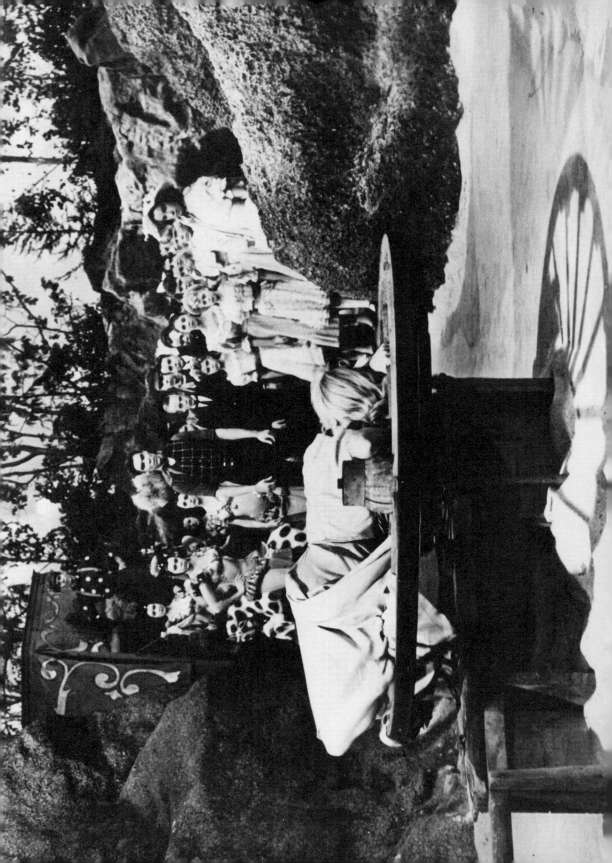

some respects, it does not offer her a permanently satisfactory role since its innocent egalitarianism takes no account of her awakening sexuality. Because of this she separates herself from the boys who also seem too mundane to understand the magic of the carousel when it arrives. What needs to be stressed in the episodes that follow (her relationship with and then rejection by the barker, and, in the primary narrative world, her accommodation both with the image of her lost father and her society), is that the movements that take place are much more subtle than those moments of symbolic transition to womanhood in many popular films. In these the 'tomboy' phase, which can be read as a refusal to accept male/female sexual differentiation with its subsequent inferior placing of the female in the patriarchal order, is often banished by a total transition to a stereotypical cultural womanhood, often symbolised by a beautiful dress, make-up, the adoption of coquetry and so on. But here there is no such dramatic turnabout and, indeed, her love dance with the barker, while entering her into the female polarity of the heterosexual universe, may be read in its stylistic connotations as searching for a mode of sexual relations which crosses the conservative-romantic (the balletic) with the individualist-modern (freer modern dance) elements, and female passivity with female activity. This style of de Mille's, evident too in the dance between Curly and Laurey in *Oklahoma!*, mixes energetic runs with lifts in which the male holds the female half the time in poses in which she looks upwards and outwards from him, as distinct from inward-turning embraces, poses which ask to be read as images of the female extended rather than subjugated by the male. This is significantly different from what is imaged in the relationship between Billy and Julie, and while substantial numbers of viewers today would find themselves distanced from, or feeling the necessity to make an effort to distance themselves from the qualities Julie stands for, the film at its less constraining levels also seems to be looking for ways out of traditionally absolutist roles.

Other parts of Louise's fantasy act out a dream based on the dominance of her absent father on her imagination, a dominance which is seen to have both positive and negative qualities – positive in the way related above, negative in that it seems to have left her fruitlessly rebellious and unhappy, perhaps only able to replay in her erotic life the scenario of his abandonment of her. The young barker who romances her is obviously a surrogate or substitute for her father, which may explain the odd intensity of her gestures

Freudian dreamwork in the musical. In the fantasy ballet Louise sprawls on the wheel that represents her father's carousel, intimidated by the forces of convention and desire, which threaten to tear her apart.

when he kisses her after their dance, her look of disgust and action of wiping her lips clean. This Oedipal theme with its sexual traces is also present in the way Billy imagines, in the song 'My boy Bill', his daughter coming to a sort of infantile sexual maturity and then rejecting her many suitors, even though they are only toddlers, for the embraces of her father, and again in the otherwise gratuitous scene where Billy, posing as a friend of her father's, talks to her in the garden in such a way that she mistakenly thinks he is going to molest her sexually.

We may feel that Billy's second departure from his daughter – at the end of the narrative – in which he is able to endorse the country doctor's words about independence from what one's parents were, allows father and daughter to relate to each other in terms other than obsession and guilt respectively. One of the ways in which the film is as moving today as when it was made is in its double sense that, to make play with the words of the famous song, you walk alone but always with an internalised ancestry, the inescapable family romance.

10

On a clear day you can see forever (1970) – Minnelli and the introspective musical

Minnelli and the self

Early proponents of authorship in the American cinema seized upon Minnelli and, alone among the directors whose work focused on the musical, he has received sustained attention. Later criticism of the extremes of *auteurism* may alter the emphasis on Minnelli's solitary control, and favour unconscious over conscious factors, but hardly undermines the obvious presence in his work of a highly developed set of interests and aesthetic dispositions.

If his musicals at MGM in the '40s and '50s (with *On a Clear Day* actually made at Paramount after a decade of inactivity in the musical genre) form a definitive group in the history of the genre, it is for two interconnected reasons. The first is Minnelli's theme of the imaginative, artistic self who seeks, in a variant of the tension between the Romantic artist and society, for transcendence in an inimical world. The second is the range of aesthetic strategies released by and incorporated in the different versions of this conflict. In each case Minnelli inflects with his own peculiar interiority traditional elements of the musical. Its happy celebration of the individual – but in so many cases the individual reduced to the good-natured average Joe or Jane – becomes in his hands the celebration of the artist or dreamer whose estrangement from social forms holds at a distance the traditional musical's often easy optimism about the integration of individual desire and group needs. Equally, its urge for colour, movement and design takes on in his films a refinement that displays the inherent aestheticism of the genre, never more evident than in his appropriation of the French Impressionist and neo-Impressionist painters in the dazzling palette of the ballet in *An American in Paris* – not merely surface *chi-chi* as some have felt, but a utopian transformation of the world by its images, turning Paris into the ideal shapes and colours of the Douanier Rousseau, Toulouse-Lautrec, Utrillo, etc.

The protagonists of Minnelli's musicals, struggling to match the outer world to their inner desires, are often literally artists, professionally engaged in making representations of the world, but this is not a necessary condition of his films. Tommy Albright in *Brigadoon*, Gigi in *Gigi*, Ella in *Bells Are Ringing* and Daisy Gamble and Marc Chabot in *On A Clear Day* are, respectively, an American businessman, a trainee courtesan in turn of the century Paris, a Manhattan telephonist, another Manhattan girl and a psychologist. The point is that all the figures are in a real sense similar to Minnelli's artists, also having alternative visions of a different order of being. To take apparently unlike instances – Tommy in *Brigadoon* and the heroine of *Gigi*: Tommy's dissatisfaction with his superficial life in New York brings him to the fantasy, or the reality – Minnelli typically never grants rationality precedence by untangling the web – of the Scottish village of *Brigadoon*, which wakes only once every hundred years. At the film's end Tommy enters, while his friend the more cynical Jeff cannot, a haven from the jarring hell of Manhattan. In *Gigi* there is a more pronounced sense of a dense societal medium which cannot be escaped as it is in *Brigadoon*. Gigi's life is circumscribed by codes of manners and behaviour at every level as her sub-versive childish vivacity is destined to pass into the socialised female creature – an aesthetic achievement undoubtedly, but wholly within the ideological confines of the Parisian world. The hope in the film is that what she has lost in the process has rubbed off on her husband, Gaston. The form of Gigi's desire has to be more restricted than Tommy's and is identified with romantic love, which is part, but not the whole of organic, pastoral *Brigadoon*. Her vision of a different order is to question the place in the world defined for her by her courtesan family with their values of sex as commodity. Whether, however, the circumscribed kingdom of love she enters with Gaston will be magical, the film does not answer. It has been suggested that the 'happy endings' even in Minnelli's early musicals have a kind of strain about them, as if they recognised that the merging of desire and reality might be more difficult than the fable tells, and close inspection might well make us feel that the solitary self rather than the couple, process rather than final arrival, is the true subtext of these films.

Literal theatre, the theatre of society, the theatre of the self – towards the end of his output Minnelli's interests move closer and closer to the last, though always in tension with a socialised world felt in some sense as restric-tive. And in the last films, the resolutions of the narratives (reacting to and taking advantage of changes of fashion and the increasing interiority released on many different fronts in the 1960s) start to leave the traditional musical's forms based on the marriage of lovers. Although Ella will marry Jeff in *Bells Are Ringing* (1960), the real resolution of the film is in her more extended discovery of the creative force her play-acting as telephonist has been in her clients' lives. In *On A Clear Day*, as we shall see, the film's end finds the 'true' lovers separating, and though Daisy, it seems, will marry her step-brother Tad, her self-discovery is the real focus. And in the little-seen *A Matter of Time* (1976), the young Nina's relationship with the elderly Countess falls entirely outside the categories of sexuality, a strange elective affinity between different minds and lives.

There is another important tendency in the later films, shared by *On A Clear Day, Bells Are Ringing, Gigi* (and behind them, *Brigadoon*), which is the leaving behind of literal artist figures – though Nina breaks this pattern – to concentrate less on the narrower possibilities of salvation through art and more on the activity of the everyday imagination. Thus not only does *On A Clear Day* end without the consummation of romantic love (the 'show' that will 'run for ever' as Gaby tells Tony Hunter in *The Band Wagon*) but also without the crystallised stasis of the work of art as fulfilment. The only 'show' at the end is the 'show' of Daisy herself, in the continual process of becoming that cannot finally be located or objectivised in the traditional forms.

A brief synopsis of the narrative of *On A Clear Day* shows how it fits within and extends the patterns just noted. Daisy Gamble (Barbra Streisand), gauche but gifted with extraordinary powers to make flowers grow and to anticipate thoughts and events, needs to give up her addictive smoking to meet the executive ambitions of her fiancé Warren. Breaking into a university class held by the psychologist Marc Chabot (Yves Montand), in order to get his help, she is accidentally hypnotised and revealed as a super-sensitive subject. Later, while Chabot gives her therapeutic hypnotism, she regresses to one of a large number of previous existences she claims to have lived but which, of course, she does not recall outside the trance. Melinda Tentrees, her *alter ego*, is a brilliant Regency belle who has unscrupulously fought her way into society's upper bracket from a London orphanage, made a wealthy marriage and then, shedding her elderly husband, made a second, love, marriage with the handsome but feckless Robert Tentrees. In this relationship, however, she is the more vulnerable party. Chabot, against his rational judgement, becomes fascinated with Melinda and uses the excuse of curing Daisy to meet her again, becoming increasingly jealous of Robert and impatient with Daisy, the 'caterpillar' obscuring the 'butterfly' Melinda.

It is gradually revealed in the world uncovered by hypnosis that Melinda

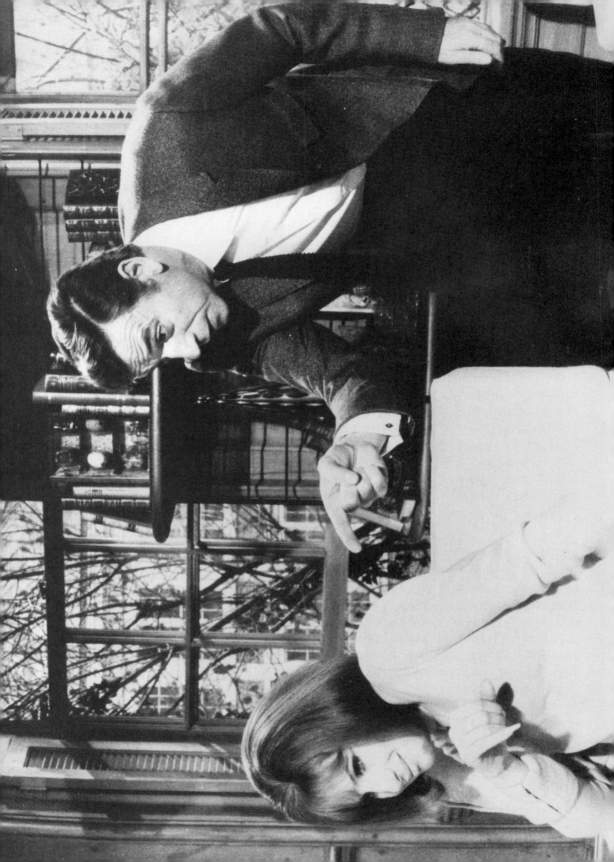

is to be executed for treasonable offences which have involved her using her extrasensory powers corruptly, and has been abandoned by Robert. Meanwhile, in the contemporary world of New York 1970, Chabot's growing interest in the irrational causes an academic scandal which threatens his job at the university. Chabot is saved from having to decide whether to compromise his new-found beliefs by the quixotic decision of the university's patron to fund ESP research.

Chabot says goodbye to Melinda, who seems also to have fallen in love with him. Daisy however accidentally hears the interview tapes which reveal that Chabot is attracted to Melinda but despises her medium. She leaves angrily and resists his attempts to bring her back to him by hypnosis. When she finally does return, he disappoints her by saying that he is returning to his wife. But then he tells her that she is 'a bloody miracle' and sends her away celebrating the incalculable self that he has come to recognise and she to discover. There are suggestions that they will marry in future incarnations in Virginia in 2038. In the meantime it seems that Daisy, free of Warren, will marry her step-brother Tad (Jack Nicholson), a wealthy flower child.

It is well-known that Minnelli's musical projects were largely hand-picked, and *On A Clear Day*, written by Allan Jay Lerner, the collaborator most attuned to him, with music by Burton Lane, underwent a considerable transformation from the Broadway original, a process that heightens all of what we have described as the Minnellian themes, inventing them when they are not present. These involve major changes in the hypnotic regression sequences, so that the powerful Melinda of the film bears little relation to her prototype. The relationship between Daisy and the psychologist is also sub-stantially altered, displacing the conventional love resolution with the invention of a new character, Daisy's step-brother, Tad (Jack Nicholson). This part, which uses some of the overspill of Nicholson's image from *Easy Rider* (1969), was apparently much cut before the release print which also excluded a love song that he sang to Daisy, presumably utilising the sitar he carries round with him. The invention of Tad, who acts out a rather comically stereotyped search for self-discovery – think, for instance, of the following dialogue: (Daisy) 'What are you doing?' (Tad) 'Same old thing. Looking for myself' – at a lower level than Chabot and Daisy, is characteristic of other changes that push the film in the direction of the introspective, of fantasy and wish-fulfilment rather than concrete relationships. The omission of some

---

On A Clear Day . . . : The contemporary musical's growing interiority. The two not-quite-lovers are psychiatrist and patient, Dr Marc Chabot (Yves Montand) and Daisy Gamble (Barbra Streisand).

and the restructuring of other stage numbers, as well as the invention of two
new ones for the film ('Go to sleep, girl' and 'Love with all the trimmings')
abet this by making Chabot and Daisy/Melinda the only two (or is it three?)
characters in the film who sing, thus creating a kind of chamber musical
intimacy. An instance of the restructuring that takes place is the way the song
'She wasn't you' (originally 'He isn't you'), which on stage belongs wholly to
the inner trance plot where it is sung to Melinda by her lover, is fantasticated
by being sung to Chabot by Melinda, from one spatio-temporal realm
(Regency England) to another (Manhattan, 1970) and this kind of complica-
tion, an extreme of the Minnellian delight in the entanglements of illusion
and reality, masks, roles and essences, is heightened at every point in the
screen version.

   In what has been said so far we have emphasised the understanding of *On
A Clear Day* to be gained from seeing it within the context of Minnelli as
author. Contextualised more widely, it can also be seen as a paradigm of an
important but slightly less obvious aspect of the contemporary musical discussed in the surrounding chapters – the late-generic transition not just to
extreme self-consciousness and parody on the one hand and harsher subject
matter on the other, but to a deepening of the musical's traditional theme of
the discovery of a truer self beneath the outer self of inhibition and pretension. In the traditional musical the progress from the one to the other is
essentially simple, a shuffling off of a form that patently does not fit, like
Don's silly pretensions to be a non-musical star in *Singin' in the Rain*. We
could say of most characters of early musicals that they are interesting
without being complicated. They appeal – Dick Powell, Alice Faye and the
rest – by virtue of their energy for happiness. Even Astaire, a more complex
persona, never much gives the sense of being troubled by doubts as to what
he is or is not. But in some later musicals there is a sense, not necessarily
synonymous with *destructive* irony, that knowledge of the self may be a more
difficult or deeper thing. It is there, fugitively, in films like *Carousel* and
Oklahoma! with their psychologised dream ballets, in the slightly muted
complexities of *It's Always Fair Weather*, and in aspects of films like *Sweet
Charity* and *Cabaret*. It is perhaps most fully present in a film such as *The Wiz*
(Sidney Lumet, 1978, starring Diana Ross), which is not just an all black
reworking of *The Wizard of Oz* (1939), but a set of interiorised variations on
what is already a myth about inner states. In this interesting film – attuned to
catch feelings about specifically black American alienation and ambitions,
and whatever the larger white audience might find representative in them –
there is absolutely no love plot attached to the heroine. Instead the story
centres on a grown-up Dorothy being forced to encounter the world below

125th Street in Harlem for the first time, to be finally told by the good witch Glenda (Lena Horne), that home is 'not just a place where to eat and sleep . . . if we know ourselves, we're always at home – anywhere'. It may be that *On A Clear Day*, which came into being because of the brief boom in musicals that followed on *The Sound of Music*, but whose commerical failure was part of the bursting of the bubble, was in some ways ahead of its audiences, though there is some evidence that its publicity was badly handled and it was clearly a film that suffered more than most from ignorant notices (including a *Time* review that must have cost it many viewers). However, as will be suggested below, it is likely to impress those interested in the musical genre for a long time.

'A nasty case of mysticism'

When she urges Professor Chabot to continue with his 'act' after disrupting his psychology class at Stuyvesant University, Daisy Gamble is not only established as a scattily vulgar intruder on serious academic business, but also as a means of questioning Chabot's approach to his subject of psychology. Chabot is committed to reason, but like characters in other Minnelli musicals, he will discover a buried self that it will be Daisy's (unconscious) role to nurture. The challenge of this other self is inscribed in the *mise-en-scène* before Chabot knows it, in the bizarre diagrams on the blackboard behind him at his first appearance, with their references to mysteries like astrology. (The professor has presumably been lecturing on the prehistory of psychology.) Later, in the same classroom, after he has begun to believe in Daisy's abilities, the diagrams behind him look impeccably scientific, as if to assert his discovery of science as mystery rather than reductionism. There is also a mysterious painting which hangs in his apartment, a sort of expressionist cloudscape, another reminder of the sky which represents infinite knowledge in the film's imagery. Like the flowers Daisy makes grow toward the light, he will bloom under her cultivation, as will she under his, shedding restrictive values. Once released, these powers teach him that he, not Daisy, has been playing the 'tricks' of which he accuses her.

As Chabot, ceasing to doubt in Daisy's extrasensory powers, becomes by the conventional world's standards a beacon of abnormality, the film's verbal element teases the conventional opposition of normal/abnormal until, at the end, celebrating Daisy's abnormality, Chabot calls her 'one of the few truly normal people to have existed'. The so-called normal world of Stuyvesant University and Chemical Foods Inc. flinches from the paranormal.

Dr. Hume Mason (Bob Newhart, with his comic persona of 'the button-down mind') speaks on its behalf when he demands that Chabot should declare that his research is devoid of any 'mystic implications'. A TV newscaster reflects this attitude, reporting 'a nasty case of mysticism' at Stuyvesant.

These allusions comically insinuate the film's central metaphors, invoking traditions of mysticism, the idea that there is a reality which lies beyond the reach of reason and to which there can only be supra-rational access. This, as we have said, is a theme latent in several other Minnelli musicals, most obviously *Brigadoon*. Biographically it may be the residue of Minnelli's Catholicism, though it should be noted that it is in his collaboration with Allan Jay Lerner, the writer of *Brigadoon* and *On A Clear Day*, that the theme is most foregrounded. In *On A Clear Day* it seems to be released and inflected by shifts in the larger psychic history of the American (and other advanced western) middle classes in the 1960s – the resurgence of interest in various non-institutionalised forms of religion, particularly eastern mysticisms, concepts of 'growth', 'flower power' (which Daisy's abilities literalise), and the interest in reincarnation that surfaces every so often and which can be examined in a popular best-selling book like *The Search For Bridey Murphy* (Morey Bernstein, 1956). Chabot, the hero as psychologist, not only brings to the fore the interest in the unconscious that runs through Minnelli's films (especially *Yolanda and the Thief* (1945) with its Dali-quoting décor), but places this wider shift in sensibility towards ideas of intuitive self-discovery against the sterile rationalism for which academic psychology is seen to stand. The ruling academic orthodoxy of behaviourism associated with B. F. Skinner is conflated with 'the sweethearts of Sigmund Freud' (Dr Conrad Fuller's phrase) in a generalised attack on scientific rationalism. One of the film's felicitous jokes advances this by casting Simon Oakland as Conrad Fuller, a colleague of Chabot's sympathetic to ESP. Simon Oakland will be recognised by many as the Freudian psychologist who diagnosed Norman Bates at the end of Hitchcock's *Psycho* (1960). Thus the Freudian rationalist is transformed.

The mystic proclaims that the real self is not the one which endures the banalities of everyday life; rather, that this self can only be discovered outside the confines of space and time. Released from these constraints, the mystic perceives things in their essence. Such essences, figured in the birth of the flowers from the underworld (unconscious?) in the first narrative image of *On A Clear Day*, and in the ineffable cloudscape of the last, are revealed to Chabot by his contact with Daisy. The exceedingly mundane reactions of contemporary reviews to Yves Montand's supposed unsuitability in the role might seem to bring the film down to earth with a thump, but the point of his casting is worth considering along, rather than against, the grain of the film's thematics. Montand, whose 'serious' acting status was established in films like *The Wages of Fear* and *Les Sorcières de Salem*, began as a singer in the French music halls. Though used uninterestingly alongside Marilyn Monroe in Cukor's musical *Let's Make Love* (1960), it is arguable that in *On A Clear Day* he is used more creatively, with the more 'philosophical' singing style of the Parisian *chanson* placed against the Streisand style, and the employment of certain traits of his 'serious' persona which seem a little off-centre in terms of the traditional musical. While this transatlantic mixture of Streisand and Montand is as intriguing as the more famous one of Chevalier and MacDonald, Montand's 'Frenchness', which does not fulfil the dominant stereotype created by Chevalier, seemed to disorient reviewers. This slight off-centredness, locatable perhaps in a slightly stubborn, fazed quality he has in the film, was seen simply as bad casting and performance, but such qualities are not out of place given Chabot's unsteady progress towards enlightenment. In a film where most of the names have meaningful connotations, the fact that Chabot (a name heavily emphasised when Daisy pronounces it 'Shabbot' and he corrects her, spelling it) is French for the bullhead fish may not be irrelevant.

Chabot's journey past rationalism is not a straightforward one since it begins by using, but ignoring, Daisy, in order to be with the dazzling Melinda. Chabot's love for Melinda (and what she feels for him) are complicated by unexpected releases of feeling, but there are real senses in which both are rather predatory romantics – Chabot imposing his own fantasies of glamour on the contemporary woman he mocks. While, at face value, this might seem an instance of the Minnellian protagonist imposing his higher fantasy on the recalcitrant world, it turns out not to be since Daisy is equally the sympathetic centre of the film. Fascinating (and even eventually touching) as Melinda is, Chabot's love for her is doubly regressive – a journey back in chronological time to a life characterised beneath its surface, perhaps even more than the twentieth century, by bigotry and privilege, and a love which, in its commitment to values of suavity, sophistication and fatality, is imprisoned in outworn notions of female sexuality.

Daisy, the girl who says she has 'no character', not even 'characteristics', seems, unlike Melinda, wholly blighted by circumstance. But the film traces in her a progress that is more liberating than Melinda's material and sexual journey. Daisy, whose love of flowers, signals her inner gifts, is – despite initial appearances – ripe for detachment from the dull world of her 'top 2 per cent fiancé', Warren, whose name suggests the earth from which her flowers, emblems of soul or freed consciousness, escape, a pattern of connotation also contained in the name Dr Hume (earth) Mason (stone). Daisy, though, as her name says, is a creature of light, etymologically the day's eye, the flower of the sun, an emblematic meaning released in the way her parade of late sixties dresses gives over to her final costume of a blazing orange and white (the former echoed in Tad's achingly yellow jumper). Chabot offers her the way of illumination, literally turning a lamp on her as a prelude to hypnotism, unlocking her mind to a world beyond Chemical Foods Inc. Passing through analogues of the traditional mystical progression such as a kind of 'dark night of the soul' each endures near the end of the narrative, the pair arrive at what in traditional terms is the unity of the soul with God, which we expect to be secularised in a variant of the traditional musical's marriage.

This is at one level denied as Chabot says he is returning to his wife, mentioned now for the first time, and on another asserted in the suggestion that he and Daisy will marry as John and Laura Caswell in Virginia in 2038. Like much in the film this teases the spectator – is it literal? is it metaphorical? – in a way that is unresolvable. But if we ask the question why Chabot in 1970 lets Daisy go, the answer is more approachable. There are certain suggestions in fact that Chabot may have invented the wife whose existence deflects Daisy. If so, his act may be seen as not simply a wholly selfish desire to preserve his feelings in an ideal state free of mundane compromise (though this may be part of it). Rather, it seems to imply Chabot's recognition that the process of marriage, subjecting their lives to ordinary time as well as possessive demands such as Warren's or sensual contempt like Robert's, would destroy what they have glimpsed, though at the same time the desire to marry is projected into the future. Though the ending does not quite take leave of marriage and romantic love, preserving it as a spectral possibility – it almost does. Here at the end a typically Minnellian ambiguity crosses traditional mystical themes (Daisy as Beatrice to Chabot's Dante), metaphysical wit (absence, nonconsummation, as the generator of desire), intimations of feminism (Chabot releases Daisy to discover herself in herself, not in the other) and a wry recognition of the force of romantic love as (even in its impossibility, perhaps especially in its impossibility) the generating force of insights beyond itself.

Streisand/Daisy/Melinda

At first sight such structures of meaning may appear pretentious – too much for the simple life-affirming conventions of the musical to bear. If, as we believe, they are not, it is because of the detailed sensuous embodiment of these meanings in the narrative and numbers. At this point it is salutary to be reminded that for most audiences – as distinct from film theorists and proponents of Minnelli as *auteur* – *On A Clear Day* was an opportunity to watch Barbra Streisand, the most popular female star of the 1970s. Almost without exception the contemporary reviews view it solely from that perspective, typically finding its plot impossible and Streisand its only redeeming feature: 'Barbra shines even in a fog', etc. Unfortunately, this concentration on Streisand, which might have pointed to the centre of the film, led only to simplistic attitudes. Nevertheless, Streisand's performance *is* at the centre and the interaction of her persona with the other elements of the film constitutes one of its dynamics, if not its chief dynamic.

Leo Braudy acknowledges Streisand as the foremost star of the contemporary musical, but sees her as a talent devoted to 'narcissism' and 'self-indulgence', the almost monstrous exemplar of the historical breakdown of the genre's ability to mediate self and society. This is a reductive and imperceptive view. More truly, her two most interesting musicals, *Funny Girl* and *On A Clear Day*, exhibit in related ways that peculiar contemporary mixture of urban romanticism and extreme self-consciousness that is perhaps the defining factor in her fascinating persona – 'Who's the American beauty rose/ With the American beauty nose?', as she sings in *Funny Girl*. Even *Hello Dolly!*, though in many ways a more stereotypical film, offers her great scope in its transformation of the role of Dolly Levi in Thornton Wilder's *The Matchmaker* into a Streisandesque vehicle, so that Dolly's hectic self-assertion and rapid-fire wit generate, perhaps even beyond the demands of the film, feelings of complexity, even of self-protectiveness and inner doubt, touching as well as assertive.

Those familiar with *Funny Girl* may remember its opening where Streisand as the star Fanny Brice enters an empty theatre, swathed from head to toe in leopard skin, and pauses to view herself in the mirror, greeting her image with 'Hello, gorgeous!' This, which might superficially be seen as proof of an image founded in self-love, is not simply the remark of a solipsistic self. Rather it is a paradigm of much of what the Streisand persona projects when creatively used – objective self-scrutiny, egotism, a wit that is dominating yet insecure, frailty and strength, emptiness and the desire for fulfilment, entrapment in the self combined with an outreaching generosity. If the musical is often about the release of a potential self, Streisand raises the motif to a self-conscious (rather than simply self-indulgent) intensity, complicated by all our contemporary awareness of role-playing and doubt as to what constitutes the essential self. Those who find her so charismatic do so, we suggest, not just because of her 'kookiness' or 'zaniness', but because of the intricate problematics of the personality she projects (for which such terms are shorthand) – the split between the urge to assert 'This is the true me!' and a range of vocal and kinesic behaviour that asserts multiplicity and fragmentation. The latter qualities are extremely ambiguous – exhilarating because they embody the performer's speed and adaptability, frightening because they may give the lie to the search for unitary essence beneath them. And all that has been mentioned is, of course, no abstract succession of effects, but very concretely grounded in the popularly available tradition of self-dramatising New York Jewish wit.

A parallel mobility is the chief defining characteristic of Streisand's highly individual singing style. This style is at the furthest extreme from the seamless texture of the singing of, say, Ella Fitzgerald, but also differs markedly from styles (e.g. Liza Minnelli's) located more unitarily in 'show business' rhetoric. For one thing there is a whole register of the wistfully innocent (the way we were?) in Streisand's delivery, quite different from anything in Liza Minnelli's. This singing style is marked not just by emotional mobility, but by something like an actual multiplicity of voices. But the precise effect of this fragmentation depends on the sense that it is not a series of superficial embellishments but the correlative of the mobility discussed above, bound together, though not simply unified, by the under-lying emotionality of her performance. Thus the impression of truthfulness to self-conscious psychological complexity that is conveyed depends on the combination of the apparently opposite qualities of scepticism and fervour. This, one might hazard, performs a particular function for the large middle-class, highly educated majority of her audience. At its most overt this style is exhibited near the beginning of *Funny Girl* when she sings 'I'm the greatest star' – a cascade of parodies, self-scrutinising routines and self-mockery, combined with aspects of the most intimate conversational delivery and others of strident emotional drive.

The conventional criticism that she overburdens songs with a style of relentlessly going 'over the top', producing an exaggerated disparity between an almost operatic intensity of rendition and vehicles too superficial for such treatment, is beside the point. Her musico-dramatic abilities in fact function best when there is a tension between a number's basic simplicity and the extreme metamorphoses it undergoes. 'Happy days are here again' (on *Barbra Streisand's Greatest Hits*) is a good example of this in its transforma-tions of tempo and mood, variations of phrasing and verbal emphasis, the

---

Daisy or Melinda? Character or glamour? Fascinating fatality or Streisand zaniness?

sudden charging of a word with unsuspected emotion (e.g. 'doubt' in 'There's no one who can *doubt* it now'), and ability to push beyond cliché into areas where 'show business' rhetoric becomes strangely personalised. A song such as 'Second-hand Rose' (on the same LP but performed in part in *Funny Girl*), illustrates how what seems a simple comic number is complicated in her hands by the presence of two idiolects rather than a single one, while in 'I'd rather be blue', in the same film, because of a similar doubleness, the untranslatable phatic irony of 'I can't do withoutcha/*Houcha-magoucha*' becomes strangely touching.

Streisand's casting as Daisy/Melinda is thus more integral to *On A Clear Day* than might at first appear, since in splitting its heroine into two separate selves it could be said to give concrete objective form to the underlying thematic of the typical Streisand performance. To say that the elements of pathos, innocence, self-doubt and lovable 'kookiness' are placed with Daisy, and those of the operatic, erotic and arrogant with Melinda is too simple, since over the course of the narrative such placements are to undergo some change, but the scheme suggests some of the reasons why the 'fit' between Streisand and the part is so good. Clearly the use of Streisand as a comedienne both in and outside the musical is also largely based on a comedy of dual consciousness, more intricate variations on the ur-Streisand line from *Hello Dolly!* (via *The Matchmaker*): "Horace Vandergelder, you go your way' (pointing her finger) 'and I'll go mine' (points again in same direction).'

Some of these characteristics appear in subtle form in the number 'What did I have?', soliloquised by Daisy when she discovers the tape recordings. The song, as these lyrics show, is centred on the thematic we have been exploring.

> I don't know why they redesigned me.
> He likes the way he used to find me.
> He lacks the girl I left behind me –
> I mean he – I mean me –

Almost any part of her delivery of the number repays close observation, but a moment open to reasonably straightforward observation is her singing of the questions

> What did I have
> That I don't have?
> What did he like
> That I lost track of?
> What did I do that I don't do
> The way I did before?

The first question is delivered in a remarkable (extremely hard to characterise) slur that seems to signify a kind of self-mockery, without expelling genuine feeling – or is it that the mockery merely attempts to hide the feeling? The second is asked in a sweetly plangent mode where the phrasing (the pronounced break between 'lost' and 'track of') affectingly mirrors the statement. The third, deeper, more intense, is full of surprises of articulation and a distinctive, mannered boom on certain syllables. Comparison with the quieter, more even performance from the stage original by Julie Harris (the vocal side of which is available on the original cast album), heightens one's sense of the extra drama of Streisand's performance, a drama further heightened by the film's invention of a terrific up-tempo conclusion to the number (a characteristic of many of her arrangements), so that the song runs from its breathily poignant beginning to an explosion of energy, turned in the very last phrases into the quiet psychological interiority of headnotes.

The numbers: mystical time, interior space

The conceits that underlie the film are based on paradoxes of time within timelessness and timelessness within time, on the dissolution of ordinary space and chronology, and even the unity of the individual: 'A mind filled with the total memory of life' is what Chabot tells Daisy she will find in herself. One of the delights of the film is the way its subterranean intimations intersect with the mundane world, and vice versa. For instance, Chabot suggests to Daisy that they should go out to dinner and she rattles out in reply a nervous monologue full of the verbal tics that so annoy the Professor.

> Where I live there's – uh – restaurant – um – called Enrico and Barnadi's but – um – no one ever said Daisy, do you want to go to Enrico and Barnardi's – mm, mm – No, they say, Daisy, we are going to Enrico and Barnardi's. Want to come along?

Placed by a window she plays idly with a white silk square, holding it so that it catches the breeze from outside and swells. Putting it on her head dreamily she begins to look like Melinda, even more so when she assumes a characteristic Melinda-like position. For a moment Daisy and Melinda exist as a palimpsest, one figure imprinted on the other in a dissolve, before the image resolves into the aristocratic Melinda draped on a couch. As she sings goodbye to him – 'He isn't you' – the montage binds together two different spatio-temporal orders, Melinda singing and accompanying herself on a harp in Regency England, looking offscreen left at Chabot, hands in pockets in his apartment, looking offscreen right at her. Here time past and time present intersect. Elsewhere the pattern is varied. Time past intrudes into time present, for instance, when Chabot sings 'This is a dream, Melinda', a reverie which, into the mainstream of the images – a moody Chabot pacing about his room – summons up almost subliminally quick single shots of Chabot and Melinda waltzing at the Brighton Pavilion. Or rather, it is even more vertiginous, because Chabot's visions are of replacing Robert as her partner, a fantasy within what may be a fantasy, and the consistency of the past world that intrudes into the present is broken by the fact that he waltzes in modern evening dress. Elsewhere time past becomes the dominant reality as in 'Love with all the trimmings' in which Melinda and Robert meet at the Prince Regent's banquet, a number occasionally interrupted by narrative moments in which Chabot questions Melinda, through Daisy, about the events she is recounting. And time future merges into time present in the images of the clouds of eternity as Daisy sings the final version of 'On a clear day you can see forever'.

Two of the most spectacularly inventive numbers of the film, Daisy's song, 'Hurry, it's lovely up here', to the flowers, which begins the film, and 'Come back to me' near its end, where Chabot tries to force Daisy to return to him by hypnotising her from a distance, are, among other things, extra-ordinary developments of the number as 'mystical' moment, disrupting and altering the usual relations of time and space. In doing this they employ, in a particularly brilliant and self-conscious manner, the technological resources of the cinema to produce their 'magic'. In the first case, the mysterious growth of Daisy's flowers under her tutelage is actualised by time-lapse photography, usually associated with scientific documentaries or wonders of nature films, not with the fiction film. 'Hurry, it's lovely up here' compresses the growth of the flowers from seeds to blooms from months into seconds, working the most 'scientific' uses of film into the most 'poetic', showing the eye what it cannot see, and establishing the alternative anti-clock time of mythic discourse, of passage and growth, death and rebirth, darkness to light. 'Come back to me', the most explosive kinesic spectacle of the film, though located in mundane time and place (present-day Manhattan), dis-plays the cinema's, and in particular the musical's, power to fragment and recompose reality rather than function merely as a recording device. Here it produces a psychological reality, the half-hypnotised Daisy's perception of Chabot's voice taking over the voices of everyone she comes across – a cop, a young boy, a cookery instructress, an elderly couple, a French poodle (a joke about Montand's nationality and accent). It is very much a conscious play on the possibilities of dubbing and montage in the tradition of Mamoulian's *Love Me Tonight* and an aural variation ('I only have ears for you') on the number in Berkeley's *Dames* where Dick Powell sees images of Ruby Keeler everywhere. A particular repeated image of Yves Montand singing in relative close-up on the roof of the Pan-Am Building, is a previously unattainable shot, possible in *On A Clear Day* only through the combination of telephoto lenses and cameras adapted to helicopter flight by the recently invented Tyler Mount. It adds to the sense one sometimes gets in the film that Minnelli, acknowledging the demise of his career in the passing of the studio system, has consciously worked into the film consummating images of the cinema as the inscriber of the imagination's values. Certainly such an interpretation is supported by Thomas Elsaesser's reading of Minnelli's films as, at one level anyway, an allegory of the movie-making process. Unlike *Brigadoon*, *On A Clear Day* never objectifies its final release in a place that its characters enter into. Rather than that, it presents a *subtilising* of the former film, leaving its beautiful fantasy world when Chabot turns from Melinda back to Daisy for the present time and place, but a time and place made numinous by the breaking down of compartmentalised time and space that has happened throughout the film, particularly in the numbers. In this sense the basic structuring of the numbers, built in various ways around ambiguities and reshifting of time and place, carries meanings that are central to the film.

The same might be said of the way the film's interest in isolation is embodied in the kind of number it employs. Instead of the musical's usual mixture of (i) (song and/or dance) address of one character to another; (ii) duets – usually for lovers; (iii) trios or other small groups – usually for friends; (iv) massed numbers expressing societal togetherness; and (v) some moments of soliloquy, *On A Clear Day* exhibits a marked – indeed almost total – shift towards soliloquy. This tendency, already strong in *Gigi*, is taken further here where the numbers are, almost without exception, refinements on the possibilities of soliloquy, e.g. address to the self; address to an *alter ego;* address to an object of fantasy; address by that object of fantasy to the self; address to things rather than characters (which can be classified as a species of self-communication). Situations which may seem, at first sight, to count as direct communication by one character to another turn out on inspection to be more ambiguous than not. It is not just that the film lacks communal numbers, or has relatively few ensembles. The only occasions in *On A Clear Day* where more than a single voice sings are the vocalisings of the offscreen chorus that sings the lyrics of the title song and comments wordlessly once when Daisy metamorphoses into Melinda. The two places in the film where one character clearly addresses another in song (leaving aside the ontological questions raised by the first) are where Melinda sings 'He isn't you' to Chabot, and where he sings 'On a clear day you can see forever' to Daisy. But what is noticeable here is that in neither case does the addressee reply to the singer, so that the song is always the utterance of a more or less isolated person. All this is consistent with the narrative's diminished interest in the couple as the unit of self-discovery, something carried through in minor details such as Tad's description of the marriage of his and Daisy's parents as a fight that was stopped in the third year. Significantly, both of the numbers invented for the film, though in some sense sung by one character to another, fulfil the pattern that has been outlined. In 'Go to sleep, girl' the character that Daisy sings to is in fact an *alter ego*, a projection of her more conventional self (also played by Streisand) – in fact the *fourth* 'character' given representation by Streisand in the film. The most sensuously beautiful of all the numbers, 'Love with all the trimmings', is another one that first of all moves towards and then veers away from the dissolution of subjectivities in duet. Melinda's impassioned song of desire for Robert as they view each other across the banquet table is, at one level, the most straightforward expression and reciprocation of desire in the film. But, at another, it is also one of the most fugitive, and certainly the most interiorised. In a film of soliloquies it is in fact the most wholly interiorised, since Melinda does not sing, but acts with realistic gestures on top of which a voice-over sings. Thus, the scene, on the surface so overt, is in fact built on a disparity between the overt and the covert. While what Melinda's looks and gestures say to Robert is in one way provocatively obvious, in another way they are a failure of communication since her inner, unprojected song, which mixes sexuality with metaphysical desires incomprehensible to Robert, never reaches him. This duality is expressed in the verbal conflict of the lyrics which mix traditional pejorative metaphors of love as appetite ('Love flavoured to entice', etc) with lines like

> My dearest love, who existed
> In a dream till this evening
> When a wave came and swept me out to sea,
> None of the loves you have known
> Could prepare you
> For the love raging in the heart of me.

Here the love of the often unfeeling and materialistic Melinda for Robert attaches her to the main current of the film, in that it is the projection of a pre-existing desire upon a wrongly chosen object that cannot bear its force. Finally, the film seems to say, there is no object short of a vision of the mystery of the whole universe on to which these feelings can adequately be projected, and the film therefore provides an eliding chain of metaphors rather than a final resting point – romantic love, Daisy's flowers, verbal statements like 'On a clear day you can see forever', the cloudscape which is overlaid at points in the film, the endlessly interiorised chinese box graphics of the title sequence. The film's eschewing of dance, though at one with a larger drift in that direction in the post-studio era musical (at least in its unmotivated forms), can also be seen as particularly appropriate in as much as dance in the popular styles of the musical usually functions as a concrete embodiment of relationship.

Though the constant ontological doubts as to who is addressing whom (a real person? a fantasy? a version of the self?) cultivated by the numbers seems to subside as the film reaches its end and Chabot addresses Daisy herself rather than Daisy as Melinda in the final numbers 'Come back to me' and 'On a clear day', these numbers preserve the emphasis on the solitary self. The last number in particular plays against the expectation that it will resolve into a love duet, by refusing to do so, by having instead one voice follow the other to indicate a more oblique relationship, a togetherness in isolation as Chabot and Daisy part. Whether read as a metaphor for self-affirmation or as a more mystic progression, the film ends with Daisy singing and celebrating herself.

Hair (1979) and the contemporary musical

The post-studio, auteurist musical

It is slightly invidious, having so carefully approached the contemporary musical through the growing dissonances of *It's Always Fair Weather*, *Carousel* and *On A Clear Day You Can See Forever*, to find ourselves restricted by space to a few general notes on a period which for quality – though not quantity – has been comparable with any in the history of the genre, and the close discussion of a single film, *Hair* (besides *On A Clear Day*) from a list of films that we would posit as the most significant of the last fifteen years. Significance in our terms is defined as an exploration of the conventions and possibilities of the musical rather than simply box-office success. *Saturday Night Fever* and *Sweet Charity* are, in our view, both films of great significance, though the latter was a financial disaster and the former a great success. What they share, within profound dissimilarities, is some quality of innovation which is able to extend our view of what the genre can do. In the case of *Sweet Charity* we have perhaps the first musical to treat within highly developed perspectives of irony the traditional material of romantic love; with *Saturday Night Fever* we have a film that suddenly managed to invest the genre with a new social setting and class ethos. Our short list of innovative films reads as follows:

Funny Girl (Wyler, 1968)
Sweet Charity (Fosse, 1968)
Finian's Rainbow (Coppola, 1968)
Cabaret (Fosse, 1972)
Nashville (Altman, 1975)
New York, New York (Scorsese, 1977)
Saturday Night Fever (Badham, 1977)
Hair (Forman, 1979)
All That Jazz (Fosse, 1979)

One From the Heart (Coppola, 1982)
The Cotton Club (Coppola, 1984)

There are admirable films not listed here which have certain qualities that have kept the film musical a developing form – for instance, the wit of *The Rocky Horror Picture Show* (1975), the elegant pastiche of Bogdanovich's *At Long Last Love* (1975) and the vivacity of *Fame* (Alan Parker, 1980), but our sense is that the main line of development can be seen in the list above. Any of these films would reward the most careful analysis – indeed the subject of the contemporary musical really demands another book, since not only are the films so interesting, but, even more than with the classical musical, criticism has largely failed to come to intelligent terms with them. Where it exists, writing on the new musical tends to be caught in an unacknowledged double bind. Thus to many writers the musical is identified with a total optimism and unqualified resolution, which makes the films we have listed look aberrant and uneasily problematic since they are all, in one way or another, marked by a swing against the more transparent affirmations of earlier films. Critics desire the easier happiness of the old models, but when such films appear they find that they do not do justice to a modern reality. But, if that really intrudes into the musical, it is thought to be unwelcome in such a utopian genre. Jane Feuer, in a book we have acknowledged several times, is one of the few writers to take a more satisfactory approach. She is able to see that the contemporary musical is dominated, like other genres in their late periods, by an increase in self-reference (something always present in the musical, but now accelerated and often leading to self-inspection and self-criticism). Just as the western film in recent years has questioned its heroes, reversed its traditional allegiances, and chipped away at its founding mythologies, so the contemporary musical has tested its conventions and questioned its founding premises.

These mythologies, clustering round ideas of romantic love and the power of art to influence reality, and expressed through those five useful categories listed by Dyer as carriers of utopian feeling – 'community', 'energy', 'abundance', 'transparency' and 'intensity' – have been undermined in various ways. But it is essential to note that this undermining is far from simple. It is not just that the new musical works with harsher and more intractable narrative material than the old, thus giving the lie to the old affirmations. If that were all there is to be said, the contemporary genre would have little call on our attention since the disruptive, the open, the unfinished, the inhuman, can be given to us more powerfully elsewhere. The point is, rather, that when we look at the most interesting recent musicals we are watching something more complicated than the explosion of the old sentimental mythologies. What we see is the encounter between a utopian urge (without which the musical, as we know it, would be unrecognisable) and a dystopian reality given prominence, even predominance, in a way that it never was before. It is the dynamic of the encounter that is essential, the tension between two conflicting impulses as the utopian drive makes of a more pressing reality what it can. If the bias towards affirmation has to respect the difficulties of less malleable interpretations of reality, the impulse to de-idealisation in turn respects the power and nostalgia (and in some sense the truth) of the old mythologies. This is why the major new films – even one as caustic as *Nashville* – cannot simply be seen in terms of irony and deconstruction. Using Dyer's categories again, another way of putting things might be that two of the most important elements in the traditional musical move into the background in many of the films we are talking about. These are 'transparency' and 'community', the signs of perfect relationships between, in the first case, individuals, and, in the second, individuals and institutions. 'Energy' and 'abundance', more impersonal categories, remain in the foreground, but the chief inflection is that much of the weight of affirmation is placed with what Dyer calls 'intensity' – the celebration of feeling, even though that feeling may have painful or negative aspects. This has, of course, always been important in popular art, which rather than being simply optimistic, insists on encountering experience with affirmation. Popular music, for instance, often deals with loss and heartbreak, but in a way that makes us feel affirmative, makes us feel somehow that the value of the experience outweighs its negative aspects.

If we look at contemporary musicals with these points in mind, it is possible to see change and development rather than confusion; a change and development speeded up by the fact that since the decline of the studio system (with which the musical, as the most expensive and multi-faceted of the genres was closely tied up for its economic viability), the musical, rather than being a staple product (that aspect of it having shifted to television 'variety' and pop videos) has become a place where directors accorded the status of authors have worked by deliberate choice. A representative instance of this is Martin Scorsese's *New York, New York*, where much of the force of the film comes from the crossing of the familiar desires of the genre to assert romantic love, the greatness of the performing life and the metaphor that equates performing with loving, with Scorsese's special sense of the violence within confused human relationships. The result is a film that asks to be read as much in terms of *Raging Bull* and *Mean Streets* as *Singin' in the Rain* and *On The Town;* or, rather, it is the latter rewritten through the sensibility of the former. Equally Bob Fosse's *All That Jazz* can be seen as a radical rewriting of *42nd Street* in which a peripheral character – the ailing, obsessive theatrical genius Julian Marsh – moves to the centre to become Joe Gideon, the director whose art embodies values, emotions and disciplines which do not mirror, but seem to be won at the cost of, the relationships in his personal life. The film can affirm his art, his energy, his wit, even his despair, but cannot pretend to hold the fragments together, just as the final affirmation of *New York, New York* is for the impersonal magnetism of the atomised and competitive city, rather than the bonds of relationship. And Coppola's brilliant *The Cotton Club*, released after the bulk of this book was written, meditates on the public, political dimension of the musical (where *One from the Heart* pursued its more personal thematics). It makes explicit the connection between the worlds of entertainment and crime (acknowledged, but a minor defeatable presence in earlier urban musicals – e.g. *42nd Street, Swing Time*, and *It's Always Fair Weather*), as well as opening up the traditional musical's submerged racial issues. The cuts between the cathedral christening and the gangland massacre that end *Godfather I* become the parallelism between the flying feet of a tapdancer and the rattle of machine guns wiping out Dutch Schultz and his gang.

Milos Forman's *Hair* (1979) is both highly representative and rather exceptional among contemporary musicals: representative in that it is an obvious example of the auteurist musical, a film made by a director whose reputation was made in other fields and, indeed, in another country, and who chooses to work in what is, with the western, the most quintessentially American of genres; representative too in its embracing of such harsh subject matter as the Vietnam war (though such direct political reference stands out beside the more private dissonances of the majority of contemporary musicals, *Cabaret* being the most obvious exception). But *Hair* is exceptional in that it is less marked by self-conscious strategies interrogating the generic limits of the musical (though in some measure it is concerned with doing this, as in the incorporation within numbers of brutal military scenes), than by a more overt and untempered optimism than most recent musicals have felt able to assert, so that as well as 'intensity', 'transparency' (in the relationships between Claude and Berger, the members of the tribe, and Claude and Sheila) and 'community' (not just in the smaller community of the hippie group but in the film's attempts to assert subconscious bonds between the apparently wholly divergent dominant and counter-cultures) seem possible again. By comparison the assertion of these values in *Finian's Rainbow* is whimsical and fabular rather than straightforward. Also, as a rock musical *Hair* mediates between the older musical language of the genre (associated with Irving Berlin, Cole Porter, George Gershwin and others) and the newer, more orgiastic modes of rock, in this pointing the way to future probable developments in the narrativised musical film.

Stage into screen: 'Let the sunshine in'

The differences between the late sixties stage and the 1979 film versions of *Hair* are considerable. From the point of view of content, while the lyrics of the songs, those retained from the show, are left largely untouched, the dialogue is almost wholly altered. This is largely because the form of the musical has been given a shape beyond all recognition from its original conception. Whereas the stage show had been a kind of dramatised spatial metaphor using song and dance to capture the mood of an alternative culture celebrating and lyricising love, inter-cultural harmony, alternative philosophy, mysticism and peace through the indistinguishable members of a 'tribe', the film, by contrast, is far more interested in the rhythms and tensions created by narrative. Where the show, observing stage conventions, is closer to a Happening, the film, to a certain extent equally a victim of convention, is keen at least initially to hold its audience (deprived of the qualities of immediacy and empathetic interaction between performers and audience), through the complexities of narrative structure. Consequently, where in the show the leading characters are already members of a tribe, their transformation from conventional citizens to hippie drop-outs taken for granted and unexplained, here we can at least see how two of them, Sheila Franklin and Claude Bukowski, progress from convention to disaffiliation and release. As we watch them struggle in their different ways against the pressures of their background, the film is able far more interestingly than the show to note not only the positive aspects of their metamorphosis but also the more problematical ones as well.

The film is not at every point wholly committed to an unqualified attack on the bourgeoisie and on the dominant traditions of mainstream life in America. It is clear as we look at the tolerant way much of conventional America is viewed that we are looking through the lens of a camera not directed by a crusading advocate of counter-culture. Milos Forman and his scriptwriter, Michael Weller, are in any case making a film about youth in revolt not on independent or underground resources, but with the backing of a major financial group. So the values of the counter-culture, however sympathetically portrayed they may be, are necessarily mediated through conventional constraints and attitudes, and as we look at the treatment of convention in the film we are allowed to see that it has a legitimacy, defined as perhaps largely misguided, of its own.

The stage show, by contrast, has a less tolerant outlook; it has the look sometimes of a medieval miracle or mystery play. Representative figures such as Margaret Mead make their appearances, like angels or devils from medieval drama. The thoughts and feelings behind the numbers are designed to work on the audience in a conceptual way that takes little notice of drama's more usual reliance on action. The film works differently in this respect, for here we do see not only the private struggle of some members of the tribe when conventional scales begin to fall from their eyes, but also the developing relationships within the group itself. Moreover, as film can break through the spatial barriers of the stage, we are taken into the country, into the city, into the worlds of the upper (Sheila's home) and lower (Berger's home) bourgeoisie. We can see for ourselves in a way that film form can much more easily accommodate, both the advantages and the limits or repressions of the safe, conventional world. Of course, Berger's father, sitting in the time-hallowed attitude of all conservative fathers reading their newspapers after a day's work, is irritatingly unreasonable when he screams at Berger to cut his hair, when he bellows that he will give him all the money he needs if he will only clean himself up a bit. But, the film seems to ask, from his position in life, brought up to believe in cleanliness, order, duty, hard work, what else could he have been expected to say? At least he is prepared, as is Berger's long-suffering mother, quietly desperate to put her son's pants in the wash, to give him the money he needs. In a flash the film can very succinctly make a point that would have been laborious and protracted on stage.

In the film the conventional American family's shortcomings are high-lighted, but there is a sense in which the origins of its constraints and idiocies are here recognised to lie in the crippling, all-powerful grip of ideology. Yet the film goes beyond more establishment-bashing in looking circumspectly at the mixed influence of all ideologies however perfect they may initially seem. An ideology concocted out of Zen, pot, Freud, Marcuse, Reich and free love, the film seems to argue, may not finally be the answer either, but it at least provided '60s youth with the means of overthrowing the received values of their parents. And so as the representative youths, Claude, Berger, Sheila, Jeannie, Hud and Wolf, try to live the nomadic life of the hippie we see not only how they improve on their parents (in standing up against the Vietnam war for instance), but also how they themselves sometimes suffer from ineradicable human vices, like myopia or cruelty, that are not neces-sarily attributable to ideology. The little drama written for the film around Hud and his girlfriend and son is not only an example of the film's even-handedness but also proof of commitment in contrast to the show's patterns to both action and psychology.

However, of the elements that do survive from the show, none is more prominent than the anti-war feelings. Yet even here the emphasis of the film is slightly different. US policy in Vietnam is of course still the prime target of criticism. The belligerent spirit of the times is beautifully epitomised in the film through Nicholas Ray's splendidly Olympian playing of the general visiting the recruiting barracks. He stands on the parade ground at one point, a mouthpiece for militaristic ideology, burbling some stale words of encouragement to the troops, thriving inwardly we feel, if his expression is to be trusted, on the anticipated stench of napalm and rotting corpses. And yet, for all the vitriolic feelings the film stirs up against the US government's Vietnam war-mongers, represented here by the general, there is a growing awareness of the possibility of a greater imminent tragedy, the Armageddon of nuclear war. At the very end of the film, as a massive crowd gathers outside the White House, three flags are raised aloft in different parts of the field: the US national flag, the flag of the southern states, and the CND flag. Though the expression on the faces of the crowd is serene, relaxed and, as it were, celebrating what is potentially good about American life (the two American flags are in part proclamations of this), the horrors that led to US involvement in Vietnam are seen now, dystopically, from the perspective of the fears of an even greater, unthinkable catastrophe.

The praise of folly

'And you're telling me I'm ridiculous!' — Berger.

After the lake incident, which makes him finally disgusted with the attitudes of the tribe, Claude decides to keep his appointment with the recruiting officers. He accuses Berger of being ridiculous. Berger agrees, adding that he is not only ridiculous, but also ludicrous. His exuberant acknowledgement of this epithet as a description of his life-style and moral values aptly summarises the ethos and *raison d'être* not only of Berger himself but also of the whole tribe, and beyond them the disaffiliated youth of '60s counter-culture. Following in the radical traditions of primitive Christianity and third-century Greek cynicism, both movements which in some senses embraced an ideal of folly, the tribe takes pleasure above all else in seeming ridiculous, ludicrous or absurd to straight society. The film brilliantly captures that mood of good-natured, insolent and disarming reasonableness so evocatively described by Theodore Roszak in *The Making of a Counter Culture* and *Where the Wasteland Ends*.

The confrontation between Claude (John Savage) and Berger (Treat Williams) is one of several scenes in the film where there is an emphasis on the distinctive absurdity of the tribe. Absurdity here, of course, has nothing to do with Camus and Sartre. Indeed part of the whole imaginative project of the disaffiliated young was not only to question the shibboleths of conventional society but also to interrogate that society's very language, its ways of seeing, and even philosophy, of the conventional kind, itself. Allen Ginsberg's poem, *Wichita Vortex Sutra*, quoted in *Hair* in the lyrics of the number '3500', is much concerned with the same point:

> Three five zero zero is numerals
> Headline language poetry, nine decades after Democratic Vistas
> and the Prophecy of the Good Grey Poet . . .

The light-hearted side of the tribe's irreverence is displayed when Sheila's clothes are hidden by Berger, Wolf and Hud, a prank as much inspired by their desire to plunge Sheila and Claude more deeply into the spirit of pure revelry as to expose Sheila's (Beverly D'Angelo) bourgeois primness. On emerging almost naked from the lake, with Claude, whom she has joined for a swim, she demands to know where her clothes are. Jeannie, who has witnessed the whole scene, responds typically with a giggle. She is the unsophisticated fool of the group, a good-natured, happy-go-lucky buffoon, short on eloquence, but overflowing with understanding and tolerance. Her giggle, repeatedly the sign of these virtues, is here used further as an endorsement of irreverence, nudity and fun, but is misinterpreted as such by Sheila who replies with sarcasm and indignation, 'Oh, funny, funny . . . You guys are so mature'. Through Sheila we see the spectacle of the discomforted bourgeoisie. Her use of 'funny', uttered disapprovingly to mean everything that is *infra dig*, reminds us that the bourgeoisie, whose spokeswoman she currently is, has lost its sense of humour, its capacity to find pleasure in innocent childish games. *Homo ludens* is all but suffocated beneath the sophistications and sobrieties of a materialistic world. The word 'mature', also used ironically here, betrays the work of ideology, for in not finding maturity in the tribe Sheila reveals that her world is characterised by a celebration of all that is old, mature, stodgy. This is refinement to the point of decreptitude. And it is precisely against this grown-up, virtually senile, sensible outlook and set of values that the predominantly youthful counter-culture is rebelling. Sheila, in transit from bourgeois old age to hippie youthfulness, suffers still from premature senility and solemnity, from which the insufferably straight Steve will never escape. For the moment Claude, too, ails from the same affliction. Part of his indignation towards Berger, Wolf and Hud at this point arises from his lingering addiction to the conventional. Though growing narrower, the chasm that separates Claude from the tribe is noticeable in this extremely revealing exchange of dialogue:

Berger:	You're not still serious about that shit are you?
Claude:	That's none of your goddam business.
Berger:	No, it is my goddam business. What do you want? You want to be a big hero with a gun? Big macho dude in a uniform? Is that what you want man, huh?
Claude:	I can't talk to you.
Berger:	Hey, I'm standing right here Claude. I'm right here. Talk to me!
Claude:	I happen to think you're ridiculous.
Berger:	I am, man, I am ridiculous. I'm totally ridiculous. I'm ludicrous. I don't want to go over there and kill people and murder women and children.
Claude:	Just go ahead and you be ridiculous, and I'll do what I have to do.

Aside from the fact that the disaffiliated positively revel in seeming ridiculous to the conventional society, the most striking feature of Berger's lines is the way in which he follows Socratic tradition and argues, as Roszak puts it, *vis-à-vis* a discussion of Paul Goodman's book *Gestalt Therapy*, co-written with Frederick Peils and Ralph Hefferline, *ad hominem*. The counter-culture 'philosophers' personalise all argument, and attempt in the process to debunk the myth of objective consciousness. Consequently, Claude is being invited not to shelter beneath the covers of inherited wisdom or the hand-me-down notions of correct behaviour. 'Talk to me!', is an attempt to make Claude realise that the issue is not unquestionable, pre-ordained or undebatable. In the new ethos of 'conviviality', to use Illich's term, his business is everyone else's.

The road to ideological rebellion takes in an important early stage where people learn to recognise a duty to respect and help others. Nowhere is what the counter-culture sees as the cancer of individualism attacked with greater determination than in the scene where Claude decides to use the money his father gave him to secure his own release from prison, following the fracas at Sheila's party, and is then persuaded to give the money to Berger so that he can try to arrange the release of the whole imprisoned tribe.

In that scene the origins of Claude's individualism are seen to lie in the predictable patterns of sacrosanct right-wing values. Claude is going to celebrate the cult of individualism by going out to slaughter the Vietnamese like some 'big macho dude'. His response has the unmistakable flourish of a John Wayne: 'I'll do what I have to do' he adds. Listening to this cliché of many a

B western proves too much for the tribe who begin, for the first time angrily, to harangue Claude, for nothing is more odious to them than defining doing what 'a man's gotta do' as the extermination of innocent peasants in South-East Asia.

But the ridiculous, ludicrous attitudes of the hippies are not confined to assaults on machismo, so in the tender scene between Hud and his girlfriend and child we see how the innocent as much as the wicked of America are dangerously vulnerable to the assaults of dominant values.

This incident allows the film to focus on at least two important issues: the first is the ethos of tenderness, the caring, extended family pattern of hippie life, and the second is the treatment of blacks in the film. *Hair* is perhaps the first musical to treat blacks as ordinary human beings, not as in *Carmen Jones*, *Cabin in the Sky*, or *Stormy Weather,* like a race apart, nor brought in, through isolated figures, as almost freakish talents, as in *High Society* or *The Five Pennies* where Louis Armstrong appears in cameo spots. Hud and his girlfriend are, in *Hair,* just as much a focus of the tribe's life and activities as, say, Wolf or Jeannie. Moreover, a black singer introduces the film's first number, 'Aquarius', a black woman stands at the centre of the group in the finale, Hud's 'spade' song is a parody of all racist attitudes to blacks, and black singers and/or dancers are involved quite naturally in many other numbers. 'Black boys are delicious' gives as much time and space to black men and women as to white; white boys give black girls 'goosebumps', and black girls give white boys the taste for a 'chocolate-flavoured love'. So as the film concentrates on Hud's cruel abandoment of his girlfriend and child we respond not in any 'special' way, just in the way we would have done to Claude or Berger had either of them been in the same position.

The film, like the hippie counter-culture generally, does bear the traces of the Black Movement's influence, yet one should not, as Roszak warns, be too anxious to look for excessive interaction. The hippie counter-culture, as he and Unger argue, was predominantly a white middle-class movement. As well as digging into exotic eastern resources like Zen, hippie drop-outs took something from the radical politics of the so-called Movement (the New Left's revolt against conventional politics and its situating of debates outside the usual arena of Democratic/Republican contests). What they borrowed from Black Power was not the hip, cool drug culture characteristic of the world of progressive jazz. Neither was it the craving of some elements in Black Power merely to take over the reins of power in an unchanged materialistic system. It was, instead, the nobler conviction that dominant white culture had alienated all Americans, black and white, from their true heritage. Black is beautiful, taught the prophets of Black Power, a slogan

which encouraged minorities to stand up and be proud of their colour, culture and racial origins. So blacks and every other racial minority were recognised by hippies as having something to contribute to the melting-pot of modern American life. *Hair* celebrates the dignity of all races, not only blacks, but Asiatics too: when, for instance, Claude lies in bed at his barracks in Nevada, the song his stream of consciousness sings is matched with visual images of a Vietnamese girl. A Vietnamese girl dancing is also intercut with the black woman who sings 'The age of Aquarius' near the beginning of the film. These images remind us that the Vietnamese are people, their traditions as worthy of respect as anyone else's, that only the tyrants of dominant white culture have conspired to challenge their right to live, to denigrate their heritage.

So, within the context of the celebration of alternative cultures, the treatment of Hud and his abandoned family has an increased poignancy. Hud's extraordinariness is as normal within the tribe as his girlfriend's ordinariness within the parameters of the conventional world outside. While he is dressed outlandishly in a calf-length, black, military-style coat, bell-bottomed trousers with feathers at the edges, and sports a head-band, long dangling ear-rings, and overgrown frizzy hair, she wears a conventionally chic middle-class white duffle coat, belted at the middle, and elegant, knee-length boots. Her hair is pulled back and tied in a bun, in a fashion not in the slightest touched by the new Afro styles symbolising the newly raised con-sciousness of American blacks. The clash between their dress and cosmetic styles, which she is the first to notice, is an indication too of their conflicting ideological attitudes. While the girlfriend is still, though black, prepared to follow conventional lines, Hud has tried to move away. He no longer answers to 'Lafayette', as Muhammed Ali became deaf to 'Cassius Clay', and we infer from his rejection of the name that he associates it with the white history of America, the war of independence against the English. Hud, as he now prefers to be called, a choice that suggests, though, a certain poverty of imagination, has signified through change of name, costume and tribal affiliation, a desire to seek alternative answers to a whole generation's questions about the meaning of life.

Yet as we watch the drama of his renunciation of his girlfriend and the way of life she represents, we are not allowed to focus on peculiarly black issues. Instead we look at a youth's disgruntled but confused, perhaps somewhat imbecilic and modish espousal of an alternative lifestyle. 'Do you understand about cosmic consciousness and all that kind of shit, because

---

Hair: Transgressing racial boundaries; lyricising a 'chocolate-flavoured love'.

that's what I'm talking about baby?' is a question that does not have the ring of the true *philosophe*.

Hud's flight from technocracy is less towards sex, though for a time it is not certain whether he or Wolf is the father of Jeannie's baby, and more towards some ill-defined 'cosmic' ideal of spiritual fulfilment defined by Roszak, *apropos* the movement generally, like this: ' . . . the willingness to consider as instructive examples all the human possibilities that lie within our intellectual horizon – including those that conventional wisdom tells us are hopelessly adolescent.' Astrology, Zen and mysticism provide the background of ideas, but in *Hair* they are all humanised, given a setting in which characters struggle to put their borrowed ideas into the practice of their lives. So in *Hud* we are given not a sentimentalised vision of black revolt into hippiedom, only an ordinary, rather dim young man, mouthing the jargon of the counter-culture, enjoying some of the trips, both psychedelic and geographical, that his companions have helped organise. This black hippie in fact provokes through an act of selfishness towards a woman and son for whom he no longer feels any responsibility one of the film's most moving numbers. As he walks away from them both, his little son looks blankly and silently, not comprehending the finer points of his parents' row, while the rejected woman, hurt and bewildered by her lover's transformations of heart and image, begins to sing the magnificent and heart-rending 'How can people be so heartless/How can people be so cruel?/Easy to be hard,/Easy to be cold', a song delivered with maximum power straight to the audience. The song was originally Sheila's in the stage version but here it aptly describes both the numbing pain a woman feels when the man she loves walks out on her, and the child's feeling of loss and bewilderment when he sees his father apparently happier to be somewhere else. The grief at the heart of the song, the pity of the situation, the cruelty of Hud's response, followed by Berger's urgent desire to reconcile the trio – an achievement reserved for the end of the film – provide some of the film's many moments of mature handling of life's more complex issues.

Not for the first time, Berger's soothing act of humanity represents the counter-culture's belief in a higher order of reason, the reason of the heart, the reason that knows, well after rational argument has been spent, that nuclear bombs are criminal, that knows intuitively what is right and wrong in the way people face up to their moral responsibilities. In his hair, in his motley, ragamuffin's costume, in his frank, unintimidated facial expression, in his innocent lack of posturing, he is folly personified, a male reincarnation of the goddess described by Erasmus as turning 'all things sacred and profane . . . topsy turvy', the antithesis of Company Man, a soul undefiled by technocracy. This image of '60s folly is on one occasion – during the ride in the convertible to Nevada to visit Claude – given an unconscious parallel with early Christianity, when Berger's hair, like that of the others, is as if haloed by the early morning sunshine.

The contrast between what Berger stands for and all that he has left behind is clearly expressed at Sheila's party. When the tribe invades the world of the upper bourgeoisie on the occasion of the party the differences in dress between the hippies and the bourgeois provide the most obvious clue to the ideological gulf that divides them. On the bourgeois side everyone is immaculately dressed in tuxedoes and sequins, while the hippies are in their usual, loose, scarf-obsessed ethnic gear. And yet, for all the exterior conventionality, all is not what it seems. As we note later on, Berger has conventional longings, as the film's doubles motif makes clear, while in the bourgeois world, too, the stirrings of revolt are noticeable. As Berger begins his number, dancing on the richly-laden feasting table when all the dinner guests are assembled, he provokes not only Sheila's approving interest but that of an unidentified middle-class matron as well, so much so that she actually joins in the dance on the table with him.

Sheila's mother is a matron, by contrast, who has progressed too far along the road to death-dealing convention. 'You've got a helluva nerve, young man' she bays at him but we know that the hippies have more than nerve. 'I got *life*, mother', Berger triumphantly replies, speaking now for the counter-culture, to a woman whose fixed expression of solemnity and aggression tells us all we need to know about her comfortable but cheerless life of social ease and ready animosity, a woman, moreover, whose secretly pot-smoking daughter, is already preparing unconsciously to take the final vows of hippiedom.

When Berger, at the end of the 'I got life, mother' number stands above her, the call of the counter-culture beckons to Sheila in a way that defies resistance. The last image of the number shows Sheila seated at one end of the table, looking up at the apex of the triangle formed by Berger's parted legs, which are seen from the back, but only from the waist down. His open legs form two sides of the triangle, the third is formed by an arrangement of flowers bestraddled by his legs on the table. In the triangle, and seen as it were above the flowers as she looks up towards its apex, which is Berger's crotch, is Sheila, trapped by the power of the counter-culture and perhaps above all, since her lifted gaze recalls the celebration in an earlier number of 'Fellatio', by the promise of a wild erotic life, that has hitherto been beyond her realm of experience. Sexual liberation is both Sheila's destiny – though her heart will be won by Claude, not Berger – and the counter-culture's most thrilling vision of utopia. Through this careful image we are reminded how, following Freud, Reich and Marcuse, the hippies assumed sexual liberation could help cure the pathological craving for power and the dehumanised lust for wealth so characteristic of the technocratic society.

Claude and Berger: 'An old-fashioned melody'

The most important change from the stage *Hair* is the reworking of the character and significance of Claude, or, to give him his full name, Claude (a suggestion of dandyism?) Hooper (an Anglo-Saxon strain) Bukowski (a symbol of European immigration). In the show Claude, not Berger, becomes the exemplary sacrificial victim of the Vietnam war. A Polish American from Flushing, he assumes there the accent of industrial Lancashire in a tribute to those English heroes of the counter-culture, the Beatles. This and his martyr's end apart, he is largely undistinguishable from the others in the tribe. In the film, however, he is something entirely different. As a farm boy from small town Oklahoma coming to New York for his call-up, he belongs to a world seemingly the antithesis of the urban rebellion of Berger and his followers. When he tells them on meeting them for the first time that he hails from Oklahoma, Berger throws up his arms in despair, and Jeannie, as if referring to a past light years away, urges him not to worry since she once came from Kansas too. At the simplest level the narrative traces Claude's exposure through a day and a night in New York to the values of the counter-culture embodied in Jeannie, Hud, Wolf and, above all, Berger, an exposure that comes too late to save him from the draft to which he chooses to submit. Sent to Nevada for training, he writes to Sheila, the rich girl he has fallen in love with and who, like him, is being pulled into the ambiance of the tribe by Berger's charisma. Berger, Sheila and the rest of the tribe drive to Nevada and, so that Claude can spend a few hours with Sheila, Berger takes his place in the barracks. While he is there, orders come for the move to Vietnam, and Berger is flown out to his death in place of Claude.

At the most obvious level the film follows Claude's education, never quite completed in the main body of the film, always likely to regress conservatively. Yet as Claude goes through his military training and writes in the barracks to Sheila, some deeper part of his consciousness is revealed to have been profoundly affected by what he has recently experienced. The number that conveys this is structured in an extremely intricate way, moving like the others between various sites: here there is a juxtaposition of images depicting brutalised army training, a Vietnamese girl appearing in a vision singing

'My body is walking in space/My soul is in orbit/With God face to face', more scenes of Claude in training or lying in bed, holding the letter he will send to Sheila. This is not a performance number in the usual sense we associate with the Hollywood musical, more a series of narrative events given further significance by musical overvoices which at the end of the sequence affirm, 'Our eyes are open, our eyes are open'. This opening of Claude's eyes is the culmination of the education he receives from Berger, by spiritual force the chief of the tribe. The lessons of this education include those of poverty (he meets the tribe when they beg from him), of almost religious dimensions (the number 'Ain't got no . . .', which negates 'home . . . shoes . . . money . . . class' etc), the assertion of the most fundamental possessions, as distinct from mere property ('I got my hair . . . head . . . brains . . . ears . . . eyes . . . nose . . . mouth'), an introduction to the realities of ethnic America (Hud's ironic song of racist names and occupations for his future son, and Berger's introduction of Hud to Claude as the 'Boogyman'), and the ecstasies of expanded consciousness through tripping on drugs ('Hashish' and the LSD vision in Central Park).

But the dynamics of the film are not as simple as that. The film's narrative may in certain respects place Claude as the representative of the narrow conservatism of Middle America, but from the very beginning it insists on complicating this presentation by associating him with an ideal of uncorrupt pastoral America. The film's first number proclaims the coming of 'The age of Aquarius', 'When the moon is in the seventh house/And Jupiter aligns with Mars/Then Peace will guide the planets/And Love will steer the stars'. This is prophecy, but the prologue finds intimations of such values already extant in the hinterland from which Claude emerges. In this beautiful opening early morning pastoral sounds precede the first visuals. Then, as dawn breaks and the mist clears, we see a clapboard house. Out of it emerge two figures who climb into a small truck and drive away. The camera pans with them but, as they drive past a small wooden church, it does not follow them, and lingers instead on the building. At a bus stop on a country road a father and son (Claude) get out. As the bus arrives the father embraces the son roughly, insisting that he takes a gift of fifty dollars for emergencies. The presentation of this awkward, affecting, almost inarticulate moment has nothing satiric or condescending in it. We may feel that the characters are in some sense limited in the expression of their feelings by background and ethos, but they also represent a simple, innate decency, which if unknowing is also very real. Then, when Claude boards the bus for New York we are led in a succession of bountiful images through a foreshortened journey across an

America that still seems burgeoning with peace and promise: pastoral landscapes, houses clustered by a lake, agricultural produce heaped in a town market, a huge motorway placed in complementary juxtaposition to the pastoral, a shot from the front of the bus that follows a quaint horse and buggy down a road and, finally, New York's vast urban landscape, significantly first seen not just in itself but in a beautiful and elaborate composition which views it beyond the river in the foreground and through a screen of trees. This last image seems to repeat the notion that the city, the sign of escape from and eventual tyranny over nature, need not be in complete antithesis to the agrarian ideal shared by both the old republic and the counterculture.

These images seem to say that Claude and Berger, the straight and the eccentric, Middle America and the blasphemous youth culture, spring from the same roots, if only conservative America would see it. We seem to be told that, after all, the hippies are not so strange and deviant, that they represent ideals which have existed in previous manifestations of American history and culture. Their communalism shares much of the spirit of the many religious and secular sects that abounded in America particularly in the nineteenth century. Their quietism, liking for passivity and paradoxes, and their breakdown of western dualism in the oriental religions they eclectically fuse with other concerns, is something found in the nineteenth-century tradition of orientalism influencing American thought, most notably in the Transcendentalists, in Emerson and Thoreau. Even the most scandalous of their allegiances, the cultivation of 'expanded' states of consciousness through the use of hallucinogenic drugs (with the salute to the dubious guru of that part of the movement, 'Timothy Leary, dearie', in the final 'sunshine' number), could be seen as a variant on the idea that somehow the inhabitants of the New World are privileged to possess an Adamic consciousness in what should have been the New Eden. If this is impossible in the society that they have inherited, it can be restored chemically.

Relation as well as difference, then, is highlighted in the scenes where Claude first encounters the tribe. The environment into which the newly-arrived Claude walks, lean, gaunt, short-cropped, with something of the younger Gary Cooper about him, is itself a paradoxical fusion of meanings. Surrounded by the skyscrapers and noise of the city, Central Park is a pastoral locus that combines both agrarian communal ideas and the pressures of city life out of which revolutions come. The lyrics of Claude's soliloquy as he goes to the draft office express this unification of city and nature into a third ideal state, a 'City' as in St Augustine's *City of God*, compounded of both:

> Where do I go?
> Follow the river.
> Where do I go?
> Follow the gulls.
> Follow the wind song,
> Follow the thunder,
> Follow the neon
> In young lovers' eyes,
> Down to the gutter,
> Down to the glitter,
> Into the city
> Where the truth lies.

If Claude has come to New York to learn, the tribe in their way are seeking Claude's world, or at least the true impulse at the back of it; and if Claude in his puzzled, taciturn way is brought under their spell, equally they seek him out, not just as someone to rescue but because, it seems, they are drawn to virtues and presences they obscurely recognise in him. A good deal of this intricate exchange and mutual recognition of values is suggested in their second encounter. Having seen Sheila and her friends riding by on horses, the hippies pool their resources in hiring a horse to ride in the park. When it bolts, Claude, with a country boy's expertise, mounts it as it flies past, performing an exuberant series of vaults as he gallops along, winning the praise of Berger and his companions: 'You really are a cowboy!'. This eulogy, unlike Berger's initial reaction to Claude's revelations about his Oklahoman origins, is not delivered ironically. Claude's ease with the animal world is something the tribe recognises and admires. The term 'cowboy', like others in the film used both verbally and visually (such as the 'United States' and the emblem of the American flag), has underneath its more rapacious and discredited connotations a bedrock of purer, more idealistic meaning that the film wants to recover: the cowboy as natural man in unison with nature, the fugitive from the institutional repressions of dominant culture. The symbolic value that horses have near the beginning of the film both in Central Park and in rural America is further underlined by the way that during the first number. 'The age of Aquarius', the mounted policemen's horses elaborately prance as if in sympathy with the hippies' dance duet. The mounted policemen become for a moment centaurs, as do Claude and the hippies, an ideal fusion of dancing animal and unrepressive mind.

This is a little reminiscent of the exuberant wit of 'Black boys are delicious', transformed far beyond the play's clever parody of the Supremes and transgression of racist sexual attitudes. The number cuts between loca-ions: girls, both black and white, watch boys of both colours in the park, while draft board officers, both black and white, inspect draftees of various pigmentations, some with Mr Universe shapes, one, a Woody Allen look-alike with pink varnish on his toenails. Part of the number presents us with the ribald joy of females asserting their sexual desires openly, and the pleasant surprise of the male being addressed as beautiful love object. But there is also the significant comedy of the way the officers, officially inspec-ting the draftees' bodies in ways from which all tenderness and eroticism has been excluded in order to decide whether they are fit killing machines (rather than the 'love machine' the girls are singing to), give voice to the repressed eroticism of their unconscious and celebrate the beauty of the young men: White girls: 'Black boys are so damned yummy.'/White officers: 'They satisfy my tummy.' There is an optimistic sense throughout the film that a fuller self waits to be liberated even in those who act as cogs of the institutions which deal out death.

The sequence that most fully encapsulates the film's will to reconcile the new and the old, the bent and the straight, comes when Claude, having been introduced to the milder pleasures of pot in 'Hashish', is led through the gates of perception at the acid feast in Central Park. It is again typical of the film's intricacy that this moment, rather than being just a simple spilling out of psychedelic images, is expanded into the equivalent of the dream ballet sequences in various earlier musicals, chief among them the miniature sym-bolic dramas choreographed by Agnes de Mille in *Oklahoma!* and *Carousel*. In fact *Oklahoma!*, which it will be remembered is Claude's home state, is alluded to in the moment where the Tantric goddess who performs the marriage of Claude and Sheila in his fantasy receives a shawl which mysteri-ously floats down from the sky, rather as Laurie, during the ballet sequence in *Oklahoma!*, receives her bridal veil. Like the earlier dream ballet, this one is an involved expression of oppositions and reconciliations that are features of both narrative and number in the film, and are associated with the two-way relationship of Claude to the tribe. Prominent among these are eastern and western religions, monogamous love and a freer sexuality, contact between the older and young generations, America past and present (and future), ideal and real.

The sequence is rooted in Claude's subjectivity, loosened up as it is by the dose of LSD he has taken in a moment that parodies the Eucharist as the host (a sugar cube) is dispensed on to the communicants' tongues by a 'priest' wearing a westerner's hat but with a face painted like an Indian's. The film makes no moral judgement on the drug culture, but uses the acid visions to construct a heady and fantastic sequence that takes off into the mystic through a heightening of Claude's own preoccupations with what has happened to him since meeting the tribe.

The basic subject matter of the fantasy, Claude's marriage to Sheila in his home-town Catholic church, has been, on the realistic narrative level, suggested by Jeannie's remark to Claude that he might marry her as a way of avoiding the draft. Claude's thoughts, of course, drift towards Sheila and, with the LSD taking effect, he gives way to fantasy. The rock band on stage in the park has a singer dressed incongruously in white tails and, in reply to the question 'What do you love?' he sings 'An old-fashioned melody'. A series of disorientating zoom shots makes the transition into Claude's trip, and the singer, still singing 'An old-fashioned melody', is found dressed for a wedding with Sheila's family and guests whom we recognise from the earlier disrupted party at Sheila's home. A marvellous matching cut from two hippies dancing to a pair of youthful socialites staidly waltzing seals the transition from one world to another while setting up the expression of the relationship of the two central lovers.

Suddenly we are transported back to the idyllic wooden church of the film's opening. Its doors open to reveal a dark, cavernous interior into which Claude ushers Sheila who seems in some respects reluctant to enter. Moments later they make their marriage vows, not in front of an ordinary priest, but a kind of Tantric sexual goddess of the kind that appealed to the counter-culture by reconciling the carnal and the spiritual. This goddess figure who moments earlier had pranced around divesting herself of a pair of pants, jettisoned with a nifty and rather comical kick, then sits surrounded by Catholic emblems on a platform rising, then descending, leaving her mystically levitating before the young couple. The vows made, the couple kiss and, when they part, Sheila is revealed as magically pregnant.

In Central Park, Claude smiles ecstatically. His idyll is, however, interrupted as, instead of organ peals, the music that celebrates the wedding is 'Hare Krishna', sung by a troupe of dancing girls who frustratingly come between him and Sheila, as if in admonition of the old-fashioned melody of his monogamous desires. This moment is the key to the increasingly hectic remainder of the vision where Claude searches for an elusive Sheila who evades him by changing shapes and roles. Metamorphosis holds sway as the goddess figure also changes shape, veering between her carnal Tantric self and a primly upright Madonna in blue who, however, is affected enough by the sensuous ambiance to cast a sly grin at a copulating couple. Towards the end of the number Berger approaches Sheila and teaches her how to levitate.

Comically flapping her arms in an effort to fly, she suddenly rises and dance-floats in the air, finally flying into the symbolic fires where Claude, now also flying, follows her. A cut to a close-up of his face in the park shows him beatifically responding to the lesson of shared sexual conviviality that has been taught him, though in a final, slightly jarring note we are made to feel that the lesson may be hard to accept. The last vestiges of his vision find Claude left in the church alone, with Berger and the others dancing out of the door.

At the simplest level the vision indulges and then chastens the old-fashioned melody of Claude's desire to marry Sheila, which contradicts the less exclusive ties he is introduced to by the family of the alternative society. But at every point it works through that particular situation to present images of larger lessons and reconciliations: of ways of thought, of cultures and of the generations. In an image which reflects much of the content of the number, the horse associated with Claude, which has mysteriously entered the church at the pronouncement of the wedding vows, walks by a huge icon of a lotus flower. It is as compelling an image of the number's embracing of east and west as could be imagined.

Towards the end of the sequence, Berger begins to dominate Claude's consciousness. While Claude searches for Sheila, we see Berger dancing on the table as he did at Sheila's party, and the swinging chandelier associated with him from that scene reappears. It is Berger who teaches Sheila to levitate, and who dances everyone out of the church. Here, as elsewhere, a kind of relationship of doubles is established, something forcibly suggested even before the vision begins, for when the 'priest' doles out his impregnated cubes, he gives his last one to Claude, running out as he reaches Berger, so that we feel that Claude has been given what is Berger's.

It is Berger who introduces Claude to the new ways, finds out where Sheila lives and then persuades Claude to gatecrash the party, arranges, though the plot misfires, for Claude to take Sheila home on his last night, and who makes the decision to visit Claude in Nevada. In the number 'Manchester, England, England' Berger stands as a sort of master of ceremonies over a born-again Claude, announcing that it is his 'first' day in America, making him utter the words of radical self-assertion 'And I'm a genius, genius' and define the relationship of himself and the divine outside the terms of western dualism and inside the terms of an eastern dissolution of subject and object: 'I believe in God/And I believe that God/Believes in Claude, that's me'. During the early part of the number Berger and Claude physically almost unite, the bigger, shaggy-haired, almost bare-chested hippie holding from behind the conventionally-dressed Claude, whose eyes glaze and head lolls under the power of Berger's presence. In the course of all this Berger actually lifts Claude off his feet, before separating himself from his pupil who then himself repeats the assertions that Berger has taught him. The sense that Berger and Claude undergo some kind of exchange is heightened by the way that Sheila, who eventually becomes Claude's girl-friend, is shown as being under the sway of Berger's spiritual–sexual power, not just in the image dwelt on at the end of the previous section but through-out the film. For instance, in the scene where Berger gets into the car with Steve and Sheila he playfully puts his hand on her knee. Other moments of identity occur during the ride with the rest of the tribe to Nevada, and when Jeannie cuts his hair. The sense seems to be that Sheila belongs to Berger, less for patriarchal reasons than symbolic ones. Though she becomes Claude's girlfriend it is Berger in Claude, or the Claude released by Berger that she loves. The climactic moment of these series of interchanges (not all, as we have remarked, one way, for Berger seems to love Claude for reasons of his own), is of course where Berger has his hair cut, puts on a military uniform and literally exchanges with Claude his clothes, name, identity and finally his death for Claude's life, a hippie Sidney Carton practising what he preaches. As Claude drifts into Berger's world, so Berger, as it were, finds the Claude in himself. Even before the swapping of uniforms he seems impelled to visit the sites of dominant culture, perhaps, we might feel, to proselytise with 'I got life, mother', but perhaps also as a more subterranean expression of links with the straight world which he seeks.

Reconciliation within a celebration of the now distant counter-culture seems to us the dominant mood of the film. What is apparent is that *Hair* – though it is other things as well – belongs to that sub-type of late seventies and early eighties film which, across the borders of several genres, struggles to provide out of the traumas of Vietnam, the heyday of the counter-culture, mass political agitation (anti-war, anti-racism), the defeat of liberalism and the assertion of regressive anti-liberal populism, images of possible reconcili-ation. *Hair* looks for an image of America as the family it was, or was in ideals and dreams, though never in actuality save in the delusive quietude of the complacent liberal consensus shattered by the events of the sixties. In this it might be compared to the Clint Eastwood films *The Outlaw Josey Wales* (1976) and *Bronco Billy* (1980), both films of counter-families with vagrant heroes who form new groups around them out of those rejected by or fleeing the traumatised great society.

Hair, in Berger's sacrificial death, gives us meanings, too, that can not only be read as the death of the counter-culture's aspirations of taking over the mainstream, a dream whose impossibility was dramatised in Nixon's

landslide over the mildest liberalism of McGovern in 1972, but also as hopes that its effects on American culture embodied in Claude and Sheila will be lasting. If the attempts at reconciliation sometimes take the easiest way out, as in the final grouping of the tribe where Wolf and Jeannie and a baby, presumaby theirs, are placed together on one side of the frame, with Hud and his girlfriend together at another, its determined refusal to be cynical, in the modern sense of the term, is often moving as it searches among the icons of American mythology for their uncontaminated sources. Milos Forman's vision of America in *Hair* owes something to his own position as a European outsider caught up, sometimes perhaps naively, in the mythology of American innocence and potential, but its strength is that it is not eccentric, that it rediscovers, in common with many other major contemporary musicals, the genre's capacity for affirmation in the face of contemporary reality. In what it says and in the beauty and vivacity of the formal means with which its says it, *Hair* tells us why film makers still reach out for the most aesthetically complete and utopian form that the cinema has developed.

'Let the sun shine in'. The age of Aquarius prefigured in the faces of the young; 'Old Glory' revivified at centre frame – the emblem of the 'United States of Love'.

Notes on sources

1 Introduction

The review by Clancy Sigal which we quote was published in *The Guardian* (26.11.81) and attacked the British Film Institute publication *Genre: The Musical*, ed. Rick Altman (London, 1981). The passage in which Renoir is quoted by Truffaut is from *The Films in My Life* by Francois Truffaut (translated by Leonard Mayhew, Harmondsworth, 1982). Richard Dyer's influential article was first printed in *Movie* 24, and is reprinted in Altman, *op. cit.* Jane Feuer's work, alluded to – like Dyer's – throughout this book, though with more areas of disagreement, is *The Hollywood Musical* (London, 1982), also a British Film Institute publication. None of the essays on particular films in the Altman anthology can compare with Andrew Britton's '*Meet Me in St Louis*: Smith or the ambiguities', never reprinted from its fairly obscure source, *The Australian Journal of Screen Theory*, 3 (1978), which was as influential in the genesis of this book as Dyer's article. In saying that Britton's discussion is the only large-scale piece of work on a musical, we do not mean to slight useful and sometimes distinguished work of a more fragmentary or modest kind (e.g. Lucy Fischer's piece on *Dames*, referred to in chapter 3, Robin Wood's piece on *Swing Time*, referred to in chapter 5, or the same writer's 'Art and ideology: notes on *Silk Stockings*', reprinted in Altman, *op. cit.*), but rather to make the point that musical texts have had little sustained attention. Raymond Bellour's long article on *Gigi*, 'Segmenting/Analysing' (also reprinted in Altman, *op. cit.*), is not really an exception since it is more interested in the film as an instance of 'classical' narrative than as a musical.

While these publications represent the analytic wing of criticism of the genre, John Kobal's *Gotta Sing: Gotta Dance: A History of the Movie Musical* (London, 1971, revised edition, 1983), is the biggest and best looking of the determinedly unanalytic 'coffee-table' publications. The passage cited to illustrate the weakness of the popular history approach is from *The Hollywood Musical* by Ethan Mordden (New York, 1982).

More generally, a rationale of the critical movement towards theory can be found in Jonathan Culler's *Structuralist Poetics: Structuralism, Linguistics and the Study of Literature* (London, 1975). The passage from Freud about the search for beauty, etc. in works of art is found in the early part of *Civilisation and its*

Discontents (translated by Joan Riviere, London, 1930). Robert Scholes' remarks about the poetic elements of language are found in *Structuralism in Literature* (New York, 1974), basically a paraphrase of what Roman Jakobson writes in 'Linguistics and Poetics' in *Style in Language*, ed. Thomas A. Sebeok (Cambridge, Mass., 1960).

2   Reading a musical: *Easter Parade*

Easter Parade has never been the subject of any kind of sustained published analysis. Information about its production may be found in Hugh Fordin's *The World of Entertainment: Hollywood's Greatest Musicals* (New York, 1976), which also notes its production costs and first run takings ($2,503,654 and $6,803,000 respectively).

The Irving Berlin songs for the film consist of some which predated *Easter Parade* and some written for the film, information that can be found in Fordin, *op. cit.*

In talking about star personae we acknowledge a general debt to Richard Dyer's *Stars* (London, 1979). A debt to Northrop Frye's great work *Anatomy of Criticism* (Princeton, 1957) is acknowledged in our text and is particularly evident in the 'mythic' elements in our reading of the film. Freud's *The Interpretation of Dreams* (edited and translated by James Strachey, Harmondsworth, 1976) and *The Psychopathology of Everyday Life* (edited and translated by James Strachey, London, 1966) are also alluded to. Terry Eagleton's *Literary Theory: An Introduction* (Oxford, 1983) is useful on questions of ideology and is the source of a quoted passage. An important work on this topic by Althusser is *Lenin and Philosophy and Other Essays* (translated by Ben Brewster, 1971). On dissatisfaction with organic models of works of art, see Eagleton, *op. cit.*

3   *Gold Diggers of 1933*

On films of the Depression period we have found very useful Robert Sklar's *Movie-Made America: A Cultural History of American Movies* (London, 1978), and Andrew Bergman's *We're in the Money: Depression America and Its Films* (New York, 1971). Our position has been clarified by strong disagreement with the thrust of a chapter by P. H. Melling, 'The mind of the mob: Hollywood and popular culture in the 1930s' in *Cinema, Politics and Society in America*, eds. Philip Davies and Brian Neve (Manchester, 1981) which argues against any positive representation of social and political realities in Hollywood films of the period.

For Warner Brothers in the '30s our main sources of information have been Nick Roddick's *A New Deal in Entertainment: Warner Brothers in the 1930s* (London, 1983), though this book rather perversely ignores the musicals, and the *Velvet Light Trap* 17 (Winter 1977) issue on Warners in the '30s.

Our main documentary source for Busby Berkeley has been *The Busby*

Berkeley Book by Tony Thomas and Jim Terry with Busby Berkeley (London, 1973). A typical interview is the one in *Cahiers du Cinéma in English* 2 (1966), 'A style of spectacle: an interview with Busby Berkeley by Patrick Brion and René Gilson'. Lucy Fischer quotes the following from Busby Berkeley, 'Rencontre avec le grand 'Architecte du Musical' ', in *Cinéma* 103 (Feb. 1966): 'I never had the intention of making eroticism or pornography. I love beautiful girls and I love to gather and show many beautiful girls with regular features and well-made bodies'.

Useful information about the making of the film at the centre of this chapter is found in the Warners–Wisconsin screenplay of *Gold Diggers of 1933*, ed. Arthur Hove (Madison, 1980), and information about its predecessor in *42nd Street*, ed. Rocco Fumento (Madison, 1980), though both editions are extremely naive in their readings of the films.

Mark Roth's brilliant reading of the Warners musicals, 'Some Warners musicals and the spirit of the New Deal' is handily reprinted in *Genre: The Musical*, ed. Rick Altman (London, 1981). His argument has weaker, more tendentious parts, such as the rating of the success of the films by the sole criterion of the forcefulness of their director figures – a method that relegates *Gold Diggers of 1933* to the position of a less successful film. But the article is a major piece of work to which we are indebted.

The major example of feminist criticism of Berkeley is Lucy Fischer's 'The image of woman as image: the optical politics of *Dames*', reprinted in Altman, *op. cit*, far superior to Paula Rabinowitz's article 'Commodity fetishism: women in *Gold Diggers of 1933*,' *Film Reader* 5 (1980), which stands, with its pretentious mishmash of vulgar feminism, Freud and Marx as a cautionary example for film analysts. For instance, in order to make the text comply with her simplistic thesis that the numbers actively diminish the heroines of the narrative, Rabinowitz reads the 'Forgotten man' number in terms of the degradation of the Joan Blondell figure, a reading of such oddity that it must be doubted whether anyone else – of any gender – has ever made it.

The essay by Freud quoted is 'The Uncanny' ('Das Unheimliche') in the standard edition, Vol. XVII, translated and edited by James Strachey (London, 1955). Susan Sontag's 'Notes on "camp" ' is found in *Against Interpretation* (London, 1967). A recent instance of a statement of non-integration in the Berkeley musicals is found in *Film Art: An Introduction* by David Bordwell and Kristin Thompson (Reading, Mass., 1979). Jean-Louis Comolli's article 'Dancing images: Busby Berkeley's kaleidoscope' in *Cahiers du Cinéma in English* 2 (1966) is referred to as an exemplar of the formalist approach to Berkeley and is also the source of the idea of a '*système* Berkeley'. The passage quoted from Hebert Marcuse occurs in *Eros and Civilisation* (London, 1969).

4 *The Merry Widow*

John Russell Taylor's remarks on operetta can be found in his collaboration with

Arthur Jackson, *The Hollywood Musical* (London, 1971). The information
about the different language versions comes from *Ernst Lubitsch: A Guide to
References and Resources* edited by Robert L. Carringer and Barry Sabath
(Boston, 1978). Carringer and Sabath also draw attention to Lubitsch's power
over such matters as omitting Thalberg's name from production credits. This
book contains some interesting analytical as well as bibliographical material.
We very much agree with their assertion that the themes of his European
comedies become more significant and subversive in the more puritan American
ambiance, but find their more detailed comments on the counterplay of the
American and the European too simple to be satisfactory.

For information on Mayer's promotion of the film through press photo-
graphs of himself, Thalberg, and Chevalier together, see Bob Thomas,
Thalberg: Life and Legend of the Great Hollywood Producer (New York, 1969).

The Merry Widow was subjected to a number of cuts in the American
version. These were restored in the BBC TV version and the one shown at the
NFT, London, in 1983. The cutting of the garter with 'many happy returns'
written on it is typical of the type of cuts made. See on this whole matter, Eleanor
Knowles, *The Films of Jeanette MacDonald and Nelson Eddy* (London, 1975).
Lubitsch's protests at the censorship, publicised in *The Motion Picture Daily*,
The Hollywood Reporter, *Variety* and *The Film Daily* are mentioned by Carringer
and Sabath, *op. cit.* Details on the censorship code, which came into force in
1934 during the making of the film, are available in Cobbett Steinberg, *Reel
Facts* (Hammondsworth, 1978).

Our assertion that Lubitsch made of himself a precursor of the 'director as
superstar' can be shown by reference to contemporary reviewers, such as
Mordaunt Hall, writing on *One Hour with You* in the *New York Times*, 24 March
1932. He mentions Lubitsch by name six times. André Sennwald's review, in
the same paper, of *The Merry Widow* also names him six times (twice as the
affectionately grand 'Herr Lubitsch'). The screen titles of Lubitsch's films associate the works with him, as in 'Maurice Chevalier in Ernst Lubitsch's *The
Smiling Lieutenant*'. Lubitsch was actually made head of production at
Paramount from February 1935 to February 1936, though, as the short period
indicates, he was not considered a (financial) success in the role. After this, he
went to be head of his own unit.

Financial details on the very expensive *The Merry Widow*, MGM's second
costliest film to date, after *Ben Hur*, are in Samuel Marx, *Mayer and Thalberg.
The Make-Believe Saints* (London, 1976). He writes that the film showed losses
of $113,000 on world returns, after five years. In other words, like some later
musicals, such as *Hello Dolly*, costs outweighed good audience figures, though
Thalberg's philosophy tolerated prestigious films which did not make a great
deal of money, but won respect for the studio.

On the representation of the sexes in the movies, see Larry May, *Screening
Out the Past, The Birth of Mass Culture in the Motion Picture Industry* (Chicago,
1980); Marjorie Rosen, *Popcorn Venus. Women, Movies and the American Dream*
(London, 1973); and Molly Haskell, *From Reverence to Rape* (Baltimore, 1974),

who writes:

> In the early years of the Depression, Hollywood was offering the public frivolous upper class entertainments, and for once the time lag between the real world and Hollywood's apprehension of it was a blessing . . . He brought with him his own milieu: an imaginary European *crème de la crème* already cut with Lubitsch vinegar, to which he added American blood. By cross-breeding American and European types, and by shifting expectations, he set up reverberations within the plot and within characters that went beyond the usual stereotypes . . . for Lubitsch, women are as often in the driver's seat as men, and roles are oppressive only in so far as life, and love, are imperfect and no one person is wholly adequate to the needs of another. [Also evident is] his sense of the mutiplicity of a woman's role as a primary condition of her being.

A good article on *The Merry Widow* is by Nancy Schwartz, 'Lubitsch's Widow: the meaning of a Waltz', *Film Comment* 11, 2 (1975). On dual-structure narratives in musicals, see Altman's own article, 'The American film musical: paradigmatic structure and mediatory function', in *Genre: The Musical* (London, 1981). For Tiomkin's remarks on film music, see James Limbacher, *Film Music: From Violins to Video* (Metuchen, New Jersey, 1974). And on Herbert Stothart specifically, see Clifford McCarty, *Film Composers in America: A Checklist of Their Work* (New York, 1972), and Aljean Harmetz, *The Making of 'The Wizard of Oz'* (New York, 1977). Wilfrid Mellers' *Music in a New Found Land. Themes and Developments in the History of American Music* (London, 1964) is, though generally useful, narrow-sighted over Hollywood musicals.

5   *Swing Time*

Very useful information on Astaire's dance styles, both individually and in partnership, can be found in Jerome Delameter's *Dance and the Hollywood Musical* (Ann Arbor, 1981). The quotation we use from Astaire about his adaptation to film comes from Morton Eustis, 'Fred Astaire: the actor/dancer attacks his part', *Theatre Arts* 21 (May, 1937). On dancing in the musical, see also Arlene Croce, 'Dance in film', in *Cinema: A Critical Dictionary. The Major Film-Makers*, 2 vols, edited by Richard Roud, I (London, 1980). For a contrasting view, taken by Gene Kelly, see Albert Johnson, 'The tenth muse in San Francisco (4)', in *Sight and Sound* 26 (summer, 1956):

> There seems to be a common misapprehension that dancing and the motion picture are well-suited to each other . . . they are not. The dance is a three-dimensional art form, while the motion picture is two-dimensional . . . the difficulties we have in transferring a dance onto film are simply those of putting a three-dimensional art form into a two-dimensional panel.

On Astaire's dance style see also Arlene Croce, *The Fred Astaire and Ginger Rogers Book* (New York, 1972). We find this book, which has a chapter on each of the films, helpful in some parts, weak in others, and somewhat overrated. The problem with much of Croce's discussion is that its specific details usually pull away from the text of the film. So, for instance, while nothing is said about the role of Mabel in *Swing Time*, we are told that Helen Broderick was the mother of Broderick Crawford, and had a song written for her by Cole Porter.

On the Fred–Ginger partnership see also Robin Wood, 'Never never change, always gonna dance', *Film Comment* 15, 9 (1979). Fred Astaire's auto-biography, *Steps in Time* (New York, 1959), is interesting almost exclusively for the revelation that he was uncomfortable in evening wear. Graham Greene's comparison of Astaire to Mickey Mouse comes from *The Pleasure Dome: The Collected Film Criticism 1935–40*, edited by John Russell Taylor (London, 1980). Alan Williams' article on background music is 'The musical film and recorded popular music' in *Genre: the Musical*, edited by Rick Altman (London, 1981).

6 *The Jolson Story/Jolson Sings Again*

There is no analytical writing on these films at all. For information about their commercial success, see Cobbett Steinberg, *Reel Facts* (Harmondsworth, 1978), Clive Hirschorn, *The Hollywood Musical* (London, 1981) – a formidably accurate and compendious source book – and David Pirie, *Anatomy of the Movies* (London, 1981). *Jolson Sings Again* is listed by Steinberg as the number one grossing film for 1949, while Pirie lists *The Jolson Story* ninth on his all-time (inflation-adjusted) list of commercially successful musicals.

Our 'average legend' (Freud's phrase in *Moses and Monotheism*) of the 'classical' musical biopic is based on intensive study of fifteen films, namely: *Night and Day, Rhapsody in Blue, The Eddy Duchin Story, The Jolson Story, Jolson Sings Again, The Buddy Holly Story, Love Me or Leave Me, The Five Pennies, The Glenn Miller Story, Lady Sings The Blues, Gypsy, Funny Girl, Yankee Doodle Dandy, The Great Waltz* (1938) and *Melba* (an operatic musical biopic). Our general remarks on biography and the biopic owe in various ways to a stimulating British Film Institute publication *Lust For Lives: An Examination of Biopix* (compiled by Cary Bazalgette, Jim Cook, Caroline Merz and Mike Westlake, undated).

On Jolson specifically we have consulted two biographies, Michael Freedland's *Al Jolson* (London, 1972) and Robert Oberfirst's *Al Jolson: You Aint Heard Nothin' Yet* (New York, 1980). These, however, are extremely problematic as factual sources, devoid of documentation and written in 'showbiz' rhetoric. There are numerous statements of Jolson's egotism and problems in resolving the performer's with the offstage life. Henry Pleasants in *The Great American Popular Singers* (New York, 1974) quotes statements by Eddy Cantor, George Jessel and Pearl Sieben which must be granted consider-able authority. An interesting instance of popular journalistic treatment of the Jolson–Keeler marriage is found in *Hollywood and the Great Fan Magazines*, ed. Martin Leven (London, 1970).

On Jolson's singing style (and associated matters) we have used Pleasants' analysis (*op. cit.*), and consulted Wilfred Mellers' *Music in a New Found Land: Themes and Developments in the History of American Music* (London, 1964), Ian Whitcomb's *After The Ball is Over* (Harmondsworth, 1973), Giles Oakley's *The Devil's Music: A History of the Blues* (revised edition, London, 1983), and Robert C. Toll's *Blacking Up: The Minstrel Show in Nineteenth Century America* (London, 1974). Robert L. Carringer in his edition of the screenplay of *The Jazz Singer* (Madison, 1979) usefully discusses Jolson's delivery of 'Toot, toot, tootsie'.

Material consulted on American Jews and European immigration included Irving Howe, *World of Our Fathers* (New York, 1976), Lester D. Friedman's *Hollywood's Image of the Jew* (New York, 1982), and the chapter by R. A. Burchell and Eric Homberger, 'The immigrant experience' in *Introduction to American Studies*, eds. Malcolm Bradbury and Howard Temperley (London, 1981).

The Andrews Sisters' spoof of 'Sonny boy' is on *The Best of the Andrews Sisters*, MCA Records, MCDW246. Detailed information about Jolson's discography is found in Oberfirst, *op. cit.*

Studies of the relation between films and society that helped us in various ways are Will Wright, *Sixguns and Society: A Structural Study of the Western* (Berkeley, 1975), Keith Reader, *Cultures on Celluloid* (London, 1981), Larry May, *Screening Out the Past: The Birth of Mass Culture and the Motion Picture Industry* (Chicago, 1980), and Peter Biskind, *Seeing is Believing: How Hollywood Taught Us to Stop Worrying and Love the Fifties* (London, 1984).

7   *Summer Holiday*

Information on the cost ($2,258,235) and first-run receipts ($1,609,000) of the film, as well as its production history, come from Hugh Fordin, *The World of Entertainment: Hollywood's Greatest Musicals* (New York, 1976). Four numbers were deleted: 'Never again' (Frank Morgan), 'Omar and the Princess' (song and ballet with Mickey Rooney and Gloria De Haven, publicity stills of which are in the British Film Institute stills collection), 'Wish I had a braver heart' (Gloria De Haven), and 'Spring isn't everything' (Walter Huston).

The film's source, Eugene O'Neill's *Ah, Wilderness!*, has been written about interestingly by Jacob H. Adler in 'The worth of *Ah, Wilderness!*', *Modern Drama* III (1960), and by Thomas F. van Laan in 'Singing in the wilderness: the dark vision of Eugene O'Neill's only comedy', *Modern Drama* XXII (1979), as well as in the various biographies and critical books on O'Neill. O'Neill's own comments about the play stress its selfconsciously idyllic vision: 'a dream waking . . . a nostalgia for a youth I never had . . . the way I would have liked my boyhood to have been' (quoted in Travis Bogard, *Contour in Time: The Plays of Eugene O'Neill* (New York, 1972), and 'To me, the America which was (and is) the real America found its unique expression in such middle-class families as the Millers . . .' (quoted by van Laan).

For background material relating to the tradition of pastoral literature and art in America we are indebted – as is obvious in the text – to the following: Leo Marx, *The Machine in the Garden: Technology and the Pastoral Ideal in America* (New York, 1964), Morton and Lucia White, *The Intellectual Versus the City: From Thomas Jefferson to Frank Lloyd Wright* (New York, 1977), which alerted us to passages in Jefferson, Crèvecoeur, Henry James' *The American Scene* and Henry Adams' *The Education of Henry Adams* alluded to or quoted in the text. Another – twice-quoted – source is the massive sociological survey *Middletown in Transition: A Study in Cultural Conflicts* by Robert S. Lynd and Helen Merrell Lynd (New York, 1937).

Andrew Britton's '*Meet Me in St Louis:* Smith or the ambiguities', *Australian Journal of Screen Theory*, 3 (1978) is a key discussion of a closely related film. Lindsay Anderson's *About John Ford* (London, 1981) is quoted on Ford's pastoral films. Tom Milne's *auteurist* account of Mamoulian, *Mamoulian* (London, 1969), gives a pleasant reading of the more unproblematic elements in *Summer Holiday*. 'Distanciation' is a concept employed by Paul Willemen in 'Distanciation and Douglas Sirk', *Douglas Sirk*, eds Laura Mulvey and Jon Halliday (Edinburgh Film Festival, 1972).

The fascinating business of the Reading fiasco and, more generally, the film's poor reception in England, was established by reference to holdings in the British Film Institute library. Sample opinions were: 'One part is musical, another poetical, another allegorical, another hysterical' (*Evening Standard*); 'bilious, technicoloured nightmare' (*Daily Worker*); 'Simple, isn't it? Not half' (*Graphic*); 'A degrading picture' (*The Observer*); 'Mickey Rooney suggests . . . an aggressive and ageing jockey' (*Daily Express*); [Mickey Rooney looks like] 'a refugee from a ventriloquist's knee' (*Evening Standard*); 'pleasant moments, dull patches, and one sequence I found repellent' (*Daily Telegraph*); '. . . to turn this delicate, pedigree masterpiece into the mongrel, semi-musical indelicacy of *Summer Holiday* . . . last but not least, immodesty has been added. The sequence in which Mr Rooney turns for comfort to a chorus girl . . . is of a singular, voluptuary beastliness which stimulates nothing except nausea' (*News Chronicle*).

8   *It's Always Fair Weather*

For biographical material, and for Donen's remarks about Kelly, we have relied on Clive Hirschorn, *Gene Kelly: a Biography* (Chicago, 1974); see also Donald Knox, *The Magic Factory: How MGM Made 'An American In Paris'* (New York and London, 1973). On Kelly's use of dance, see Jerome Delameter, *Dance in the Hollywood Musical* (Ann Arbor, 1981). Information about the cutting from the film of the Michael Kidd number, 'Jack and the space giants', and about casting problems, – the desire for but unavailability of Jules Munshin and Frank Sinatra, comes from Hugh Fordin's, *The World of Entertainment: Hollywood's Greatest Musicals* (New York, 1976). Fordin's remarks about *It's Always Fair*

Weather are rather dismissive, as are John Russell Taylor's in his collaboration with Arthur Jackson in *The Hollywood Musical* (London, 1971). Michael Wood's original and helpful remarks can be found in *America in the Movies, or 'Santa Maria' It Had Slipped My Mind* (London, 1975). See also, Leo Braudy, *The World in a Frame: What We See in Films* (New York, 1977). On the representation of women in film see Molly Haskell, *From Reverence to Rape* (Baltimore, 1974) and Marjorie Rosen, *Popcorn Venus: Women, Movies and the American Dream* (London, 1973). For comments on the use of TV in the USA see Erik Barnouw, *Tube of Plenty* (New York, 1975).

Production costs of the film were $2,620,256. First run receipts were $2,485,000 (see Fordin *op. cit.*).

9   *Carousel*

We have relied heavily for biographical information on the following: Richard Rodgers, *Musical Stages: an Autobiography* (London, 1976), Frederick Nolan, *The Sound of Their Music* (London, 1978), Deems Taylor, *Some Enchanted Evenings: The Story of Rodgers and Hammerstein* (New York, 1953), and Joshua Logan, *Josh! My Up and Down In and Out Life* (New York, 1976). For further insight into production conditions, see Michael B. Druxman, *The Musical: From Broadway to Hollywood* (New York, 1980). William Ludwig is quoted as saying that in *Oklahoma!* they were not allowed to break out of the proscenium, to take advantage of the camera. He also claims that Rodgers and Hammerstein exercised great control over Zinnemann, while making a contradictory statement that Agnes de Mille invented new elements of the ballet for the film.

Contemporary journalistic reviews of *Carousel* as a film heralding the decline of the musical can be seen, for instance, in *The Times* or *Time*. *The Times* review of 23 April 1956 reads: 'The cinema is not to blame if *Carousel* represents the decline, the decadence of American musical comedy. The brave, authentic impulse which found so exciting an impression in *Oklahoma!* and *Annie Get Your Gun* is here dried up and has to be stimulated artificially'. *Time*, 19 March 1956, writes 'The melodies have all their clovered freshness still, but if film fans lick their lips over anything else about this movie version of the Broadway musical, it will be because they can't tell sweet from saccharine'.

On pastoral see William Empson, *Some Versions of Pastoral* (London, 1935); on dreams see Sigmund Freud, *The Interpretation of Dreams*, edited and translated by James Strachey assisted by Alan Tyson (Harmondsworth, 1976).

10   *On a Clear Day You Can See Forever*

There is no serious writing on *On A Clear Day*, but there is a long tradition (dating back to the early days of *auteur* criticism) of work on Minnelli's films, both musical and non-musical, which has influenced us. In particular, we acknowledge Thomas Elsaesser's 'Vincente Minnelli', reprinted in *Genre; the Musical*, ed. Rick Altman (London, 1981), and Richard Dyer's summarising piece 'Minnelli's web of dreams' in *Movies of the Fifties*, ed. Ann Lloyd (London, 1982). The reading of Minnelli's films as allegories of the movie-making process comes from the former article.

On Barbra Streisand our attitudes have been sharpened by disagreement with the negative assessment of her in Leo Braudy's *The World in a Frame: What We See in Films* (New York, 1976). Of the songs analysed in our text 'Happy days are here again' and 'Second-hand Rose' are included on *Barbra Streisand's Greatest Hits* (CBS 63921). The original version by Fanny Brice – much more ethnic, pointing up the duality of the Streisand version – is included on *40 Years of Golden Oldies* (Arcade Records). The vocal side of the original stage version of *On A Clear Day*, with Julie Harris, is available on RCA LSOD-2006.

The film's press reception (consulted in the British Film Institute Library) was for the most part strikingly unintelligent. 'Musical escapism – there is no other word for it – reaches a new numbing level with *On A Clear Day* . . . for its story is simply and wholly an elaborate excuse for some extravagant period flashbacks' (*Daily Telegraph*); 'It is one of those hybrids between a musical and a straight play, in which people in prosaic situations burst foolishly into song and then continue as if nothing has happened' (*Spectator*); 'All the film lacks is that indefinable something, the alchemist's gold of the musical, which lifts one out of mere pleasure into exhilaration' (*Observer*). '*Barbra shines even in a fog* . . . Barbra Streisand is one of the great comic talents of the movies. She rises above everything. And she rises above *On a Clear Day You Can See Forever*' (*People*).

11 *Hair*

For Jane Feuer's remarks on the musical's self-consciousness, see *The Hollywood Musical* (London, 1982). Richard Dyer's categories are to be found in 'Entertainment and Utopia', in *Movie 24*.

Invaluable sources on contemporary American history and culture are: Theodore Roszak's two books, *The Making of a Counter-Culture: Reflections on the Technocratic Society and Its Youthful Opposition* (London, 1970), and *Where The Wasteland Ends. Politics and Transcendence in Postindustrial Society* (New York, 1972), Irwin Unger, *The Movement: A History of the American New Left, 1959–1972* (New York, 1975), and Godfrey Hodgson, *America in Our Time* (New York, 1976). These are essential reading on topics like the hippie counter-culture, the rise of Black Power, the backlash of the 'silent majority' and the liberal consensus of the '40s and '50s. Also, see Paul Goodman, Frederick Perls and Ralph Hefferline, *Gestalt Therapy* (New York, 1951). On nineteenth-century American socialistic utopian communities, see especially Edmund Wilson, *To the Finland Station* (London, 1940). Allen Ginsberg's poem 'Wichita Vortex Sutra' can be found in *Planet News 1961–1967* (San Francisco, 1968). It is worth trying to locate the issues raised by *Hair* within the context of

Milos Forman's other 'American' themes in films like *Taking Off* (1971), *One Flew Over the Cuckoo's Nest* (1975), and *Ragtime* (1981).

For a favourable review of *Hair* see the July 1979 review in *Time*:

> It achieves its goals by rigorously obeying the rules of classic American musical comedy: dialogue, plot, song and dance blend seamlessly to create a juggernaut of excitement . . . If portrayed literally, Claude's odyssey to self-awareness would be as hokey as Hollywood's 'trip' movies of the '60s like *Easy Rider*. Instead, *Hair* presents the decade in the terms of balletic myth. The passions of a generation are poured into a single setting, Central Park, on a single enchanted night.

See also, on the ethos of an era, Ivan Illich, *Tools for Conviviality* (London, 1973).